❧ LINCOLN'S PROCLAMATION ❧

THE STEVEN & JANICE BROSE LECTURES *in the* CIVIL WAR ERA

William A. Blair, editor

Lincoln's
PROCLAMATION

EMANCIPATION RECONSIDERED

EDITED BY

William A. Blair & Karen Fisher Younger

THE UNIVERSITY OF NORTH CAROLINA PRESS

Chapel Hill

Designed by Courtney Leigh Baker
Set in Whitman by Keystone Typesetting, Inc.
Manufactured in the United States of America

The paper in this book meets the guidelines for permanence
and durability of the Committee on Production Guidelines
for Book Longevity of the Council on Library Resources.

The University of North Carolina Press has been a
member of the Green Press Initiative since 2003.

Library of Congress Cataloging-in-Publication Data
Lincoln's proclamation : emancipation reconsidered / edited by William A. Blair
and Karen Fisher Younger.
p. cm. — (The Steven and Janice Brose lectures in the Civil War era)
"This collection arose from a symposium on the Emancipation Proclamation held at the
Pennsylvania State University in April 2007 as part of the Steven and Janice Brose Distinguished
Lecture Series sponsored by the George and Ann Richards Civil War Era Center"—Introd.
Includes bibliographical references and index.
ISBN 978-0-8078-3316-2 (cloth : alk. paper)
1. Lincoln, Abraham, 1809–1865—Views on slavery—Congresses.
2. Lincoln, Abraham, 1809–1865—Relations with African Americans—Congresses.
3. United States. President (1861–1865 : Lincoln). Emancipation Proclamation—Congresses.
4. Slaves—Emancipation—United States—Congresses. 5. African Americans—Social
conditions—19th century—Congresses. 6. Southern States—Social conditions—
19th century—Congresses. 7. Border States (U.S. Civil War)—Social conditions—
Congresses. I. Blair, William Alan. II. Younger, Karen Fisher.

E457.2.L8435 2009
973.7092—dc22
2009016601

13 12 11 10 09   5 4 3 2 1

To

STEVE AND JAN,

for

THEIR VISION

CONTENTS

ACKNOWLEDGMENTS

It seems like a long time now since the email message came from Susan Welch, dean of the College of the Liberal Arts at the Pennsylvania State University. She had heard from an alumnus who had an inquiry very different from any we usually get at the George and Ann Richards Civil War Era Center. She said that alumnus Al Lord had a friend who at the time owned a wartime printing of the Emancipation Proclamation. It originated as part of a forty-eight-copy run known as the Leland-Boker edition, which was signed by Abraham Lincoln and turned over to the Union League and the U.S. Sanitary Commission for fund-raising at the Great Central Fair held in Philadelphia in June 1864. Lord wanted to know if we would be interested in having it on loan for, oh, perhaps a year. Would we be able to take advantage of such an opportunity?

Some decisions are easier to make than others, and this one was certainly a snap. Because the original manuscript of the proclamation burned in the Chicago Fire, second-generation (or later) printings, especially ones created during the conflict and signed by the chief executive, were about as close to the real thing as one could get. Taking into account the time it takes for synapses to fire, mere milliseconds lapsed before we said, "Yes!" We then had to scurry to find a secure place to display such a valuable document. The Richards Center is not a museum but a collection of faculty and graduate students within the department of history, established to promote broad studies of the Civil War era and share these findings with the public. Something told us that hanging the Emancipation Proclamation in the hallway of a classroom building through which students and the public passed regularly was not exactly the best idea.

We are grateful to William Joyce, head of Special Collections at the University Libraries, for arranging the space to hang the proclamation in the exhibit room for the university's archives. And we thank the library personnel in general—especially Dean Nancy L. Eaton and Jim Quigel in special collections—for their hospitality in allowing us to lead alumni, the public, and school groups through a usually much more quiet space in order to further the education about the transformation of freedom in the United States.

With the right facility secured, we were able to accept custody of the document, which was transported by Al Lord, a 1967 graduate of Penn State. Lord combines a passionate enthusiasm for history, especially regarding Abraham Lincoln, with a passionate enthusiasm for his alma mater. He was able to secure the document thanks to his friend and associate William Chaney. The generosity of both individuals is part of the reason this book exists. But here we also have to add Seth Kaller to the list of those due gratitude. He was the dealer whom Chaney used for the proclamation. During the year it was on loan, the proclamation found a very appropriate buyer: the National Constitution Center in Philadelphia. Kaller ensured that the proclamation appeared at our symposium, and he brought for display numerous other valuable documents that had graduate students, faculty, and members of the public salivating. Most of us discovered at least one document that we had never seen before. We cannot thank him enough for his sensitivity and his expertise.

The challenge of temporarily housing such a historical treasure as a wartime printing of the Emancipation Proclamation is finding good ways to share it. Besides conducting talks in the library for various groups—including public school teachers from around the country—we decided to put together a symposium on emancipation, at which the document would be displayed. Emancipation was more complicated than many people know, and it seemed more than fitting to continue to explore this subject, especially with the coming of the bicentennial of Lincoln's birth in 2009. Plus, it seemed wise to revisit this seminal event in the history of the United States, which continues to have repercussions more than a century later, especially as scholars have found new ways to see emancipation in a broader context within an Atlantic world. We invited top scholars to reconsider various aspects of the proclamation and to share their findings with anyone who cared to come. Ultimately, about one hundred incredibly dedicated people gave up a Saturday in April 2007 to listen to and question the speakers. We are grateful to them for their interest and for their lively exchange during the final question period.

We also benefited from having considerable expertise here at Penn

State with which to organize such a conference. Mark Neely continued to show why he is one of the best practitioners in the field of Civil War scholarship. Whenever Mark says, "I think I might have something," you should leap at the chance to listen, for it usually will result in a meaningful piece of work that makes you chew on what he says. He never ploughs old ground and is a model for scholarly productivity and professionalism. Nan Elizabeth Woodruff and Amy Greenberg, both faculty affiliates of the Richards Center and very important to different initiatives, served as moderators and as hosts during the public event. We are enormously thankful to them for the good work that they do.

It is also a fact of life that there would have been no symposium, no fiscal management, no book exhibit, no conference room, no lunch, and virtually none of the details of essential, ongoing aspects of normal life without the capable oversight of Barby Singer. Her title is staff assistant at the Center, yet we all know that she really runs the place. She had the help of graduate students for a limited part of her duties on the day of the symposium, but we realize how much she did to make this event, and our ongoing programs, a success.

We could not have organized the symposium or this book without generous support from several quarters. One was the National Endowment for the Humanities. In 2005, the federal government—through the NEH—decided that the Richards Center was an institution worth investing in by awarding a challenge grant under the *We the People* initiative. The grant recognized the Richards Center for its leadership as a "national resource" for the teaching and studying of this seminal period of our history. The NEH understood that we have a broader mission than studying four years of warfare. At the Richards Center, our central focus remains interpreting the struggle for freedom. We have an incredible array of scholars, graduate students, and programs that assess multiple aspects of the transition from slavery to civil rights.

Another area of support came from George and Ann Richards, who have been a delight to be associated with. They had faith in what we hoped to accomplish and provided the ability for us to attract others to our cause. We will never forget George's mantra: "Dream big dreams and we will figure out how to get there." We hope that this is one step along the way.

Finally, we must give credit where credit is due. This book lives within a series sponsored by Steven and Janice Brose. We thank the University of North Carolina Press, especially David Perry, for the enthusiasm shown for our efforts. But without the Broses we could not have launched a series to help stimulate fresh insights into a seminal part of U.S. history. Their support has provided a crucial foundation for the edifice on which this book rests. We happily dedicate this volume to them.

❧ LINCOLN'S PROCLAMATION ❧

INTRODUCTION

In Lincoln Park, about a mile east of the U.S. Capitol, resides one of the few outdoor representations of emancipation in the country. Every day, thousands of commuters pass it on their way to work or play. The observant ones would notice two figures on the pedestal: Abraham Lincoln stretching his hand over a crouching slave who wears freshly broken shackles. One simple word sounds the message of this monument, "Emancipation." It is a handsome work of art, standing twenty-four feet from top to bottom. Nonetheless, it is easy to overlook this piece of stone in a city filled with numerous other monuments, many of them much more imposing. But this quiet statue that anchors one side of the park, surrounded by Victorian-era homes in the Capitol Hill District, is worth attention. It contains the achievements and the contradictions that marked the coming of freedom for enslaved African Americans in the United States. One person can see the comforting figure of Lincoln, the Great Emancipator; another can view the statue with less comfort, wondering why the slave must kneel to a paternalistic hand.[1]

Lincoln remains arguably the most popular president in American history, yet his legacy is not without controversy; the most hotly debated part of the sixteenth president's achievements always has been his Emancipation Proclamation. Part of the reason is that the proclamation, and the process of ending slavery in this country, traveled an uneven road that lends itself to multiple interpretations. With the Constitution acknowledged as protecting slavery, the president faced limits on what he could do with executive powers. So he freed slaves in the Confederate states and not in the loyal border regions. Additionally, emancipation came about through the efforts of many hands, including military officers, legislators, abolitionists, and slaves whose resistance forced changes in government policies. Yet the limitations of the proclamation were not confined to the border states of Missouri, Kentucky, Maryland, and Delaware. Even in the

Confederate South, most African Americans remained enslaved until the end of the war, and the institution was not banished from American life until the passage of the Thirteenth Amendment in 1865. Emancipation, consequently, wore many faces and took many forms, with its nature shaped by numerous people, by place, and by time.

Lincoln's own words and gestures have added to the complexity of sorting through his motivations and which people or situations to credit for this landmark change in the meaning of freedom. In 1862, he answered an open letter by newspaperman Horace Greeley with the statement that any action he took was to save the Union and not to end slavery. Two years later, he framed a letter that outlined his position on slavery and the war in which he again stated that slavery was secondary to the cause of Union. He took the reasonable position that he could not destroy the government in order to abolish the institution, then added about his own role: "I claim not to have controlled events, but confess plainly that events have controlled me."[2]

Yet this was somewhat disingenuous on Lincoln's part. In August 1863, he had reaffirmed his commitment to the proclamation, refusing to concede emancipation as a bargaining chip for the South to rejoin the Union. He did this again in 1864 when he would not trade emancipation for peace as Union representatives met with Confederates in Canada. The news of his terms angered Democrats who had supported the president, thinking even this late in the conflict that emancipation would only be a temporary measure, limited to the former slaves who had fought for or been freed by contact with the Union army. Democrats conceived of no further revolutionary measures to end slavery forever. If they had had their way, millions of people might have remained enslaved after the war.[3] The president remained committed to emancipation despite political pressures to do away with the policy or to limit its extent to only the slaves freed during the war.

The problem of how to consider Lincoln's proclamation thus originated in the war. Diehard abolitionists were cheered that he came around to issuing the proclamation but were less happy with the time it had taken to act and the limited extent of the provisions. Democratic supporters and opponents of the administration were either consoled by the president's cautious approach or outraged at what appeared to be a revolutionary measure that stretched the Constitution, setting potentially dangerous precedents for the protection of property. People looking at the emancipation process could find evidence to support multiple positions: Lincoln as lukewarm on slavery and committed more to Union; Lincoln as moderate and controlling the contours of abolition; Lincoln as radical who encouraged enlistment of African Americans as soldiers, which made them active agents of abolition.

These varied impressions existed when, on the eleventh anniversary of Abraham Lincoln's assassination, April 14, 1876, a distinguished group of government officials—including President Ulysses S. Grant and Supreme Court justices—gathered for the dedication of the Freedmen's Memorial to Abraham Lincoln. This is the statue that currently sits in Lincoln Park. The effort to memorialize Lincoln and emancipation began with a $ 5 donation from Charlotte Scott, an African American woman, and gained momentum largely from contributions by African Americans— many of them veterans of the U.S. Colored Troops.

Although initiated by African Americans, the memorial created mixed feelings within the black community as the final design and crucial decisions were made by a white committee. Frederick Douglass, the preeminent black American of the mid-nineteenth century, agreed to speak at the dedication of the monument. Like other African Americans, he was dissatisfied with the design of the monument, not the recognition of the martyred president. Douglass thought the monument trivialized the role of the enslaved in bringing about their own liberation by depicting former slaves as dependent upon Lincoln's generosity. Douglass was overheard to say that the statue "showed the negro on his knees when a more manly attitude would have been indicative of freedom."[4] What had emerged was a monument that, to African Americans, portrayed black people as submissive and ignored their contributions to their liberation. It was a depiction most representative of the perceptions of white Americans at the time (and despite these perceptions Lincoln was a popular figure among African Americans).

A few white committee leaders, however, did express apprehension that the monument was not entirely appropriate. Their input caused certain changes to be made in the statue. One modification was to clench the fist of the slave's shackled right hand. The other was to make the figure more realistic by using as a model a man named Archer Alexander, who had been a slave in Missouri. Ironically, the face symbolizing freedom belonged to a man who had been exempted from the president's Emancipation Proclamation. The slave-owning border states that remained

Emancipation Monument, Lincoln Park,
Washington, D.C. Sculpture by Thomas Ball.
Photograph by William A. Blair.

loyal to the Union—Missouri, Kentucky, Maryland, and Delaware—were unaffected by the proclamation, which attacked the institution wherever the Union army advanced in Confederate territory from 1863 onward. Douglass in his oration never referred to this figure, which to him was the opposite of what he would have portrayed as manly.

When Douglass did speak, he must have raised some eyebrows among the white leaders who gathered for the ceremonies. Douglass told the audience about Lincoln: "He was the white man's president, entirely devoted to the welfare of white men." Douglass indicated that Lincoln was as willing as any president to protect slavery where it existed. "You are the children of Abraham Lincoln," he added. "We are at best only his step-children, children by adoption, children by force of circumstance and necessity."[5] Douglass said that though the black race recognized that Lincoln shared in the prejudices of his time, they also exonerated him because he mobilized the country not only to save the Union but also to win the support of the broader public for the abolition of slavery. And Douglass resolved the contradictory impressions of Lincoln better than most—then or now—when he said: "Viewed from the genuine abolition ground, Mr. Lincoln seemed tardy, cold, dull, and indifferent; but measuring him by the sentiment of his country, a sentiment he was bound as a statesman to consult, he was swift, zealous, radical, and determined."[6] Douglass recognized the different impulses that coexist within all human beings.

Despite the ambivalence among black Americans over the unveiling of the Freedmen's Memorial, Lincoln more often than not enjoyed acclaim among the majority of scholars until the middle of the twentieth century when historians such as Richard Hofstadter ridiculed the proclamation as having "all the moral grandeur of a bill of lading." The most strident critic, then and more recently, has been Lerone Bennett Jr., who accused Lincoln of being a white supremacist who resisted emancipation.[7] These scholars have questioned Lincoln's commitment to African Americans, contending that he acted only for white Americans to save the Union, without a keen regard for antislavery. The proclamation's flat prose coupled with the fact that it did not free a single slave who was not already entitled to freedom under legislation passed by Congress the previous year suggest to these scholars that African American freedom lies not with Lincoln and the federal government but with the masses of African Americans who fled to Union army camps at the start of the war and forced Lincoln's government to deal with them.[8] Recently, the trend has been toward defending the president's racial views and considering him, in the words of one scholar, a "masterful anti-slavery leader" who consistently took a radical stance toward ending the institution.[9]

Others in between these poles have acknowledged the president's role in emancipation, crediting him for contributing to the end of slavery, while recognizing that abolition was not the product of one man but of many hands, including those of slaves and free black people.[10] More recently, the pendulum seems to be swinging back to favoring Lincoln's approach to emancipation. Historians such as Allen Guelzo have argued for appreciation of Lincoln's antislavery commitment by considering his support of the proclamation even when members of his own party asked him to consider trading it for peace with the Confederacy. Even Guelzo, who favors interpreting the Emancipation Proclamation as radical, opens his book with a wry comment on the measure—calling it "surely the unhappiest of all of Abraham Lincoln's great presidential papers."[11] By that he means that the proclamation seems to be best remembered for what it did not do and for being written in a complex, legalistic way that guarantees it will rarely be quoted. Whatever one's opinion about Lincoln, and despite the incredible number of works on him and on the abolition of slavery, emancipation remains a fertile subject for exploration—because his is not the only story worth telling.

This collection arose from a symposium on the Emancipation Proclamation held at the Pennsylvania State University in April 2007 as part of the Steven and Janice Brose Distinguished Lecture Series sponsored by the George and Ann Richards Civil War Era Center. The essays in this volume intend to deepen the understanding of the proclamation by considering some aspects of the president's decision making, but to do much more as well. Lincoln remains an important figure, but we wanted to widen the focus beyond Washington and consider the proclamation on a broader stage and from a variety of perspectives, including how we remember the ending of slavery both in the United States and in the Atlantic world. In many respects, the proclamation is not the only centerpiece: the consequences and legacies of freedom provide avenues for fresh exploration, especially the engagement of black Americans in the process and the issues of citizenship and rights that were not decided by Lincoln's document. Together the essays tend to fall in line with studies that consider emancipation as a product of many hands, best understood when considering the various actors, the place, and the time.

When considering Lincoln, two aspects of his life that have attracted great and continued interest have been his racial and religious views. Paul Finkelman first sets the context of the proclamation's creation and how Lincoln arrived at this policy. He argues that critics of Lincoln miss the mark and that the president followed a brilliant strategy in his steps toward emancipation. Mark E. Neely Jr. next considers what he calls the mythology surrounding the president's support of colonization. Neely challenges the prevailing notion that Lincoln offered the voluntary exportation of freed African Americans from the country as a means of making emancipation more palatable politically to more conservative Americans. Neely does not specifically enter the debate about the president's racial views but does assert that Lincoln likely believed in colonization when many in the country did not. It was not a position, Neely maintains, that would have had a beneficial political impact, as many others have alleged. The study fits a current trend to see Lincoln's racial beliefs as more complicated than the simple dichotomy of racist or not—to portray Lincoln as holding varying, sometimes contradictory positions that also changed over time. Next, Richard Carwardine resurrects a meeting that the president had with ministers from Chicago, who encouraged the Union leader to issue his proclamation. Most scholars have dismissed the meeting as having little or no impact, but Carwardine raises good reasons for reassessing the meeting and Lincoln's attention to the religious community in general. It is possible that the president gained insights into popular opinion by keeping tabs on the mood of mainstream Protestant denominations. Carwardine does not specifically comment on the composition of the president's religious values and practices, but his analysis adds to the current tendency among scholars to see Lincoln as being sensitive to religious themes and thought, despite not being a traditional churchgoer.

The subsequent two authors examine various ways that African Americans contributed to the meaning of freedom. In "What Did the Slaves Think about Lincoln?" Steven Hahn shows how the Emancipation Proclamation can lead to an exploration of the political consciousness of the enslaved. This way of thinking about slaves—as engaging in political activities—opens new ways to consider organization within the African

American community and the forging of similar attitudes and stances that cut across plantation and nonplantation districts. Slaves may not have voted, but they could watch the reactions of masters to such things as the coming of the war and the proclamation. They could conclude that an enemy of a master might well be a friend. And the knowledge might embolden them to further acts of resistance on the plantation. Their resistance through flight might even help influence a president to consider using emancipation as a weapon against the Confederates. More to the point, Hahn attempts to restore the interpretation of W. E. B. Du Bois, who defined what the slaves did during the war as a rebellion. To reach this conclusion, Hahn brings in analysis of the slave uprising in St. Domingue, or current-day Haiti.[12]

Stephanie McCurry, meanwhile, asks us to consider the implications of gender and race, as she raises the intriguing question: how could black women establish citizenship? She points out that emancipation accomplished during wartime typically privileges military service as the means of achieving freedom. But citizenship tended to be gendered in another way in the nineteenth century—as something that could be achieved through marriage. She explains that "slave men took the martial route to emancipation, and slave women, apparently, the marital one, which is to say that women got freedom at second hand, by way of marriage and in relation to their husbands' rights." The attention on the male route to freedom has left a gap in our understanding of the experiences and perceptions of slave women—how they struggled for, and understood, their liberation. McCurry also underscores the influences of region and time, as she examines her question both early and later in the war—and within the Union-occupied Mississippi River Valley and border states. She, too, uses St. Domingue as one means of understanding the dynamics of emancipation through martial means.

Citizenship, though, had additional dimensions beyond gender. Michael Vorenberg explores the complicated, even frustratingly ambiguous nature of citizenship in the nineteenth century. Lincoln's proclamation did not deal with what happened to the slaves who were freed. Their status within the nation remained uncertain, especially because the *Dred Scott* ruling by the Supreme Court in 1857 had determined that any person of color in the United States could not be considered a citizen legally. Vorenberg shows that Lincoln did not quite take the lead on this issue. He also offers a creative and more precise way of thinking about the definition of a citizen, breaking it down into three distinct types. The Constitution is strikingly quiet about the rights that go with citizenship. Authorities at the time, such as Attorney General Edward Bates, wrestled with the differences between what Vorenberg terms legal citizenship (who belongs) and civic citizenship (what rights do they enjoy). And he adds one more kind of citizenship to consider: affective, or that loyalty which arises from within an individual.

Louis Gerteis looks at other issues that the proclamation did not resolve. He considers emancipation from the perspective of the border states, and finds that although they were exempted from the proclamation they were not unaffected by its provisions. Once the proclamation took effect, and federal authorities began to enlist African Americans in the military, slavery began to unravel as an institution. Gerteis sees the process coming slowly but inexorably in the border region, with loyal planters using all means at their disposal—including civil government— to attempt to stem the tide. But it was to no avail, largely in part because of the energy of the slaves themselves, who took advantage of the situation whenever possible. Yet their actions occurred within channels established by the government and supervised by federal authorities. Like McCurry, Gerteis shows that the most clear-cut and quickest path to freedom was through enlistment in military service. He ends his essay with new information on the establishment of Emancipation Day celebrations in the region. While these commemorative events have become better known, more often than not historians have looked either at those in the Confederate South or the North. Gerteis affirms the importance of remembering emancipation for African Americans in the border region and of the central role of black veterans.

The issue of how to remember the proclamation and emancipation remains a difficult one today. We justifiably celebrate Lincoln, but we do not commemorate the abolition of slavery—one of the most important milestones of U.S. history. William Blair ends the collection with some thoughts on the problem of commemorating freedom, especially when it also conjures the memory of slavery. When studying this phenomenon, he suggests that scholars should consider the differing layers and competing forms of civic ceremonies, in which vernacular celebrations may go unrecognized by "national" traditions. He also extends his view to the Atlantic world and finds that it is more common than not for nations to overlook emancipation as part of their civic rituals and holidays.

The essays as a whole point to a reconsideration of the conventional wisdom concerning aspects of Lincoln and emancipation. Among much of the public, emancipation remains imperfectly understood as an event with a singular viewpoint. The authors of this book remind us that the act of emancipation elicits multiple perspectives, similar to the way different people see different things in the statue in Lincoln Park. And even for historians, who have written thousands of books on the subject over the course of nearly 150 years, there remain undiscovered historical treasures, although these will inevitably modify rather than completely revise our understanding of a man who has been the subject of an estimated 10,000 books, not to mention the numerous volumes analyzing the measures that ended slavery. Even Frederick Douglass understood the daunting challenge of capturing the complexity of the president during the unveiling of the Freedmen's Memorial in 1876. At one point he observed: "Any man can say things that are true of Abraham Lincoln, but no man can say anything that is new of Abraham Lincoln."[13] Yet he tried to do so anyway; as do we.

Notes

1. For good descriptions of the origins and complicated impressions of the statue, see Kirk Savage's *Standing Soldiers, Kneeling Slaves: Race, War, and Monument in Nineteenth-Century America* (Princeton: Princeton University Press, 1997), 89–122; Kathryn Allamong Jacob, *Testament to Union: Civil War Monuments in Washington, D.C.* (Baltimore: Johns Hopkins University Press, 1998), 24–27.

2. Abraham Lincoln to A. G. Hodges, April 4, 1864, Abraham Lincoln Papers, Library of Congress, Washington, D.C.

3. Allen C. Guelzo, "Defending Emancipation: Abraham Lincoln and the Conkling Letter, 1863," *Civil War History* 48 (December 2002): 313–37; Abraham Lincoln to Charles D. Robinson, August 17, 1864, Abraham Lincoln Papers, Library of Congress, Washington, D.C.

4. Quoted in Savage, *Standing Soldiers, Kneeling Slaves*, 117.

5. Frederick Douglass, *Oration by Frederick Douglass Delivered at the Occasion of the Unveiling of the Freedmen's Monument in Memory of Abraham Lincoln, in Lincoln Park, Washington, D.C., April 14th, 1876* (Washington, D.C.: Gibson Brothers, 1876), 5, in Frederick Douglass Papers, Library of Congress, Washington, D.C.

6. Douglass, *Oration at the Unveiling of the Freedmen's Monument*, 10.

7. Richard Hofstadter, *The American Political Tradition and the Men Who Made It* (1948; reprint, New York: Knopf, 1973), 129; Lerone Bennett Jr., "Was Lincoln a White Supremacist?" *Ebony*, February 1968, 35–38; and *Forced into Glory: Abraham Lincoln's White Dream* (Chicago: Johnson Publishing, 2000).

8. Works by Barbara Fields, David Donald, and the editors of the Freedmen and Southern Society Project position the president more passively as a moderate. Among the many volumes published by the Freedmen and Southern Society Project is Ira Berlin et al., eds., *Free at Last: A Documentary History of Slavery, Freedom, and the Civil War* (New York: New Press, 1992).

9. Richard Striner, *Father Abraham: Lincoln's Relentless Struggle to End Slavery* (New York: Oxford University Press, 2006), 1.

10. LaWanda Cox, *Lincoln and Black Freedom: A Study in Presidential Leadership* (Columbia: University of South Carolina Press, 1981); James M. McPherson, *Battle Cry of Freedom: The Civil War Era* (New York: Oxford University Press, 1988), and "Who Freed the Slaves?" *Reconstruction* 2 (1994): 35–40; Harry Jaffa, *A New Birth of Freedom: Abraham Lincoln and the Coming of the Civil War* (Lanham, Md.: Rowman & Littlefield, 2000); David Blight, *Race and Reunion: The Civil War in American Memory* (Cambridge: Harvard University Press, 2001).

11. Allen C. Guelzo, *Lincoln's Emancipation Proclamation: The End of Slavery in America* (New York: Simon & Schuster, 2004), 1.

12. W. E. B. Du Bois, *Black Reconstruction in America, 1860–1880* (New York: Atheneum, 1935).

13. Douglass, *Oration at the Unveiling of the Freedmen's Monument,* 9.

PAUL FINKELMAN

Lincoln and the Preconditions for Emancipation

The Moral Grandeur of a Bill of Lading

In 1948 the great historian Richard Hofstadter began a frontal assault on the iconic image of Abraham Lincoln in American history and culture. Hofstadter's Lincoln was a cynical politician, "among the world's great political propagandists."[1] Since then other scholars have focused on the racist language in some of Lincoln's prepresidential speeches, his support of colonization long after it was discredited, and his refusal until late in his administration to support black political rights.

Most controversial of all has been the evaluation of Lincoln's commitment to black freedom and the nature and timing of the Emancipation Proclamation. It took Lincoln more than a year to propose emancipation and even then he seemed to vacillate, apparently willing to withdraw the preliminary proclamation if the rebellious states would return to the Union.[2] He did not issue the final Emancipation Proclamation until nearly two years into the war. When finally issued, the proclamation did not free all the slaves in the United States. Hofstadter offers a caustic critique of the final document. Lincoln was one of the greatest craftsmen of the English language in American political history. But here, in the most important moment of his life, he is a pettifogger, drafting a turgid and almost incomprehensible legal document that had, in Hofstadter's words, "all the moral grandeur of a bill of lading."[3] Unlike almost everything else Lincoln wrote, the proclamation itself was dull. Even historians who admire Lincoln think it was "boring" and "pedestrian."[4]

On the surface, these criticisms of Lincoln are somewhat plausible. In the end, however, a careful understanding of Lincoln's own ideology and philosophy, the constraints of the Constitution, and the nature of the Civil War suggest that such attacks ultimately miss their mark. Lincoln's strategy and policy turn out to be subtle, at times brilliant, and ultimately effective, as slavery came to an end everywhere in the nation with the ratification of the Thirteenth Amendment in 1865.

AS A COMPETENT and successful lawyer, and a student of the U.S. Constitution, Lincoln began his presidency with a strong sense of the limitations that the Constitution placed on any emancipation scheme. In his first inaugural address he urged the seven states that claimed to have left the Union to cease their efforts to secede and return to their proper political relationship within the United States. In making this case Lincoln reminded these Deep South states that slavery was safe within the Union. Quoting from a speech he made before his election, Lincoln declared: "I have no purpose, directly or indirectly, to interfere with the institution of slavery in the States where it exists. I believe I have no lawful right to do so, and I have no inclination to do so." He then reiterated the point by quoting the Republican Party platform: "The maintenance inviolate of the rights of the States, and especially the right of each State to order and control its own domestic institutions according to its own judgment exclusively, is essential to that balance of power on which the perfection and endurance of our political fabric depend; and we denounce the lawless invasion by armed force of the soil of any State or Territory, no matter what pretext, as among the gravest of crimes." Lincoln promised "that all the protection which, consistently with the Constitution and the laws, can be given, will be cheerfully given to all the States when lawfully demanded, for whatever cause—as cheerfully to one section as to another."[5]

This position reflected an orthodox and well-understood interpretation of the U.S. Constitution that had never been successfully challenged in law or politics. In 1787 the understanding of the Constitution by all parties was quite clear: the national government had no power to interfere with the "domestic institutions" of the states. Thus the states, and not the national government, had sole power to regulate all laws concerning personal status, such as those regarding marriage, divorce, child custody, inheritance, voting, and freedom—whether one was a slave or a free person. As Gen. Charles Cotesworth Pinckney told the South Carolina House of Representatives after the Constitutional Convention: "We have a security that the general government can never emancipate them [slaves], for no such authority is granted and it is admitted, on all hands, that the general government has no powers but what are expressly granted by the

Constitution, and that all rights not expressed were reserved by the several states."[6]

The development of American constitutional law from ratification to Lincoln's election reaffirmed Pinckney's understanding of the Constitution: that it created a government of limited powers and that any powers not explicitly given to the national government were retained by the states. Constitutional jurisprudence in the three decades before Lincoln took office not only had strengthened this understanding but also had expanded it to actually encroach on the powers of Congress. Except for a few constitutional outliers, such as Lysander Spooner, no antebellum politicians or legal scholars believed Congress had the power to regulate slavery in the states. In 1860 a claim of federal power to end slavery in the states was simply unthinkable for someone like Lincoln, who took law and constitutionalism seriously.

In addition to the constitutional limitation on federal power, there was also an issue of property rights. The Fifth Amendment to the Constitution declares that "no person . . . shall be deprived of life, liberty, or property, without due process of law; nor shall private property be taken for public use without just compensation." In *Dred Scott v. Sandford* (1857) Chief Justice Roger B. Taney had used this clause to strike down federal legislation banning slavery in the territories. Lincoln and most Republicans rejected the legitimacy of that portion of the decision,[7] arguing that Congress could ban slavery from the territories. But there was a huge difference between banning slavery in new territories and taking slave property from people in the states or even in federal jurisdictions such as Washington, D.C., where slavery was legal. Lincoln, like almost all lawyers at the time, understood that even *if* Congress had the power to take slaves from American citizens, it could only be done through compensation, as required by the Fifth Amendment.

When Lincoln entered office he understood that he had "no lawful right" to "interfere with the institution of slavery in the States where it exists." In his attempt to bring the seceding states back into the Union he also declared, "I have no inclination to do so." This statement in his inaugural address could be interpreted to mean that Lincoln had no personal interest or desire in ending slavery. But Lincoln chose his words carefully. His personal views on slavery were clear: he hated slavery and had always believed that "if slavery is not wrong, nothing is wrong."[8] But his personal desires could not overcome the constitutional realities of his age. Because he had no power to touch slavery where it existed, he could honestly say he had no inclination to attempt to do what was constitutionally impossible. Consistent with his long-standing Whig ideology, Lincoln rejected the idea of acting outside the Constitution. Reflecting his sense of the politically possible, Lincoln willingly reassured the seceding states that he did not intend to attempt what he could not constitutionally, legally, or politically accomplish. When circumstances changed, so would Lincoln's "inclination," but in March 1861 Lincoln had no reason to foresee such changes.

Lincoln's constitutional understandings in 1861 were hardly new. He had articulated them in the Illinois legislature in 1837, when the twenty-eight-year-old representative was one of six members of the Illinois state assembly to vote against a proslavery resolution that was supported by eighty-three members of that body. The resolution declared that the right to own slaves was "sacred to the slaveholding States." Not only did Lincoln vote against this resolution, but he also joined one other representative in framing his own resolution, asserting that slavery was "founded on both injustice and bad policy." In this protest against the actions of the majority in the legislature, Lincoln asserted the traditional understanding that the national government had "no power, under the constitution, to interfere with the institution of slavery in the different States." However, Lincoln also asserted, again consistent with traditional constitutional understandings, that Congress did have "the power under the constitution, to abolish slavery in the District of Columbia."[9] This early foray into the constitutional issues of slavery suggests that Lincoln, even as a young man, understood the constitutional limitations as well as the constitutional possibilities of fighting slavery.

A decade later, in his single term in Congress, Lincoln proposed a bill for the gradual abolition of slavery in the District of Columbia. Such an emancipation scheme would avoid the Fifth Amendment problem of taking property without due process or just compensation, because gradual emancipation did not free any existing slaves but only guaranteed that their as-yet-unborn children would be free. Lincoln read the proposed emancipation bill on the floor of Congress but in the end did not introduce it. A powerless freshman Congressman, he explained, "I was abandoned by my former backers."[10] In fact, with the acrimonious debates over the Wilmot Proviso tearing Congress apart, a serious discussion of a bill to end slavery in the district was not even remotely plausible. Nevertheless, this bill, like his state legislative resolution, underscores that Lincoln was always interested in ending slavery where he could, but that he had not adopted a radical abolitionist vision of ending slavery everywhere in the United States through federal action.

This, then, was the constitutional framework with regard to slavery that Lincoln understood as he entered the White House. He personally hated slavery—he was "naturally antislavery" and could "not remember when" he "did not so think, and feel."[11] But he understood the constitutional limitations on his actions.

Even as he understood this, he knew, as all Americans did, that slavery was the reason for secession and the cause of the war. Almost every southern ordinance of secession made this clear. Consequently, it may seem that attacking slavery should have been the first goal of the Lincoln administration. Root out the problem, destroy the institution, and the Union could be restored. Such a simplistic response did not comport with the reality of the crisis Lincoln faced. As much as he hated slavery and would have liked to destroy it, Lincoln understood that an assault on slavery required the complete or partial fulfillment of four essential preconditions.

FROM THE MOMENT the war began, Lincoln faced demands for emancipation. Abolitionists and antislavery Republicans wanted Lincoln to make the conflict a war against slavery. Northern free blacks were anxious to serve in a war of liberation. From the beginning of the war slaves escaped to U.S. Army lines where they assumed (usually correctly) that they would find freedom. But seriously committed opponents of slavery in the North were relatively few in number, and southern slaves had no political influence, at least in the first year of the war. Most northerners wanted a quick end to the conflict and a restoration of the Union. Emancipation did not fit into that formula, just as it did not fit into any generally recognized interpretation of the Constitution.

Early attempts at emancipation—such as Gen. John C. Frémont's precipitate proclamation freeing slaves in Missouri—illustrate the complexity of the issue and the delicate handling the goal of achieving black freedom required. Many abolitionists (and some modern-day critics of Lincoln) bristled at the idea that achieving freedom could demand delicacy.[12] Their position was relatively straightforward: slavery was immoral and wrong, and slavery was the cause of the war. Ending slavery would be a great humanitarian act, one that was justified by the southern states' secession. The president, however, was not prepared to accept such a facile and simplistic solution. Emancipation required the convergence of four preconditions in the context of the war effort, legal understanding, and popular ideology. Without these preconditions emancipation was both meaningless and impossible.

First, Lincoln needed a constitutional or legal framework for taking slaves—the private property of masters—and for freeing those slaves. Mere hostility to the United States by slave owners was not a sufficient reason for taking their property from them. Creating a legal framework was complicated by the different statuses of the slave states. Four of the slave states—Maryland, Delaware, Kentucky, and Missouri—had not joined the Confederacy. Their citizens still enjoyed all of the protections of the U.S. Constitution, and neither Congress nor the president had any power to interfere with these states' domestic institutions, including slavery. Lincoln did believe Congress could end slavery in the District of Columbia, the Indian Territory, and other federal territories such as Utah and Nebraska. However, emancipation in those places would presumably require compensation, since the Fifth Amendment to the Constitution prohibited the taking of private property without due process of law and just compensation. This provision of the Constitution would also hold true for ending slavery in the loyal slave states, if Lincoln somehow found a constitutionally acceptable method of doing that.

The status of citizens of the new Confederacy was much less clear. Lincoln claimed that secession was illegal and that the Confederacy could not legally exist. If this were true, then presumably the citizens of the Confederacy were still protected by the Constitution. Combatants, on the other hand, might not be as protected by the Constitution, but even here the legal issues were complicated. Personal property used in combat—a weapon, a wagon, or a horse—could of course be confiscated on the battlefield. This would be true whether the combat was with Confederate soldiers in uniform or pro-Confederate guerrillas in civilian clothes. Presumably, slaves used in a combat situation—such as teamsters—might also be seized. Beyond that the government had no power to take property from combatants.

Thus, at the beginning of the war there was no clear legal theory on which emancipation might proceed. Emancipation without such a theory would doubtless have been overturned by the Supreme Court. At the beginning of the war every one of the six justices on the United States Supreme Court was a proslavery Democrat.[13] Five of the justices, including Chief Justice Taney, had been part of the majority in *Dred Scott* and had held that the Fifth Amendment protected slave property in the territories. The sixth, Nathan Clifford, was a classic doughface—a northern man with southern principles—who could be expected to support slavery and oppose emancipation. Taney, a "seething secessionist," in fact drafted an opinion striking down emancipation just in case he had the opportunity to use it.[14] Lincoln could reasonably expect the court to strike down any emancipation act that was not constitutionally impregnable.

Second, even if Lincoln could develop a coherent legal and constitutional theory to justify emancipation, he still needed to have the political support to move against slavery. Most northerners disliked slavery but were not prepared for a long bloody crusade against it. Even Republicans such as Salmon P. Chase and William H. Seward, who had been battling slavery all their adult lives, did not think there was sufficient public support yet to attack it. Lincoln, who was already on his way to becoming a master politician, needed to create the circumstances necessary to make emancipation an acceptable wartime goal. The war began as one to save the Union, an objective that commanded support among almost all northerners. Lincoln could not afford to jeopardize that support by moving too quickly to turn on slavery, despite his deep hatred for the institution.

Third, Lincoln needed to secure the four loyal slave states before he could move against slavery. The demographics were crucial. There were more than 2.5 million whites living in these states. If Missouri and Kentucky seceded they would become the second- and third-largest states in the Confederacy. More important, they would be the largest and third-largest states in terms of the crucial white population that would provide troops for the Confederacy. The border slave states could also provide three of the four largest cities in the Confederacy—Baltimore, St. Louis, and Louisville—dwarfing all other Confederate cities except New Orleans.[15] Strategically the border states were even more important. If Maryland joined the Confederacy the nation's capital would be completely surrounded by the enemy. If Missouri joined the rebel nation there would be a Confederate army on the upper Mississippi poised to threaten Lincoln's home state of Illinois and penetrate into Iowa and Minnesota.

Most crucial of all was Kentucky. A Confederate army on the southern bank of the Ohio River would interrupt east-west commerce and troop movements, threaten the vast agricultural heartland of Ohio, Indiana, and Illinois, and endanger key cities, including Cincinnati, Chicago, Indianapolis, and Pittsburgh. With more than 200,000 slaves in the state, Kentucky was vulnerable to Confederate entreaties. An abrupt movement toward emancipation would push the bluegrass state into the hands of the enemy, which would probably send Missouri to the Confederacy as well. Early in the war a group of ministers urged Lincoln to free the slaves because, they said, God would be on his side. He allegedly responded, "I hope to have God on my side, but I must have Kentucky."[16] Early emancipation would almost certainly have cost Lincoln that crucial state, and possibly the war.

This leads to the fourth precondition for emancipation: the actual possibility of a military victory. Lincoln could only move to end slavery if he could win the war; if he attacked slavery and did not win the war, then he accomplished nothing. This analysis turns modern critiques of Lincoln on their head. Critics of Lincoln argue that he eventually moved toward emancipation for military and diplomatic reasons: because he needed black troops to repopulate his army and to prevent Britain and France from giving diplomatic recognition to the Confederacy. Emancipation is explained as a desperate act to save the Union by a man who was, as Lerone Bennett put it, "forced into glory" by circumstances.

The chronology of emancipation does not support this analysis. Both Lincoln and Congress began to move toward emancipation only after a series of U.S. victories in early 1862. Lincoln then waited to announce emancipation until after a major victory that stopped Lee's army dead in its tracks—with huge casualties—at Antietam. Early emancipation would have probably thrown Kentucky and Missouri into the Confederacy and perhaps doomed the Union cause. While emancipation may be properly seen as one of the elements of victory, it must also be seen as an outcome of the likelihood of Union success. Though likely possible without emancipation (which even the use of black troops did not necessarily require), victory would have been more difficult and perhaps taken longer. But, while victory was possible without emancipation, emancipation was clearly impossible without victory. Conditions looked bright after Antietam, when the preliminary proclamation was announced, and Lincoln assumed they would look just as positive in a hundred days, when he planned to sign the proclamation on January 1, 1863. Thus, rather than being forced into glory when he announced emancipation, Lincoln understood that moral glory—emancipation—could only be possible through military glory.

NONE OF THE four preconditions for emancipation existed in the summer of 1861. Nevertheless, the push for emancipation would not wait until all of the circumstances allowed for it. In the first half-year of the war Lincoln faced three different models for attacking slavery. Two of these models satisfied the first three preconditions: there was a legal/ constitutional basis for these two modes; they would not undermine northern support for the war; and they would not chase Kentucky and Missouri out of the Union. The third one, Gen. John C. Frémont's proclamation freeing slaves in Missouri, failed all of these tests, and Lincoln wisely overruled it.

The first model involved slaves who simply left their masters and fled to the safety and protection of the U.S. Army. In exercising self-emancipation these fleeing slaves created the need for clever lawyering and a clear government policy, even when no one in the administration was ready to develop such a policy. In his second inaugural Abraham Lincoln would assert that in 1861 "all knew" that slavery "was somehow the cause of the war." However, when the war began the administration could not focus its energies on destroying the cause of the war because of the lack of preconditions necessary to attack slavery. The slaves, however, were under no such constraints. They knew, even more than their masters or the blue-clad enemies of their masters that this war was about slavery—about them and their future. While Lincoln bided his time, waiting for the moment to strike against slavery, hundreds and then thousands of slaves struck out for freedom.

The war had hardly begun when slaves began to stream into the camps and forts of the U.S. Army. The army was not a social welfare agency and was institutionally unprepared to feed, clothe, or house masses of propertyless refugees. Initially the army returned slaves to masters who came after them. This situation undermined the morale of U.S. troops, who fully understood that they were returning valuable property to their enemies, and more important, that those enemies would use that property to make war on them. Slaves grew the food that fed the Confederate army, raised and cared for the horses the Confederates rode into battle, and labored in the workshops and factories that produced the metals and weapons necessary to fight the war.[17] As Frederick Douglass noted, "The very stomach of this Rebellion is the negro in the form of a slave." Douglass correctly understood that if you "arrest that hoe in the hands of the Negro, . . . you smite the rebellion in the very seat of its life."[18] Returning slaves to Confederate masters was hardly different than returning guns or horses to them. Initially, however, some army officers did just that.

On May 23 three slaves owned by Confederate colonel Charles K. Mallory escaped to Fortress Monroe in Hampton, Virginia, under the command of Gen. Benjamin F. Butler. A day later Butler faced the surrealistic spectacle of Confederate major M. B. Carey approaching under a flag of truce to demand the return of the slaves under the fugitive slave law. Major Carey, identifying himself as Mallory's agent, argued that Butler had a constitutional obligation to return the slaves under the fugitive slave clause of the Constitution and the Fugitive Slave Law of 1850. Butler had been a successful Massachusetts lawyer before the war and had devoted some thought to the issue. He told Carey that the slaves were contrabands of war because they had been used to build fortifications for the Confederacy. They could not be returned to Mallory.[19] As Butler reported to his superiors, he told Carey "that the fugitive slave act did not affect a foreign country, which Virginia claimed to be and she must reckon it one of the infelicities of her position that in so far at least she was taken at her word." Butler then offered to return the slaves to Colonel Mallory if he would come to Fortress Monroe and "take the oath of allegiance to the Constitution of the United States."[20]

This was the end of Colonel Mallory's attempt to recover his slaves, but it was the beginning of a new policy for the United States. Butler, in need of workers, immediately employed the three fugitives. His refusal to return what he considered contrabands of war served the dual purposes of depriving the enemy of labor while providing labor for the United States.

The policy, however, was not applied everywhere at once. By the middle of the summer slaves poured into U.S. forts and camps, where troops had conflicting orders regarding the refugees. Some officers returned slaves to all masters; others only returned them to loyal masters in Maryland, Kentucky, and Missouri. Some offered sanctuary to all slaves who entered their lines.

Clarity of sorts came from Secretary of War Simon Cameron on August 8, when he informed Butler of the president's desire "that all existing rights in all the States be fully respected and maintained" and that the

"Gen. Ben. Butler."
Courtesy of the
Library of Congress.

war was "for the Union and for the preservation of all constitutional rights of States and the citizens of the States in the Union." Because of this, "no question can arise as to fugitives from service within the States and Territories in which the authority of the Union is fully acknowledged." This of course meant that military commanders could not free fugitive slaves in Missouri, Kentucky, Maryland, and Delaware. But the president also understood that "in States wholly or partially under insurrectionary control" the laws could not be enforced, and that it was "equally obvious that rights dependent on the laws of the States within which military operations are conducted must be necessarily subordinated to the military exigencies created by the insurrection if not wholly forfeited by the treasonable conduct of the parties claiming them." Most important, "rights to services" could "form no exception" to "this general rule."[21]

The policy seemed to be that in the border slave states the military would return fugitive slaves, but not in the Confederate states. The slaves of masters loyal to the Union who lived in the Confederacy presented a "more difficult question." The solution was to have the army employ the fugitives, but to keep a record of such employment, so at some point loyal masters might be compensated for the use of their slaves. Cameron, speaking for the president, admonished Butler neither to encourage slaves to abscond, nor to interfere with the "servants of peaceful citizens" even in the Confederacy, nor to interfere in the voluntary return of fugitives to their masters, "except in cases where the public safety" would "seem to require" such interference.[22]

By late August Butler's contraband policy had become the norm. The U.S. Army could employ any slaves who ran to its lines, provided they came from Confederate states. This was not a general emancipation policy, and indeed, the army had been admonished not to deliberately attempt to free slaves. But the army would not return fugitive slaves to masters in the Confederate states, even if the masters claimed to be loyal to the United States. Shrewdly, the Lincoln administration had become part of the process of ending slavery while professing not to be doing so. To placate abolitionists the administration could point to the growing thousands of "contrabands" who were being paid a salary and often wearing the only clothing available, blue uniforms.[23]

This emerging policy began with a general's response to a Confederate colonel and was soon adopted by the Department of War and the president. It was not a direct attack on slavery, and it was not an emancipation policy, per se. It did protect the freedom of thousands of slaves who were developing their own strategy of self-emancipation by running to the U.S. Army. By the time Secretary of War Cameron spelled out the policy to General Butler, Congress had endorsed it and pushed it further along with the First Confiscation Act.

On August 6 Congress passed the First Confiscation Act, which allowed for the seizure of any slaves used for military purposes by the Confederacy.[24] This was not a general emancipation act and was narrowly written to allow the confiscation of slaves only in actual use by Confederate forces. No slave owners in the border states, even those sympathetic to the Confederacy, were put in jeopardy. Freeing slaves under the Confiscation Act might have violated the Fifth Amendment if seen as allowing a taking of private property without due process. There was no such risk in a military context. Surely the army could seize a weapon in the hands of a captured Confederate soldier without a due process hearing, or take a horse from a captured Confederate. Similarly, slaves working on fortifications or being used in other military capacities might be taken.

Ambiguous and cumbersome, the First Confiscation Act did not threaten slavery as an institution. It merely allowed for the seizure of those slaves—relatively few in number—being used specifically for military purposes. However, the Confiscation Act did indicate a political shift toward emancipation. It was not decisive, because the emancipatory aspects of the law were limited, but it did show that Congress was ready to support some kind of emancipation. Neither Congress nor the American people were ready to turn the military conflict into an all-out war against slavery; however, Congress—which presumably reflected the ideology of its constituents—was ready to allow the government to free some slaves in the struggle against the Confederacy.

This law, along with the contraband policy, can be seen as a major step toward eventual public support for emancipation. In the Confiscation Act, Congress embraced the principle that the national government had the power to free slaves as a military necessity. The logical extension of this posture could be the total destruction of slavery. If Congress could free some slaves through the Confiscation Act, or the executive branch could free some slaves through the contraband policy, then the two branches might be able to free all slaves if the military and social conditions warranted such a result.

On August 30, just a few weeks after Lincoln signed the Confiscation Act, Maj. Gen. John C. Frémont declared martial law in Missouri and announced that all slaves owned by Confederate activists in that state were free.[25] This order went well beyond the Confiscation Act. Lincoln immediately and unambiguously urged Frémont to withdraw his proclamation, pointing out that it undermined efforts to keep Kentucky in the Union: "I think there is great danger that the closing paragraph, in relation to the confiscation of property, and the liberating slaves of traitorous owners, will alarm our Southern Union friends, and turn them against us—perhaps ruin our rather fair prospect for Kentucky." Thus he asked the general to "modify" his proclamation, "on his own motion," to align with the Confiscation Act. Aware of the exaggerated egos of his generals, Lincoln noted: "This letter is written in a spirit of caution and not of censure."[26]

While Lincoln waited for Frémont to act, letters poured in from border state unionists urging the president to directly countermand Frémont's order. One Kentucky Unionist told Lincoln: "There is not a day to lose in disavowing emancipation or Kentucky is gone over the mill dam."[27] Lincoln understood the issue. He told Senator Orville Browning that "to lose Kentucky is nearly . . . to lose the whole game."[28] Lincoln hoped that Frémont—who had been the Republican candidate for president in 1856—would be politically savvy enough to withdraw the order.

Frémont, hoping to score points with the abolitionist wing of the Republican Party, embarrass Lincoln, and set himself up to be the Republican candidate in 1864, refused to comply with the request of his commander in chief. Instead of withdrawing his proclamation, Frémont asked Lincoln to formally countermand it, which would in effect allow Frémont to later blame the president for undermining emancipation. Lincoln "cheerfully" did so, ordering Frémont to modify the proclamation. Still playing politics, Frémont claimed he never received the order but only read about it in the newspapers, and he continued to distribute his original proclamation.[29] Frémont's stubbornness, lack of political sense, and military incompetence led to his dismissal by Lincoln on November 2, 1861.[30] He would get another command and fail there, and by the end of the war Frémont would be marginalized and irrelevant.

Lincoln's response to Frémont has been condemned by many scholars as illustrating his insensitivity to black freedom. Here was a perfect moment to strike a blow against slavery. Frémont was a national hero and a popular general. By supporting his abolitionist general, critics of Lincoln argue, the president could have turned the war into a crusade against slavery. Unlike Frémont, Lincoln understood that an unwinnable war would not end slavery, it would only destroy the Union and permanently secure slavery in the new Confederate nation. His comments to Frémont bear out his realistic assessment that if Kentucky, and perhaps Missouri, joined the Confederacy, the war might be lost. Frémont's proclamation jeopardized Kentucky and that led Lincoln to overturn it. The fall of 1861 was simply not the time to begin an attack on slavery, especially in the loyal border states.

Lincoln did not respond to Frémont with a lecture on constitutional law, but he might have. Freeing slaves in the Confederacy who were being used for military purposes was probably constitutional. Freeing slaves *within* the United States—which included Missouri—was probably not constitutional unless those slaves were being used in active resistance against the government. Thus, the First Confiscation Act could have been used to free slaves being used by pro-Confederate forces in Missouri for military purposes; however, this is not what Frémont wanted to do. He wanted to take slaves who were not directly being used for military purposes and were the property of people living in the United States. Because Missouri had not seceded, Confederate sympathizers who were not involved in direct combat were still protected by the Constitution. Thus Frémont's plan would have violated the Constitution by seizing property from U.S. citizens without due process or just compensation.

Lincoln was attacked by some in the abolitionist wing of the Republican Party for his response to the Missouri proclamation. Privately he assured Senator Charles Sumner that the difference between them on emancipation was only a matter of time—a month or six weeks. Sumner accepted this statement and promised to "not say another word to you about it till the longest time you name has passed by."[31] The time would in fact be more like a year, but there is little reason to doubt that Lincoln was moving toward some sort of abolition plan.

For Lincoln there were two paramount issues to consider. The first was timing. He could only attack slavery if he could win the war; if he attacked slavery and did not win the war, then he accomplished nothing. Critics of Lincoln argue that he eventually moved toward emancipation because he needed black troops to win the war. But, the alternative reading—starting with his correspondence with Frémont—is that he could only move against slavery after he had secured the border states and made certain that victory was possible. Only then could he make emancipation actually work. Rather than a desperate act to save the war effort, emancipation becomes the logical fruit of victory. Frémont's proclamation surely did not fit that bill; consequently, Lincoln countermanded it.

LINCOLN CLEARLY UNDERESTIMATED the time needed before he could move against slavery. The preconditions he needed for emancipation did not emerge in the month or six weeks he forecast to Sumner. A call for emancipation had to be tied to a realistic belief that the war could be won; there was no point in telling slaves they were free if the government could not enforce that freedom. The prospect of a military victory was not great in the fall of 1861. The embarrassing defeats at the first battle of Bull Run and Ball's Bluff did not bode well for the future. In December the Senate passed resolutions that led to the formation of the Joint Committee on the Conduct of the War.[32]

The first half of the next year, however, would be "one of the brightest periods of the war for the North."[33] In fact, this bright period began before the new year and continued for almost six months in 1862. In November 1861 Admiral Samuel du Pont had successfully seized the South Carolina Sea Islands with the important naval base at Port Royal. Once this beachhead on the South Carolina coast was established, the United States would never be dislodged from it. At least some of the war would now be fought in the heartland of the South.[34] Although Lincoln could not yet know it, this was the beginning of the shrinking of the Confederacy. In February, Roanoke Island in North Carolina was captured, and by the end of April the navy and army had captured or sealed off every Confederate port on the Atlantic except Charleston, South Carolina, and Wilmington, North Carolina. Ports such as Savannah, Georgia, remained in Confederate hands, but the rebels no longer had access to the ocean except through blockade runners, who had virtually no effect on the Confederate war effort.

In the West, the United States won a series of crucial victories, securing Kentucky for the Union. Although the Kentucky legislature had voted in September to stay in the Union, support for the Confederacy remained strong in the Bluegrass State. The state's governor, Beriah Magoffin, had resigned to join the Confederacy. In November General McClellan had told Gen. Don Carlos Buell that it was "absolutely necessary that we shall hold all the State of Kentucky" and to make sure that "the majority of its inhabitants shall be warmly in favor of our cause." McClellan believed that the conduct of the "political affairs in Kentucky" was perhaps "more important than that of our military operations." He wanted to ensure that the United States Army respected the "domestic institution"—slavery— in the state.[35]

Underscoring McClellan's concern, later that month some two hundred Kentuckians organized a secession convention and declared their state to be in the Confederacy. In December the rebel congress admitted Kentucky into the Confederacy. At times there were more than 25,000 Confederate troops in the state. As the new year opened, Kentucky was hardly secure. That changed in a ten-day period in early February. On February 6, a relatively obscure brigadier general, Ulysses S. Grant, captured Fort Henry on the Tennessee River in northern Tennessee. On the 16th he captured Fort Donelson on the Cumberland River, along with more than 12,000 Confederate troops. These twin victories established a

U.S. presence in the Confederate state of Tennessee. More important, they emphatically secured Kentucky for the Union. By the end of the month the U.S. Army was sitting in Nashville, Tennessee, the first southern state capital to fall. Instead of Kentucky possibly going into the Confederacy, it was more likely that Tennessee would be returned to the United States.

On the other side of the Mississippi, in early March Confederate forces suffered a devastating loss at Pea Ridge in Arkansas. The Confederates, led by Earl Van Dorn, had planned to march into Missouri and eventually capture St. Louis. But Pea Ridge ended any chance of Missouri becoming the twelfth Confederate state. Instead, the outcome made it all the more likely that Arkansas would be brought back into the Union. A month later the United States won an important but bloody victory at Shiloh in southwestern Tennessee. On the same day U.S. naval forces combined with the army to seized Island No. 10 in the Mississippi River, capturing more than fifty big guns and some 7,000 Confederate soldiers. In April, Memphis fell to combined navy and army operations, and on May 1, Gen. Benjamin Butler, who had developed the contraband policy while a commander in Virginia, marched into New Orleans.

This truncated history of the first months of 1862 illustrates how circumstances allowed Lincoln to begin to contemplate emancipation. By June he knew that the border South was unlikely to join the Confederacy. There would be still be fighting in that region—especially horrible guerrilla warfare in Missouri—but by June 1862 it was clear that Kentucky, Maryland, Delaware, and Missouri were secure. So too was a good piece of Tennessee as well as the cities of New Orleans, Baton Rouge, and Natchez and smaller river towns in Mississippi, Louisiana, and Arkansas. There could be no more realistic fears that an emancipation policy would push Kentucky or Missouri into the Confederacy.

Lincoln now had a reasonable chance of implementing an emancipation policy for a substantial number of slaves. Even if the war ended with some part of the Confederacy intact, the president could break the back of slavery in much of the Mississippi Valley. Once free, these blacks could not be easily reenslaved.

By the spring of 1862 Lincoln had the third and fourth prerequisites in place for emancipation: security of the Upper South and a reasonable chance of military victory that would make emancipation successful. He was also moving toward the first prerequisite: a legal theory that would justify emancipation. The theory was not complete, but it had been developing since Butler discovered the legal concept of contrabands of war and brilliantly applied it to slaves. The First Confiscation Act had supplemented it. In March 1862 Congress prohibited the military from returning fugitive slaves, whether from enemy masters, loyal masters in the Confederacy, or masters in the border states. Any officers returning fugitive slaves could be court-martialed and, if convicted, dismissed from military service.[36] None of these laws or policies had attacked slavery directly. Freeing contrabands required that slaves take the initiative of running to the army *and* that the army be in close proximity to them. The Confiscation Act only applied to slaves being used for military purposes. Most slaves fit neither category.

The second of the four prerequisites—insuring political support for emancipation—was still an open question in 1862. But the nation was moving toward emancipation. On April 10 Congress passed a joint resolution declaring the United States would "cooperate with," and provide "pecuniary aid" for, any state willing to adopt a gradual emancipation scheme.[37] The most important step in this process was the act, passed in April, abolishing slavery in the District of Columbia and providing compensation for the masters of the freed slaves. This law was consistent with Lincoln's long-standing understanding of what the Constitution allowed because the U.S. government had control over the district. The president happily signed this law, which resembled the bill he had wanted to introduce in Congress fifteen years earlier.[38] In addition, by providing compensation to the masters, this law was more likely to survive a challenge on Fifth Amendment grounds.

In addition to providing payment to masters for the slaves, the D.C. emancipation law also provided money for colonization of former slaves in Africa or Haiti. Critics of Lincoln often have focused on this one provision as proof of Lincoln's racism and his insincerity with regard to both emancipation and black rights. However, a serious analysis of this provision, which these critics rarely offer, undermines the strength of such claims.

The law provided up to $100,000 for the colonization of both free blacks already living in the district and the newly emancipated slaves. The operative language, however, was critical. The money was "to aid in the settlement and colonization of such free persons . . . as *may desire to emigrate* to the Republics of Hayti or Liberia, or such other country beyond the limits of the United States as the president may determine."[39] This language, which Lincoln had demanded, did not require or force anyone to leave the United States, and it allowed the president to prevent voluntary emigration if he was to "determine" it was not suitable. The law also limited the amount to be appropriated for each emigrant to $100.[40]

This provision was clearly a sop thrown to conservatives and racists, who feared a free black population. In 1860 the census had found over 14,000 blacks in the city, including about 3,200 slaves. The appropriation would have provided money for the colonization of only 1,000 blacks— less than a third of the newly freed slaves and less than 7 percent of the entire free black population of the city in 1860. Moreover, by 1862 the black population in the city was much larger than 14,000, which meant that an even smaller percentage of the population could leave under the appropriation. Furthermore, the $100 individual appropriation was hardly much of an incentive for any free black or former slave to move to a new country. Not surprisingly, no record exists of *any* African American taking advantage of this offer. This law in fact may be unique in American history as the only time that Congress appropriated a substantial sum of money to be given out to individuals, and none of the money was spent.

The political message of this law was significant. Congress, in an election year, was prepared to begin to dismantle slavery. Members of the House, who were to stand for reelection in the fall, were willing to run on a record that included voting to free some of the slaves. In June Congress abolished slavery in the federal territories, this time without compensation.[41] It was in this context, with the war going relatively well, with the border states secure and some emancipation taking place, that Lincoln began to work on the greatest issue of his lifetime.

AS CONGRESS MOVED to end slavery in the territories and the District of Columbia, Lincoln contemplated a much larger issue: ending slavery in the Confederacy. Before Lincoln could act, once again one of his generals began to move against slavery without authority. On May 9, 1862, Maj. Gen. David Hunter, the commander of U.S. forces in the Department of the South, issued General Order No. 11, declaring martial law in his military district, which comprised the states of South Carolina, Georgia, and Florida. The general order declared all slaves in those states to be free because slavery was "incompatible" with a "free country" and with his imposition of martial law. This action went well beyond the authority of a

"Officer David Hunter,
full-length portrait
in full military dress,
standing, holding
sword, facing front."
Photograph by E. & H.
T. Anthony (New York,
1861). Courtesy of the
Library of Congress.

general, and even had Lincoln wanted to support Hunter's program, he could not possibly have approved of a general acting in this manner without authority of the executive branch. Not only did Hunter lack authority for such an action, but he had not even consulted with his military superiors, the War Department, or the president. No president could have allowed a military commander to assume such powers, and, not surprisingly, ten days later Lincoln revoked Hunter's order.[42]

This was not like the situation in Missouri in 1861. Lincoln did not have to placate border state slaveholders. South Carolina, Georgia, and Florida were already out of the Union. Nor would such an order cause Lincoln any great political harm. Most northerners were by this time ready to see the slavocracy of the Deep South destroyed, and Hunter's action was a major step in that direction. Politically, it would not have cost Lincoln much to move against slavery, especially in South Carolina, where the rebellion began. But the need to preserve executive authority and maintain a proper chain of command, if nothing else, forced Lincoln to act. He simply could not let major generals set political policy.

Lincoln's response, however, gave a hint of his evolving theory of law and emancipation. He rebuked Hunter for acting without authority, but he did not reject the theory behind Hunter's general order: that slavery was incompatible with both a free country and the smooth operation of military forces suppressing the rebellion. Instead, he wrote: "I further make known that whether it be competent for me, as commander in chief of the Army and Navy, to declare the Slaves of any state or states, free, and whether at any time, in any case, it shall have become a necessity indispensable to the maintenance of the government to exercise such supposed power, are questions which, under my responsibility, I reserve to myself, and which I can not feel justified in leaving to the decision of commanders in the field."[43] In the rest of his proclamation Lincoln urged the loyal slave states to take up Congress's offer of March 6, to give "pecuniary aid" to those states that would "adopt a gradual abolishment of slavery." He asserted that "the change" such a policy "contemplates" would "come as gentle as the dews of heaven, not rending or wrecking anything." He asked the leaders of the slave states—those within the Union and presumably those who claimed to be outside the Union—if they would "not embrace" this offer of Congress to accomplish "so much good . . . by one effort."[44]

In hindsight, this document is a stunning example of Lincoln as a deft and subtle politician shaping public opinion in advance of announcing his goals. By this time he was fully aware that none of the Confederate states were going to ever end slavery on their own and that for the foreseeable future neither would the border states. But he was willing to continue to make conciliatory gestures, urging a peaceful and seemingly painless solution to the problem. This made him look more conservative on the issue of slavery even as he was advocating abolition and preparing the public for an eventual end to slavery. He was offering a solution to America's greatest problem with the least amount of social disruption. But he also hinted that there were alternative solutions. He did not exactly say he had the power to end slavery as commander in chief; he merely asserted that *if* such power existed, it rested with him, and that if he felt emancipation had "become a necessity indispensable to the maintenance of the government" he was prepared to act against slavery.

Lincoln was preparing the public for the future. He was in no hurry. He was carefully laying the groundwork for public support, on the basis of military necessity. At the same time, he was laying the groundwork for a legal and constitutional rationale to justify emancipation. Like any good courtroom lawyer, Lincoln was not ready to lay out his strategy all at once. He wanted to prepare his jury—the American public—for what he was going to do.

In mid-July a series of events converged to convince Lincoln that emancipation would have to come soon. On July 12 he met for the second time with representatives and senators from the Upper South, urging them to endorse compensated emancipation (with federal help) for their states. He argued that by taking this stand the loyal slave states would help the war effort by showing the rebels "that, in no event, will the states you represent ever join their proposed Confederacy." Although Lincoln did not expect the border states to join the rebellion, he apparently believed that voluntary emancipation in those states would be a blow to Confederate hopes and morale. He famously told the border state representatives and senators that the "incidents of war" could "not be avoided" and that "mere friction and abrasion" would destroy slavery. He bluntly predicted —or more properly warned—that slavery "will be gone and you will have nothing valuable in lieu of it." He also pointed out that General Hunter's proclamation had been very popular and that he considered Hunter an "honest man" and "my friend."[45] The border state representatives and senators did not take the hint, indicating to Lincoln that they believed any move against slavery was unconstitutional. Two days later more than two-thirds of them signed a letter denouncing any type of emancipation as "unconstitutional." Eight border state representatives then published letters of their own supporting the president.[46]

On July 14, the same day that the border state representatives denounced emancipation, Lincoln took a final stab at gradualism, although he doubtless knew the attempt would fail. He sent the draft of a bill to Congress that would provide compensation to every state that ended slavery. The draft bill left blank the amount for each slave that Congress would appropriate, but specified that the money would come in the form of federal bonds given to the states. This bill was part of Lincoln's strategy to end slavery through state action where possible as a way of setting up the possibility of ending it on the national level. If he could get Kentucky or Maryland to end slavery it would be easier to end it in the South. This was also consistent with prewar notions of federalism and constitutional interpretation that the states had sole authority over issues of property. Congress reported this bill and it went through two readings, but lawmakers adjourned before acting on it.

Lincoln surely knew that this bill, like his meeting with the border state representatives, would not lead to an end to slavery in the Upper South. Nevertheless, this very public attempt at encouraging the states to act to end slavery was valuable. As with his response to Hunter, Lincoln was showing the nation that he was not acting precipitously or incautiously. On the contrary, he was doing everything he could, at least publicly, to end slavery with the least amount of turmoil and social dislocation.

This proposed bill must also be seen in the context of Lincoln's actions on July 13, the day before he proposed the bill and the day after his meeting with the border state representatives. On the 13th Lincoln privately told Secretary of State William H. Seward and Secretary of the Navy Gideon Welles that he was going to issue an Emancipation Proclamation. This was not a sudden response to the border state representatives rejecting compensated emancipation. Had they accepted Lincoln's proposal it would not have affected slavery in the Confederacy, where most slaves lived. Indeed, Lincoln told Welles that for weeks the issue had "occupied his mind and thoughts day and night."[47] Indeed, that was probably an understatement. Lincoln had probably been troubled by the issue since he had been forced to countermand Frémont's proclamation, or maybe from the moment he first heard of Butler's contraband solution to runaways. Lincoln's conflicting views over emancipation—his desire to achieve it and his sense that the time was not right—were surely evident in his May 19 response to Hunter's proclamation, nearly two months before he spoke with Welles.

Lincoln told Welles the issue was one of military necessity. "We must free the slaves," he said, "or be ourselves subdued." Slaves, Lincoln argued, "were undeniably an element of strength to those who had their service, and we must decide whether that element should be with or against us." Lincoln also rejected the idea that the Constitution still protected slavery in the Confederacy. "The rebels," he said, "could not at the same time throw off the Constitution and invoke its aid. Having made war on the Government, they were subject to the incidents and calamities of war."[48]

Here Lincoln sounded much like Benjamin Butler in his response to Major Carey. Since that incident the administration had accepted the idea that the fugitive slave clause of the Constitution could not be invoked by rebel masters. But why, Lincoln might have asked, was the fugitive slave clause different from any other part of the Constitution? If rebel masters were not entitled to the protection of that clause then they were not entitled to the protection of any part of the Constitution. Thus, Lincoln had found a constitutional theory that would be acceptable to most northerners. It might not pass muster with the U.S. Supreme Court, but that issue might not arise until after most slaves had been freed.

The military necessity argument is a more curious one. Lincoln did not begin to move toward emancipation until after the United States had had substantial military success in the first five months of 1862. Thus, emancipation was not a desperate act forced by military necessity. Rather, it was an act that could only be accomplished by military success. However, in framing its constitutionality, Lincoln argued simultaneously that emancipation grew out of military power—that is his power as commander in chief—and that as commander in chief he could do whatever was necessary to win the war and thus preserve the Union.

Four days after speaking with Welles and Seward, Lincoln signed the Second Confiscation Act into law.[49] This law was more expansive than the First Confiscation Act. It provided a death penalty as well as lesser penalties—including confiscation of slaves—for treason and also allowed for the prosecution of "any person" who participated in the rebellion or who gave "aid and comfort" to it. The law also provided for the seizure and condemnation of the property of "any person within any State or Territory of the United States . . . being engaged in armed rebellion against the government of the United States, or aiding or abetting such rebellion." This would include Confederate sympathizers in the border states as well as in the Confederacy. Two separate provisions dealt, in a comprehensive way, with the issue of runaway slaves and contrabands.

Section 9 of the law stated that slaves owned by someone "engaged in rebellion against the government" who escaped to Union lines or was captured by U.S. troops would be "forever free of their servitude, and not again held as slaves." Section 10 prohibited the military from returning any fugitive slaves to any masters, even those in the border states, unless the owner claiming the slave would "first make oath that the person to whom the labor or service of such fugitive is alleged to be due is his lawful owner, and has not borne arms against the United States in the present rebellion, nor in any way given aid and comfort thereto." Like the Washington, D.C., emancipation act, this law allowed for the colonization of such blacks "as may be willing to emigrate" to other lands. This was a sop to conservatives who feared black freedom, but it would not require anyone to leave the United States.[50] Significantly, unlike the D.C. emancipation bill, the Second Confiscation Act allowed colonization but did not appropriate any money for it.

The Second Confiscation Act was one more step toward creating public opinion that would allow emancipation. It also helped clarify the legal and constitutional issues while once again affirming that under the war powers Congress or the president might emancipate slaves. The act did not, however, actually do much to free slaves. The law provided numerous punishments for rebels, but their slaves would only become free after some judicial process. Had there been no Emancipation Proclamation or Thirteenth Amendment the act might have eventually been used to litigate freedom, but it would have been a long and tedious process. The only certain freedom created from the act came in sections 9 and 10, which secured liberty to fugitive slaves escaping rebel masters. But this was not really much of a change from existing policy.

On July 22, five days after signing the act, Lincoln presented his cabinet with his first draft of the emancipation proclamation. The draft began with a reference to the Second Confiscation Act and contained a declaration warning "all persons" aiding or joining the rebellion that if they did not "return to their proper allegiance to the United States" they would suffer "pain of the forfeitures and seizures" of their slaves.[51] This language would not appear in the final proclamation but would be recast by Lincoln as a separate public proclamation on July 25.[52]

The rest of the first draft of the proclamation focused on Lincoln's intent to urge Congress to give "pecuniary aid" to those states voluntarily ending slavery and "practically sustaining the authority of the United States." This was one more attempt to get the loyal slave states to end slavery. The final sentence of this draft proclamation finally went to the main issue. Lincoln declared that "as a fit and necessary military measure" he did "order and declare" as "Commander-in-Chief of the Army and Navy of the United States" that as of January 1, 1863, "all persons held

"Culpeper, Va. 'Contrabands.'" Two African American men sit
in front of a tent behind Union lines. One is holding a soup ladle,
the other smoking a cigar. Courtesy of the Library of Congress.

as slaves within any state or states, wherein the constitutional authority of
the United States shall not then be practically recognized, submitted to,
and maintained, shall then, thenceforward, and forever be free."[53]

This was the great change for Lincoln. He was now on record as
believing that he had the constitutional power to end slavery in the
Confederacy. Lincoln had solved the first precondition of emancipation.
Kentucky, Missouri, Maryland, and Delaware were securely in the United
States, and while their leaders were not ready to end slavery, they clearly
would not be joining the Confederacy. The third condition had been met.
The fourth condition had at least been partially met. With U.S. troops

controlling most of the Mississippi Valley, a good deal of Tennessee, and the islands off the coast of South Carolina and Georgia, and most southern ports closed by the Navy, Lincoln knew that an emancipation program would be successful in freeing a substantial number of slaves, even if somehow a shrunken Confederacy survived. The only precondition left to achieve was the development of political support for emancipation, and here Lincoln was also close. Congress had been moving toward emancipation; generals such as Hunter were pushing for emancipation; and once Lincoln proposed emancipation to his cabinet only the conservative Montgomery Blair, who was from a slave state, expressed reservations. Blair did not oppose the concept but did think it would cost the Republican Party votes in the fall elections. In the next two months Lincoln would work to lay the political groundwork for gaining greater public support for emancipation.

FOR THE REST of the summer Lincoln quietly set into motion the necessary conditions for emancipation. Illustrative of this was his famous letter to the *New York Tribune* on August 22. In an editorial titled "The Prayer of Twenty Millions," Horace Greeley had urged Lincoln to end slavery. Lincoln responded with a letter declaring that his goal was to "save the Union" and that he would accomplish this any way he could. He would free some slaves, all slaves, or no slaves to save the Union. He also noted that this position was a description of his "*official* duty" and not a change in his "oft-expressed *personal* wish that all men every where could be free."[54]

The answer to Greeley was one more step to creating the political conditions for emancipation. Lincoln had now warned the nation that he would end slavery if it were necessary to preserve the Union. In fact he had been quietly and secretly moving toward this result all summer. His letter was a prelude to what he had already determined to do. No northerner could be surprised when he did it. Abolitionists could be heartened by having a president who believed, as they did, that "all men every where" should "be free." Conservatives would understand that they had to accept emancipation as a necessity.

On September 13 Lincoln replied coyly to an "Emancipation Memorial" from a group of Chicago ministers. He asserted that emancipation was useless without a military victory and would be "like the Pope's bull against the comet." He asked how he "could free the slaves" when he could not "enforce the Constitution in the rebel States."[55] Tied to this problem was the fear that emancipation would take "fifty thousand bayonets" from Kentucky out of the Union army and give them to the Confederates.[56] He also noted that he needed full public support to succeed. Thus, he urged the ministers to be patient. Emancipation could only come with military success and the ability to "unite the people in the fact that constitutional government" should be preserved.[57]

Even as Lincoln responded to the ministers, evading any commitment and refusing to reveal his plans, he knew he had almost all his prerequisites on the table. To end slavery he needed the prospect of military success, the ability to secure the border states, public support for black freedom, and a constitutional theory to justify his actions. In early September he had all of this except the first. The war had being going well since the previous December, and he needed a significant battlefield victory to have all his prerequisites in place. When he had that victory, emancipation would not be a "necessity" of preserving the Union, as he has said in the Greeley letter, but rather, it would be the fruit of victory. The victory at Antietam was the last piece of the puzzle. Lincoln could now issue the proclamation as the logical fruit of the military successes that had taken place since the previous December.[58]

On September 22 Lincoln issued the preliminary proclamation, declaring that it would go into effect in one hundred days. He chose the 22nd carefully, because it would be exactly one hundred days until January 1, 1863, thus tying emancipation with the new year. He now also had his constitutional/legal theory for issuing the proclamation, which he had laid out in the Greeley letter.

Lincoln issued the proclamation in his dual capacity as "President of the United States of America, and Commander-in-Chief of the Army and Navy." The purpose of the proclamation was "restoring the constitutional relations" between the nation and all the states. The preliminary proclamation authorized the enlistment of black troops and put the nation on notice that in one hundred days he would move against slavery in any place that was still in rebellion against the nation.[59]

On January 1, 1863, the final proclamation was put into effect. Here Lincoln made the constitutional argument even more precise. He issued it "by virtue of the power in me vested as commander in chief, of the Army and Navy of the United States in time of actual armed rebellion." This was, constitutionally, a war measure designed to cripple the ability of those in rebellion to resist the lawful authority of the United States. It applied only to those states and parts of states that were still in rebellion. This was constitutionally essential. Lincoln only had power to touch slavery where, as he had told the ministers from Chicago, he could not "enforce the Constitution." Where the Constitution was in force, federalism and the Fifth Amendment prevented presidential emancipation. The document was narrowly written, carefully designed to withstand the scrutiny of the Supreme Court, still presided over by Chief Justice Taney. It applied only to the states in rebellion. It would not threaten Kentucky or Missouri, and it would not threaten the constitutional relationship of the states and the federal government.

A careful reading of the proclamation suggests that professor Hofstadter was right. It did have "all the moral grandeur of a bill of lading." But Hofstadter failed to understand the significance of a bill of lading to a skilled railroad lawyer, which is what Lincoln had been before the war. A bill of lading was the key legal instrument that was used to guarantee the delivery of goods between parties that were far apart and may never have known each other. A bill of lading allowed a seller in New York to safely ship goods to a buyer in Illinois, both confident the transaction would work. One contemporary living in Britain, Karl Marx, fully understood the highly legalistic nature of the proclamation. Writing for a London newspaper during the war, Marx had a clear fix on what Lincoln had done, and why he did it the way he did: the "most formidable decrees which he hurls at the enemy and which will never lose their historic significance, resemble—as the author intends them to—ordinary summons, sent by one lawyer to another."[60]

So, in the end, when all the preconditions were met—the border states secured, military victory likely, political support in place, and the constitutional/legal framework developed—Lincoln went back to his roots as a lawyer and wrote a carefully crafted, narrow document: a bill of lading for the delivery of freedom to some 3 million southern slaves. The vehicle for delivery would be the army and navy—of which he was commander in chief. As the armies of the United States moved deeper into the Confederacy they would bring the power of the proclamation with them, freeing slaves every day as more and more of the Confederacy was redeemed by military success. This was the moral grandeur of the proclamation and of Lincoln's careful and complicated strategy to achieve his personal goal that "all men every where could be free."[61]

Notes

1. Richard Hofstadter, *The American Political Tradition and the Men Who Made It* (New York: A. A. Knopf, 1948), 110, 115, 131.

2. Lincoln indicated that the proclamation would go into effect only if the Confederate states did not return to the Union. He had no expectation any of the Confederate states would accept this offer, so his vacillation is more apparent than real. Had the Confederate states returned to the Union before the proclamation went into effect, he would have had no constitutional power to end slavery in them.

3. Hofstadter, *American Political Tradition*, 110, 115, 131.

4. Allen C. Guelzo, " 'Sublime in Its Magnitude': The Emancipation Proclamation," in *Lincoln and Freedom: Slavery, Emancipation, and the Thirteenth Amendment*, ed. Harold Holzer and Sara Vaughn Gabbard (Carbondale: Southern Illinois University Press, 2007), 66.

5. Abraham Lincoln, "First Inaugural Address—Final Text," in *The Collected Works of Abraham Lincoln*, 9 vols., ed. Roy P. Basler (New Brunswick, N.J.: Rutgers University Press, 1953–55), 4:262–63 (hereafter cited as *CW*).

6. Pinckney quoted in Jonathan Elliot, *The Debates in the Several State Conventions on the Adoption of the Federal Constitution*, 5 vols. (1888; reprint, New York: Burt Franklin, 1987), 4:286. For greater discussion of this issue at the Constitutional Convention see Paul Finkelman, *Slavery and the Founders: Race and Liberty in the Age of Jefferson*, 2nd ed. (Armonk, N.Y.: M. E. Sharpe, 2001).

7. Paul Finkelman, *Dred Scott v. Sandford: A Brief History* (Boston: Bedford Books, 1995); Joseph R. Fornieri, "Lincoln's Critique of *Dred Scott* as a Vindication of the Founding," in Holzer and Gabbard, *Lincoln and Freedom*, 20–36.

8. Lincoln to Albert G. Hodges, April 4, 1864, *CW*, 7:281.

9. "Protest in the Illinois Legislature on Slavery," *CW*, 1:74–75.

10. Benjamin Quarles, *Lincoln and the Negro* (New York: Oxford University Press, 1962), 30.

11. Lincoln to Hodges, *CW*, 7:281.

12. For modern critical assessments of Lincoln and emancipation, in addition to Hofstadter, see Lerone Bennett Jr., *Forced into Glory: Abraham Lincoln's White Dream* (Chicago: Johnson Publishing Co., 2000); LaWanda Cox, "Lincoln and Black Freedom," in *The Historian's Lincoln: Pseudohistory, Psychohistory, and History*, ed. Gabor S. Boritt and Norman O. Forness (Urbana: University of Illinois Press, 1988); Ira Berlin, "Who Freed the Slaves? Emancipation and Its Meaning," in *Union and Emancipation: Essays on Politics and Race in the Civil War Era*, ed. David W. Blight and Brooks D. Simpson (Kent, Ohio: Kent State University Press, 1997); Julius Lester, *Look Out Whitey! Black Power's Gon' Get Your Mama!* (New York: Dial Press, 1968); Lerone Bennett Jr., "Was Lincoln a White Supremacist?" *Ebony*, February 1968, 35–42.

13. There were three vacancies on the court when Lincoln took office that he could not immediately fill. The seats could not be filled until Congress reconfigured the circuits for justices.

14. Don E. Fehrenbacher, *The Dred Scott Case: Its Significance in American Law and Politics* (New York: Oxford University Press, 1978).

15. Peggy Wagner, Gary W. Gallagher, and Paul Finkelman, *The Library of Congress Civil War Desk Reference* (New York: Simon and Schuster, 2002), 70–72.

16. Lowell Hayes Harrison, *Lincoln of Kentucky* (Lexington: University Press of Kentucky, 2000), 135; see also David Lindsey, "Review of *The Civil War in Kentucky* by Lowell H. Harrison," *Journal of American History* 63 (1976): 136.

17. Charles Dew, *Bond of Iron: Master and Slave at Buffalo Forge* (New York: W. W. Norton, 1994), 264–311.

18. Douglass quoted in James M. McPherson, *Battle Cry of Freedom: The Civil War Era* (New York: Oxford University Press, 1988), 354.

19. Benjamin F. Butler, *Butler's Book* (Boston: A. M. Thayer, 1892), 256–57.

20. Maj. Gen. Benjamin F. Butler to Lt. Gen. Winfield Scott, May 24/25, 1861, in *The War of the Rebellion: A Compilation of the Official Records of the Union and Confederate Armies*, 128 vols. (Washington: GPO, 1880–1901), ser. 2, 1:752 (hereafter cited as *OR*).

21. Simon Cameron to Maj. Gen. Benjamin F. Butler, Aug. 8, 1861, *OR*, ser. 2, 1:761–62.

22. Ibid.

23. On setting out a pay scale for black laborers, see Special Orders No. 72, October 14, 1861, and General Orders No. 34, November 1, 1861, *OR*, ser. 2, 1:774–75.

24. An Act to confiscate Property used for Insurrectionary Purposes, August 6, 1861, *Statutes at Large, Treaties, and Proclamations of the United States of America*, vol. 12 (Boston: Little, Brown, 1863), 319.

25. *OR*, ser. 1, 3:466–67.

26. Lincoln to John C. Frémont, Sept. 2, 1861, *CW*, 4:506.

27. William E. Gienapp, *Abraham Lincoln and Civil War America: A Biography* (New York: Oxford University Press, 2002), 89.

28. Lincoln to Orville H. Browning, Sept. 22, 1861, *CW*, 4:531–32.

29. Lincoln to John C. Frémont, Sept. 11, 1861, *CW*, 4:517–18.

30. General Order No. 28, Nov. 2, 1861, *OR*, Additions and Corrections to Series 2, 3:558–59 (Washington: GPO, 1902).

31. Stephen Oates, *With Malice Toward None: The Life of Abraham Lincoln* (New York: Mentor Books, 1978), 292.

32. McPherson, *Battle Cry of Freedom*, 358–68.

33. Ibid., 368.

34. One of the important results of this was the liberation of thousands of slaves on the Sea Islands, many of whom would later be enlisted when the United States began to organize black regiments in late 1862. See David Dudley Cornish, *The Sable Arm: Negro Troops in the Union Army, 1861–1865* (New York: W. W. Norton, 1966); and Willie Lee Rose, *Rehearsal for Reconstruction: The Port Royal Experiment* (New York: Oxford University Press, 1976).

35. [Gen.] George B. McClellan to Brig. Gen. D. C. Buell, November 7, 1861, *OR*, ser. 2, 1:776–77.

36. "An Act to make an Additional Article of War," March 13, 1862, *Statutes at Large*, 12:354. This law modified an important part of the Fugitive Slave Law of 1850, which had authorized the use of the military or the militia to return fugitive slaves.

37. Joint Resolution No. 26, April 10, 1862, *Statutes at Large*, 12:617.

38. "An Act for the Release of Certain Persons Held to Service or Labor in the District of Columbia," April 16, 1862, *Statutes at Large*, 12:376.

39. Ibid., 378. Emphasis added.

40. Ibid. Misunderstanding of the colonization bill is common. John Hope Franklin, for example, asserts that the law "provided for the removal and colonization of the freedmen," when in fact it did not provide for "removal" but merely allowed voluntary colonization. John Hope Franklin, *The Emancipation Proclamation* (Garden City, N.Y.: Doubleday, 1963), 17.

41. "An Act to Secure Freedom to all Persons Within the Territories of the United States," June 19, 1862, *Statutes at Large*, 12:432.

42. "Proclamation Revoking General Hunter's Order of Military Emancipation of May 9, 1862," May 19, 1862, *CW*, 5:222.

43. Ibid., 222–23.

44. Ibid., 223.

45. "Appeal to Border State Representatives to Favor Compensated Emancipation," July 12, 1862, *CW*, 5:317–18; Gienapp, *Abraham Lincoln and Civil War America*, 110; McPherson, *Battle Cry of Freedom*, 503.

46. *CW*, 5:319; Gienapp, *Abraham Lincoln and Civil War America*, 110; McPherson, *Battle Cry of Freedom*, 503.

47. Lincoln quoted in McPherson, *Battle Cry of Freedom*, 504.

48. Ibid.

49. "An Act to suppress Insurrection, to punish Treason and Rebellion, to seize and confiscate the Property of Rebels, and for other Purposes," July 17, 1862, *Statutes at Large*, 12:589.

50. Ibid.

51. Emancipation Proclamation—First Draft [July 22, 1862], *CW*, 5:336.

52. Proclamation of the Act to Suppress Insurrection, July 25, 1862, *CW*, 5:341.

53. Emancipation Proclamation—First Draft [July 22, 1862], *CW*, 5:336.

54. Lincoln to Horace Greeley, August 22, 1862, *CW*, 5:388–89.

55. "Reply to Emancipation Memorial Presented by Chicago Christians of All Denominations," September 13, 1862, *CW*, 5:419–25 (quotations on 420).

56. Ibid., 423.

57. Ibid., 424.

58. In hindsight it is of course clear that Antietam was not the knockout blow Lincoln was hoping for, and the end of 1862 and the first half of 1863 would be a period of enormous frustration for him as the war went badly. But Lincoln could not know or foresee this when he issued the preliminary proclamation.

59. Preliminary Emancipation Proclamation, September 22, 1862, *CW*, 5:433.

60. Marx quoted in Phillip Shaw Paludan, *The Presidency of Abraham Lincoln* (Lawrence: University of Kansas Press, 1994), 187–88.

61. Lincoln to Horace Greeley, August 22, 1862, *CW*, 5:388–89.

MARK E. NEELY JR.

Colonization and the Myth That Lincoln
Prepared the People for Emancipation

The most mysterious period of Lincoln's presidency is the two months that followed the first reading of the Emancipation Proclamation to the cabinet on July 22, 1862, and the public announcement of the policy in the preliminary Emancipation Proclamation of September 22, 1862. At the cabinet meeting on July 22, the president was already prepared to issue a proclamation freeing the slaves, but he asked for comments from the cabinet members. Postmaster General Montgomery Blair urged delay, on the ground that the announcement of emancipation would hurt the Republicans in the autumn elections. The secretary of state, William H. Seward, spoke at length on the risks to foreign policy, saying Europe might fear that the supply of American cotton would be lost to them for generations. Besides, he said, the announcement would look like a sign of weakness if offered now, in the wake of the defeat at the end of June of George B. McClellan's army before Richmond in the Peninsula campaign, instead of after a military victory. Lincoln had not thought of the way the proclamation would look to the world after the recent disastrous Union defeat. He decided to wait for a victory.

Lincoln kept secret the document that he had already drafted, but in the meantime, he gave a series of public statements, all of which appeared to indicate that he was not likely to issue an emancipation proclamation. On August 14 he met with a delegation of African Americans, told them bluntly that their race was the cause of the civil war being fought by America's white people against each other, and suggested that they lead their race out of the country for good. On August 22, he sent a carefully crafted letter to Horace Greeley, the editor of the most widely read anti-slavery newspaper in the nation, the *New York Tribune*, suggesting that any policy on slavery the president adopted in future would come for reasons of state and not for moral reasons, thus taking all the idealism out of the emancipation to come. On September 13, he suggested to a delegation of Christians from Chicago that any paper proclamation issued against slavery would resemble "the Pope's bull against the comet": it would be useless as a practical matter. Thus an emancipation proclamation would, if anyone paid attention to the public record of statements to this point, be lacking idealism, would have no practical utility in really damaging slavery, and would be for the sake of a people the country was best rid of anyhow. Then, nine days after the meeting with the Chicagoans, Lincoln announced to the world the preliminary Emancipation Proclamation.

There is no making sense of such a perverse record, but on one part of the record, at least, a consensus seems to be forming among historians: the colonization plea to the African American delegation. That, nearly everyone is agreed, constituted a matter of preparation for the emancipation policy to come, a subtle political reassurance to an overwhelmingly racist white electorate and their kin that the president was working on a policy to get African Americans to depart the United States forever so that when emancipation came, as Lincoln, who had the proclamation sitting ready to issue in his desk, secretly knew it would, the white people in the country would not worry about the possibility that freed slaves would come north.

Historians now tell us, in interpreting the colonization proposal, that it was a matter of "political calculation" and "an effective tool in dealing with the politically charged issue of what would be done with slaves freed during the war."[1] The best of the one-volume biographies of Lincoln states, "Lincoln's critics, white or black, . . . did not understand that the President's plea for colonization—heartfelt and genuine as it was—was also a shrewd political move, a bit of careful preparation for an eventual emancipation proclamation."[2] More recently, in a review of a new book on Lincoln in the *New York Review of Books*, we have been told that "Lincoln the politician was a master of misdirection, of appearing to appease conservatives while manipulating them toward the acceptance of radical policies." This was "political legerdemain." The book under review voiced the same idea. In the colonization conference in the White House, according to this new book, Lincoln was "once again using racism strategically" to "make emancipation more palatable to white racists." Overall the image of Lincoln we are given is, as the reviewer said, that of "a practitioner of the art of the possible, a pragmatist who . . . recognized that" his antislavery principles "could only be achieved in gradual, step-by-step fashion through compromise and negotiation, in pace with progressive changes in public opinion and political realities."[3]

To assume that Lincoln's strange record in this mysterious period really added up to "shrewd" political preparation of the ground for a major new policy initiative is to take sides in one of the oldest debates in Lincoln historiography. Biographies published in the nineteenth century tended to depict Abraham Lincoln as a reformer biding his time until the right moment came along for emancipation. Men as different as William Henry Herndon and the coauthors John Nicolay and John Hay eagerly spread the story that when Lincoln, as a twenty-one-year-old frontier flatboatman, witnessed a slave auction in New Orleans he vowed at that time to attack slavery if he ever got the chance. Herndon's account of the event is unforgettable:

In New Orleans, for the first time Lincoln beheld the true horrors of human slavery. He saw "negroes in chains—whipped and scourged." Against this inhumanity his sense of right and justice rebelled, and his mind and conscience were awakened to a realization of what he had often heard and read. No doubt, as one of his companions has said, "Slavery ran the iron into him then and there." One morning in their rambles over the city Lincoln and two compatriots passed a slave auction. A vigorous and comely mulatto girl was being sold. She underwent a thorough examination at the hands of the bidders; they pinched her flesh and made her trot up and down the room like a horse to show how she moved and in order, as the auctioneer said, that "bidders might satisfy themselves" whether the article they were offering to buy was sound or not. The whole thing was so revolting that Lincoln moved away from the scene with a deep feeling of "unconquerable hate." Bidding his companions follow him he said, "By God, boys, let's get away from this. If ever I get a chance to hit that thing [meaning slavery], I'll hit it hard."[4] Nicolay and Hay agreed. Noting that Lincoln had made a trip to New Orleans previously, they said that the second trip "evidently created a far deeper impression on his mind than the former one. . . . The sight of men in chains was intolerable to him."[5]

Years of historical revisionism took their toll on such a view by the end of the twentieth century. Lincoln himself had said in an autobiographical statement that the man who told the New Orleans story to Herndon, John

Hanks, had left the boatmen before they arrived in New Orleans.[6] Furthermore, late in life, Lincoln, in a letter written to a Kentucky journalist named Albert G. Hodges on April 4, 1864, explained that though he had hated slavery all his life he "never understood" that the presidency "conferred" on him "an unrestricted right to act officially on this judgment and feeling." He did so act, of course, eventually, and he concluded this way to Hodges: "I claim not to have controlled events, but confess plainly that events have controlled me. Now, at the end of three years struggle the nation's condition is not what either party, or any man devised, or expected. God alone can claim it. Whither it is tending seems plain. If God now wills the removal of a great wrong, and wills also that we of the North as well as you of the South, shall pay fairly for our complicity in that wrong, impartial history will find therein new cause to attest and revere the justice and goodness of God."[7]

By the middle of the twentieth century historian T. Harry Williams saw Lincoln's Emancipation Proclamation as a surrender to political forces in his own party, namely the Radicals, whom he could not control: "The wily Lincoln surrendered to the conquering Jacobins in every controversy before they could publicly inflict upon him a damaging reverse. Like the fair Lucretia threatened with ravishment, he averted his fate by instant compliance."[8] Later historical works seemed to diminish our estimate of the strength of the Radicals, but others argued that African Americans freed themselves, essentially, and that their initiative in escaping the plantations and entering Union lines forced emancipation on Lincoln.[9] The image of Lincoln had shifted from the view taken in the days of Herndon and Nicolay and Hay. Did racism in American society somehow control Lincoln, or did Lincoln manipulate and control racism to make emancipation acceptable?

ONE THING IS CLEAR: the effects of making such comments about race as Lincoln did in his conference on colonization were disastrous for African Americans eager to swell the dwindling ranks of the Union armies. It is not surprising, of course, that African Americans rejected the policy, but it is somewhat surprising to see on what grounds they objected: in general African Americans responded by emphasizing patriotism as much as race. That was especially surprising when we see the patronizing, unfeeling, misleading, and insulting language Lincoln used in speaking to the African American delegation. For his part, Lincoln emphasized race. First, he noted the "physical difference" between white and black. Each race suffered from the presence of the other race, he pointed out. Second, Lincoln stated flatly, "But for your race among us there could not be war," with "white men cutting one another's throats." Third, he said that African Americans were "extremely selfish" for asking what material gain they might derive from emigration. They should show more self-sacrificing leadership. Fourth, he questioned the very foundation of their patriotism, saying, "One reason for an unwillingness [to go] . . . is that some of you would rather remain within reach of the country of your nativity. I do not know how much attachment you may have toward our race. It does not strike me that you have the greatest reason to love them. But still you are attached to them at all events." He then, like some small-town operator trying to sell a dubious land development scheme, promised them riches in coal deposits in Central America, a region he described as not remote, like Liberia, but instead on a great "highway."[10]

Before examining the response to Lincoln's address on colonization, it is crucial to note that even if it was a political tactic, it had cruel effects. African Americans for the most part were.looking for a signal from Lincoln that emancipation was coming. Such a sign would indicate that their place in the United States was at last secure. That would change many immediate and desperate plans. African Americans, since the announcement of the *Dred Scott* decision back in 1857, were leaving the United States all the time. On September 4, 1862, for example, less than three weeks after the president's dispiriting address on colonization, the barque *Chanticleer* set sail with six African American families aboard, sixty-eight people in all, who had sold their property in rural Illinois and Wisconsin, no doubt despairing of the future of their race in the United States, to go live in Haiti.[11] A truthful revelation of the government policy embodied in a document sitting in Lincoln's desk might have changed the course of their lives.

Second, it should also be noted that Lincoln's address on colonization appeared in print at the same time that a wave of violence against African Americans in New York, Cincinnati, Chicago, Toledo, and New Orleans was making news.[12] It may not be exactly accurate to term these events "a wave," as they seem to have had different local triggering circumstances, but to African Americans they looked ominously similar: they showed white malice toward blacks in an atmosphere of virulent race-baiting in the press and in politics. With the exception of the New Orleans melee, they all involved, apparently, conflicts between African Americans and Irish Americans, and thus they foreshadowed the horrifying race riot in New York City in the next Civil War summer—the draft riots of July 1863. Thus the warnings from the black community of the dangers of encouraging such malice should not have been ignored.

These events, which have not been much studied, included a riot that occurred in Lincoln's home state only five days before his meeting with the African American delegation. On the docks at 12th Street in Chicago a gang of white laborers offered to unload the schooner *Meridian* for $75, a very high price for a job that usually paid $15. But labor was scarce in Chicago and elsewhere because of the departure of so many working men for the armies. The captain managed to bargain the price down to $45, when a group of African Americans offered a competing bid of $13. Two riots ensued between the white and black dock workers.[13] In the previous month in Chicago the so-called "omnibus riot" occurred, the result of an attempt by a bus driver named Kelley to throw a black man named Walker off his bus, against precedent and law. A crowd gathered, but there really was no "riot," though the Republican press attempted to make out that there was one. The subsequent trial of the bus driver, which resulted in a hung jury, was conducted in entirely political discourse in the courtroom and in press coverage, with opposing attorneys and editors accusing abolitionists of exciting blacks to unseemly public ambitions and Republicans accusing Copperheads of being emboldened by recent Union battlefield defeats to spread fear of emancipation in the North.[14]

The riots in Ohio are perhaps the most famous of the lot. On July 11, 1862, Irish American stevedores attacked African American strikebreakers willing to unload New York & Erie Line boats in Toledo at prestrike wages. The riots spread all along the docks, and one bystander was killed. Trials of the rioters afterward resulted in at least one conviction of a rioter named Thomas Tiernan, who was sentenced to imprisonment and fined.[15] A week later Irish stevedores fought with African American deckhands from Ohio River steamers newly employed in the tight labor market on the thriving Ohio River docks in Cincinnati.[16]

In Brooklyn, on August 4, 1862, a series of alleged insults to white women and a shoving incident at the door of a saloon across the street from a Lorillard tobacco factory led to demands from Irish American neighbors that the factory dismiss its roughly one hundred African American workers. The manager was apparently complying when Irish American men and women stormed the factory and tried to set it on fire. Because it occurred in the New York City area, the event was much covered by the many newspapers in New York and led Henry Highland Garnet, a prominent African American clergyman, to denounce the *New York Herald* for inciting white mobs to attack black citizens. As quoted in the press, Garnet apparently said something along the lines that it was not, after all "the rascally blacks of the Five Points who were assailed, but the very best classes of colored citizens."[17] In other words, it was clear in all the incidents described here that the rioters chose as their victims African Americans who wanted to work.[18]

Knowledge of these events is important for understanding the context of the best-known response to Lincoln's address on colonization: that of Frederick Douglass, the African American abolitionist. He pointed out the incentive such expressions of racism offered to "the ignorant and base, who need only the countenance of men in authority to commit all kinds of violence and outrage upon the colored people of the country."[19] Even if Lincoln's address was a political ploy, it is wrong to ignore the social costs of such coldblooded maneuvers.

Douglass, although he had abandoned his own planned trip to Haiti and was being forged into an iron-willed American nationalist and patriot, emphasized race in his response. He was disgusted by the "pride of race and blood" shown in Lincoln's speech.[20]

Other responses from African Americans laid emphasis on factors besides race.[21] Even before Lincoln addressed the delegation in the White House, one African American in Chicago wrote in a letter to the editor that Lincoln had no right to consult colonizationists at such a moment, and said the country was "refusing its own children a home." African Americans had been eager to help from the moment of the firing on Fort Sumter, he said, "from a sincere sense of duty to . . . country, to the enslaved, his children, civilization, and in fact every noble duty which can animate mankind."[22]

Robert Purvis, the son-in-law of Philadelphia's African American leader James Forten, could hardly contain himself in his reply to Lincoln's remarks. "Great God!" he exclaimed. "Sir, we were born here." This was not the white man's country, he pointed out; it was the red man's country until expropriated by the whites.[23] Consideration of nation was almost always present.

"Frederick Douglass, head-and-shoulders portrait." The photograph was taken in the decade before the start of the Civil War when Douglass was in his late thirties or early forties. Courtesy of the Library of Congress.

The "Colored Men of Philadelphia" responded in anger and in love. They began by denying that color distinguished them as much as slavery did, forcing ignorance and poverty on them. Religion did not show that the Creator judged His creatures by their color. Stressing their status as property holders in Pennsylvania, owning houses and other property worth millions in the aggregate, they asked, "Shall we sacrifice this, leave our homes, forsake our birth-place, and flee to a strange land, to appease the anger and prejudice of the traitors now in arms against the Government, or their aiders and abettors in this or in foreign lands?" They also asked whether the strangers who would take their places would "make better citizens, prove as loyal, love the country better, and be as obedient to its laws as we have been?"[24]

Another long, formal reply came from African Americans of Newtown, Long Island. They pointed out first that they were not a different race because "God has made of one blood all nations that dwell on the face of the earth." They said they were "acclimated" to this country, the land of their birth, and then they launched into a sentimental statement of patriotism: "This is our native country, we have as strong attachment naturally to our native hills, valleys, plains, luxuriant forests, flowing streams, mighty rivers, and lofty mountains as any other people." To the president's remark about their having no reason to like white people, they responded, "Nor can we fail to feel a strong attachment to the whites with whom our blood has been commingling from the earliest days of this country."[25]

The African American war hero Robert Smalls, who had commandeered a Confederate naval vessel called the *Planter* and sailed it into Union lines, was traveling across the North on a triumphal speaking tour. When it was rumored that he had signed on for the voyage to set up a colony in Central America, he set the record straight in a public letter. He said it was untrue, described the event in which he and eight other men, five women, and three children had "conferred freedom on ourselves" in the *Planter*, and declared that he was headed back to the South to serve in the U.S. Navy.[26]

The black community was no monolith, of course. Even within Frederick Douglass's own family there were differing opinions. One of his sons expressed interest in going on the proposed expedition to Central America, and the other was apparently on the fence.[27]

Taken all in all, Lincoln's statement on colonization did not have a beneficial political effect on African Americans, and it may have put them at risk in a hostile culture.

SURPRISINGLY, IT IS almost as easy to illustrate the political ineptitude of Lincoln's colonization address in its effects on white northerners as it is on black northerners. But to do so systematically, we must understand the nature of white "public opinion" in the middle of the nineteenth century. There was no such thing, really. There was only the opinion of Republicans and of Democrats on public questions in the rigidly partisan nineteenth century.

We need to ask ourselves first, who was the colonization talk supposed to soothe? Put simply, Democrats opposed colonization and had for a long time, and Republicans were likely to go along with whatever their presidential leader proposed. People in both parties, moreover, regarded colonization as utterly impractical.

Republicans were notoriously split in the Civil War into radical and moderate factions. We know that Lincoln's intraparty political troubles would come from the radical faction. To radicals, of course, colonization was unpopular, and Lincoln gained no ground with them by proposing it. For some radicals, indeed, it was anathema. The *Chicago Tribune* responded to Lincoln's initiative proposed to the African American delegation in the White House as Frederick Douglass had, saying that the "interview between the President and the representatives of the colored race . . . constitutes the wide and gloomy background of which the foreground is made up of the riots and disturbances which have disgraced within a short time past our Northern cities."[28]

Some moderate Republicans were more receptive, but then they were going to follow the party's moderate leader, Lincoln, anyhow. In their case, proposing colonization was preaching to the choir. Even these more conservative Republicans proved lukewarm. If we look at newspaper opinion, we can see this clearly. The *Philadelphia Inquirer* begged its readers not to regard colonization as "chimerical"—hardly a thundering endorsement of the plan.[29] The *Evening Bulletin*, also a Philadelphia newspaper of conservative Republican leanings, said the president's plan deserved "a fair trial" but expressed doubts that "such emigration will ever cut very deep into the South," for African American labor was essential to the cotton states.[30]

The *New York Times* came nearer the antislavery center of the party, and it regarded the president's plan unenthusiastically as an experiment almost certain to fail. "We regard the scheme of deporting the four millions of Africans that are rooted in the Southern soil as utterly impracticable, but still the experiment of black colonization in Central America and elsewhere is well worth trying."[31]

We must turn to the potential opponents of emancipation to find those who were most likely to be seduced by Lincoln's legerdemain with colonization: the Democrats. The *New York Herald* was not a Democratic newspaper, but it was not Republican either, and it hated abolitionists with an abiding passion and expressed outspoken disdain for and crude ridicule of African Americans. The *Herald* naturally admired Lincoln's colonization address because it proclaimed a "great truth," the inequality of the races.[32] As for colonization itself, the paper stated, "We are not opposed to the colonization of the negroes, but it does not practically amount to anything." The African Americans would not leave voluntarily in great numbers, and besides, their labor was essential to the U.S. economy.[33] New

York City's *Journal of Commerce*, a thoroughgoing Democratic paper, likewise commended the president's embrace of the scientific and "common sense doctrine of the inequality of the races," but they were skeptical of the practicality of colonization.[34] Other Democratic newspapers ridiculed the idea.[35]

Prominent Ohio Democrat Samuel Sullivan Cox, in a speech made in the House of Representatives earlier in the summer and reprinted on September 9 after Lincoln's address on colonization, said that colonization was much too expensive and that African Americans would remain in the United States. Freedmen would not go to New England, for the African American, Cox said, "does not thrive there." The only suitable northern climate was to be found in southern and central Ohio—Cox's district.[36]

For the most part, Democrats said little about colonization in August and early September.[37] In Ohio, where race riots and a border with a slave state made the issue particularly keen, the *Cleveland Plain Dealer*, a Democratic newspaper, commended the plan.[38] Pennsylvania's *Harrisburg Patriot and Union* proved cool and reserved: "without at this time expressing our own opinions, which may be modified by future light, we merely confess a doubt as to the practicability of the proposed measure."[39]

Most important, the whole idea of "acceptance of radical policies" by the Democrats defies the partisan imperatives of nineteenth-century political culture.[40] When emancipation was announced in late September, the Democrats opposed the measure as virulently as might be expected. None broke ranks.[41] Again, colonization did not figure prominently in the debate and performed little role in altering the terms of the debate. Some Democrats were opposed to emancipation and colonization both. Thus the *Albany Argus*, of upstate New York, later commented on the Emancipation Proclamation itself by saying, "It is to be deplored that the Administration . . . wastes its energies on philanthropic abstractions and utopian schemes for the emancipation or colonization of the negro."[42]

Democrats were no more enthusiastic about paying for the ship's passage of 4 million freed people than they were about having them migrate northward. As the *York (Pa.) Gazette* expressed it: "Are they to be brought amongst us . . . to compete with our white laboring masses. . . . Or are they to be colonized at the additional expense of HUNDREDS OF MILLIONS exacted from the white freemen of our country? . . . All loyal men will agree to the fact that the enemies of our country *deserve to lose their negroes,* but the question will arise, should the rights of the loyal be destroyed . . . ?"[43]

Not a single newspaper that I have read commented on the Emancipation Proclamation of September 22 by saying, "we need not worry about this seemingly dangerous social experiment because the plan is to colonize outside the country the people who are set free anyway." In fact, all the newspapers, Republican and Democratic alike, responded to the announcement of the preliminary proclamation with discussions, pro or con, based firmly on the *contrary* assumption, namely, that the freed African Americans would forever form a part of the United States and would have to be somehow accommodated.[44] The colonization address had no effect whatever on the debate on the proclamation once it was announced.

There were a few colonizationists in the United States, but not even these necessarily supported *Lincoln's* colonization scheme. The president of the American Colonization Society himself, John H. B. Latrobe, pointed out that Africa was superior to Central America as a destination, though he did not see the two programs as antagonistic. And from the African American side of emigration, Henry Highland Garnet, who was pastor of the First Colored Presbyterian Church in New York City and president of the African Civilization Society and who regularly recruited African Americans to emigrate to foreign lands, spurned Lincoln's proposal as well. Garnet, like Robert Smalls, had to deny rumors he had signed on to go, and—despite the lure of federal funding for emigration that lay in the president's plan—rejected it as "little better than a filibustering expedition," that is, an attempt to establish a U.S. colony in Central America.[45]

In fact, what the colonization proposal elicited was not eager acceptance by anyone but much ridicule. Frederick Douglass called the plan "silly and ridiculous."[46] The cruel farce was best captured by the humorous essayist Orpheus C. Kerr. His real name was Robert Newell, and his pen name was a pun on "office seeker." He wrote for the *New York Sunday Mercury,* but his humorous pieces were widely reproduced across the country in both Republican and Democratic newspapers. Just after the address on colonization, Kerr wrote one of his funniest pieces on Lincoln's speech to the African American delegation in the White House. Kerr's lampoon paralleled Lincoln's language very closely and thus reveals how close to the utterly ridiculous Lincoln veered in this unfortunate conference. Thus the satirical version of Lincoln's speech began, as Lincoln had, by calling attention to race: "You and we are different races. . . . The fact that we have always oppressed you renders you still more blamable."

Kerr included the satirical piece in a series of articles about the fictional Mackerel Brigade, stationed on Virginia's eastern shore. In this piece, the brigadier general gave a speech to an assembled group of slaves, offering "bliss to a delegation from that oppressed race which has been the sole cause of this unnatural war." Kerr gave the speech a bogus biblical grounding by saying, "It is my purpose to settle the negro question in accordance with the principles laid down in the Book of Exodus." This humorous essay reminds us that, although everyone in the room at the White House meeting except for Lincoln and, presumably, the newspaper reporter, was a clergyman, Lincoln did not employ his considerable vocabulary of biblical language.

Kerr found no relevance in Lincoln's references to George Washington's sacrifices for independence (posed by Lincoln as models for the African American leaders to emulate in departing for hardships on other shores), and he also ridiculed the idea that the Central American destination was a "highway." In the end, Kerr's general said to the person who reported his words, "Colonization, my boy, involves a scheme of human happiness so entirely beyond the human power of conception that the conception of it will almost pass for something inhuman."[47]

SOME POLITICAL LEADERS did support Lincoln's idea of colonization. The core of sincere Republican colonization sentiment lay in one family, the Blairs, as historian Eric Foner discovered long ago.[48] Francis Preston Blair Sr., of Maryland, and his two sons Montgomery Blair, also of Maryland, and Francis "Frank" Preston Blair Jr., of St. Louis, were ex-Democrats of great importance to the Republican Party. Montgomery, as a member of Lincoln's cabinet, had the president's ear. But the Blairs focused their attentions on other problems during the war, and leadership of the colonization cause fell first to Lincoln himself. It is difficult to believe that without his stubborn interest in colonization the idea would have enjoyed as much life as it did among Republicans.

The practical administration of the policy was handled by the Interior Department, headed by Caleb Blood Smith, who was a politician of only average ability and whose health seems to have been in decline. Below

Smith, the key responsible official after May 1862 was a longtime profes-
sional colonization agent named James Mitchell. Mitchell arranged the
awkward meeting of Lincoln and the African American delegation of
August 1862. Such must have been among his routine duties, for he held
the patronage position of emigration commissioner in Smith's Interior
Department by May 1862.

Mitchell had previously been active as a colonization agent in Indiana,
where he served as a Methodist minister in Jeffersonville, and in Illinois
—in Lincoln's hometown, in fact. Indiana gave colonization a new lease
on life in the 1850s after the revision of the state constitution in 1851,
Article XIII of which prohibited free black people from entering the state
to settle. The Indiana legislature subsequently provided an appropriation
of $5,000 plus funds from fines for violation of the race-exclusion mea-
sures to be used to colonize African Americans out of the country.[49]
Mitchell emerged into greater prominence with the advent of these aggressively exclusionary measures. He and the cause of colonization were
now blessed with the sanction and monetary resources of the state.[50]

Indiana now needed Mitchell's advice on race, and the year after the
state's constitution was revised he issued a report entitled, *Answer of the
agent of the Indiana Colonization Society to the resolution of inquiry on the
subject of African colonization, passed by the House of Representatives of the
General Assembly of the State of Indiana, on the 3d of February, 1852.*[51]

Mitchell drew closer to Lincoln, who in 1852 was practicing law,
because Illinois had passed a similar exclusion measure in its new constitution of 1848, and Illinoisans later showed interest in following the
Indiana example. The Democratic newspaper in Springfield, the state
capital, reported favorably on colonization in the mid-1850s. It commended the Indiana system, which organized the state for colonization,
appropriated money, and required an annual report on the question.[52]

The idea of bringing the Indiana system to Illinois was in the air—
or perhaps Mitchell himself brought it there: his *Letter from the Rev.
J. Mitchell, relative to colonization* was published in Springfield as early as
1851.[53] In 1853, Mitchell announced to Illinoisans his appointment as
agent for the region with this broadside: *To the friends of colonization: The
writer being appointed to the office of general agent of the American Colonization Society for the northwest, we thus respectfully call your attention to the
interest of African colonization, and make some suggestions on which our
friends in Illinois may act as to render the cause a great service.*[54] Lincoln

could be considered one of those friends to whom Mitchell's broadside was addressed; he spoke on colonization at the First Presbyterian Church in Springfield on August 30 that year.[55] By 1854 Mitchell was the corresponding secretary of the Illinois Colonization Society.[56] He filed an official report with the Illinois State Legislature in 1855: *Letter from the Rev. J. Mitchell, Agent of the American Colonization Society, in Reply to Certain Inquiries of the House of Representatives Relative to Colonization.*[57] In it he answered the question of the best destination, if Illinois should decide to "establish a settlement on the coast of Africa for the accommodation of the colored people." He did not know how many of Illinois's 5,000–6,000 African Americans were willing to emigrate, but he described the debate within the African American community between those seeking to leave the United States and those hopeful that the conditions in the country would improve for their continued residence. Mitchell predicted that eventual emancipation was inevitable and that race war would as inevitably follow that if the races were not separated. In other words, colonization was a moral and political necessity.

In January 1854 Lincoln had to withdraw as speaker for the annual meeting of the Illinois Colonization Society because of an illness in his family.[58] He apparently took a rain check and spoke the next year on January 4. By that time, he was attempting to combine advocacy of colonization with opposition to the Kansas Nebraska Act.[59] In an otherwise stirring speech in Peoria in 1854, Lincoln found himself rambling on the subject:

> When southern people tell us they are no more responsible for the origin of slavery than we; I acknowledge the fact. When it is said that the institution exists; and that it is very difficult to get rid of it, in any satisfactory way, I can understand and appreciate the saying. I surely will not blame them for not doing what I should not know how to do myself. If all earthly power were given me, I should not know what to do, as to the existing institution. My first impulse would be to free all the slaves, and send them to Liberia,—to their own native land. But a moment's reflection would convince me, that whatever of high hope, (as I think there is) there may be in this, in the long run, its sudden execution is impossible. If they were all landed there in a day, they would all perish in the next ten days; and there are not surplus shipping and surplus money enough in the

world to carry them there in many times ten days. What then? Free them all, and keep them among us as underlings? Is it quite certain that this betters their condition? I think I would not hold one in slavery, at any rate; yet the point is not clear enough for me to denounce people upon. What next? Free them, and make them politically and socially, our equals? My own feelings will not admit of this; and if mine would, we well know that those of the great mass of white people will not.[60]

Lincoln may have spoken for the colonization society, but he was not as certain on the subject as Mitchell.

In 1857 Lincoln was elected a manager of the state colonization society, a position he held the next year on the eve of his famous campaign against Stephen A. Douglas for the U.S. Senate.[61] In Springfield at this time, colonization was apparently not a politically polarizing movement among white opinion leaders. The Illinois governor, always a Democrat until the rise of the Republican Party in the state, served as president of the society, which contained many eminent Whigs, among them Lincoln and Orville H. Browning.[62] The society had the air of an acceptable establishment charity, a cause about which good men in either political party did not speak ill and with which clergy from various Protestant denominations associated themselves.

In the end it was a good thing for Mitchell that Lincoln saw no strongly partisan quality in colonization, because the Methodist preacher was a Democrat. He was removed from a minor office when the Republicans, led by Lincoln, gained control of the government in 1861. Lincoln saw to it that his friend Mitchell regained a patronage post in the administration.[63]

Most "systematic" thinkers about race in the middle of the nineteenth century are bound to appear as crackpots today, and Mitchell is no exception. His ideas need nevertheless to be examined here, not only because Mitchell was the man in the room in 1862 who had brought the African American delegation to Lincoln, but because Lincoln had ample opportunity to gain familiarity with those ideas.[64] In December 1861 Mitchell sent the president a twenty-page letter about colonization. One never knows whether Lincoln took time to read such long pieces of mail, but if he did in this case, he certainly got an eyeful. Whatever the state of opinion in Springfield on the question had been, Mitchell stood for systematic exclusion and not for vague white Christian charity.

Mitchell began his discussion with the assertion that *"the Negro requires a strong government."* The idea was important, because Mitchell argued consistently that the presence of a population of free people of African descent was incompatible with republicanism. He rooted the need for strong government in his observation of the "natural indolence and want of energy and enterprise" of that people. Mitchell believed that mixing races only lowered the condition of the higher or stronger race. The people of Mexico, "the home of the mixed bloods of North America," stood in his mind for the future of a racially amalgamated republic. Yet Mexico, with its factional political strife, along with Central American republics south of it, stood also as possible lands to be colonized with the people of African descent from the United States. He thought the annexation of Texas had been a mistake that served mainly to bring mixed-blooded people into the United States, and he opposed other southern imperialist schemes from the same fear of mixed bloods. Race also dictated a foreign policy at odds with the Monroe Doctrine itself, for Mitchell asserted that the strong central government likely to be imposed on Mexico by the European intervention there during the American Civil War should be accepted by the United States.[65]

Five months later, Mitchell expanded the ideas laid out in his letter, put less emphasis on immediate concerns of foreign policy, and, probably because of his position in the Interior Department, managed to gain Government Printing Office publication for the final document. His *Letter on the Relation of the White and African Races in the United States, Showing the Necessity of the Colonization of the Latter. Addressed to the President of the United States* began with a warning typical of racist theorists of the time: "Terrible as is this civil war between men of kindred race for the dominion of the servant, future history will show that it has been moderate and altogether tolerable when contrasted with a struggle between the black and the white race, which, within the next one or two hundred years must sweep over this nation, unless" African Americans were colonized. He maintained that the presence of the African race in the United States undermined the institution of the family and made us "a nation of bastards." It inflicted "damage to Christian faith," and, of course, was causing "our civil contentions." The belief that a large population of African stock was incompatible with republicanism still lay at the heart of Mitchell's argument. Now he attempted to add a constitutional imperative to colonization. He contended that the clause of the Constitution guaranteeing a republican form of government to the states (Article IV, section 4) compelled "*gradual removal* of such anti-republican elements and peoples as cannot be engrafted on the national stock."[66]

In the midst of the anti–New England sentiment Democrats were then beginning to foment in much of Mitchell's Old Northwest, the Methodist clergyman also blamed New England for attacking the colonization movement and thus raising the threat of "engrafting negro blood on the masses of the Mississippi valley." For a former Democrat, Mitchell had a remarkable ability to find heroes in old Whigs. The greatest of his heroes was the old colonizationist Henry Clay, but he also admired Zachary Taylor, who before his early death in the presidency showed interest in "the Ebony line" to Africa.[67]

Particularly pronounced in this 1862 expression of Mitchell's colonizationist rationalizations was a motif of conspiracy familiar to American politics. " 'Power,' " he warned " 'is ever stealing from the many to the few,' and ambitious and designing men are ever on the alert to take advantage of actual or accidental differences in race, nationality, or religion, to divide the masses of a republic into permanent factions or bands; the effect of which, is the introduction, first, of an oligarchy, to be soon followed by a monarchy." It had long been the plan of Great Britain to "fasten the people [African races] permanently on the soil of this country." That explained England's promotion of abolitionism before the war, on the one hand, and England's contradictory favoritism to the fledgling Confederacy during the Civil War. The Puritan and the Cavalier, as he expressed the idea at one point, both aimed at saddling the country with the African race permanently.[68]

Mitchell was working hard for colonization in Washington, D.C., before the Emancipation Proclamation existed in any form. On July 1, 1862, he asked the president to exert his influence on Congress to fund colonization, not only of the people freed in the recent District of Columbia emancipation act but also and more importantly of the "contrabands" who thronged the Union armies by the thousands in captured Confederate territory. Mitchell had learned a certain amount of practicality to go along with his self-confessed "mystical" belief in colonization. He knew that the recently freed District of Columbia African Americans would show little interest in colonization as they began to enjoy their new liberty. The less fortunate escaped slaves from the Confederacy, he reasoned, were more dependent on the federal government and more fearful that their status would change with political change in Washington, and were therefore more likely to be convinced to emigrate. The gigantic colonization project would not appear to be expensive when one considered that these refugees were costing the government rations for support anyway. Mitchell sought a modest appropriation, say $100,000, enough to show colonization was in earnest. The expensive removal of population could come later with peace, when the government was not so strapped for cash.[69] He and Lincoln eventually wangled a respectable sum but not the million dollars Mitchell had thought possible.[70]

Few of the qualities that Mitchell dwelt upon in his thinking about African Americans were matched anywhere in Lincoln's rare and spare observations on that people. Lincoln did not stress laziness as a distinguishing quality and certainly never asserted that tyranny was necessary to govern them. He recognized willingly that African Americans needed the lure of freedom to make them eager to fight for the nation. And even when he speculated on degrees of nonfreedom for African Americans in the future, he contemplated the possibility of "temporary" apprenticeships only because of their "present condition as a laboring, landless, and homeless class."[71] Lincoln certainly never showed any signs of approval of the French intervention in Mexico during the Civil War, as Mitchell had in his first, private letter to the president. Nor did Lincoln engage in elaborate and fantastic musings on world conspiracies and grand racial destinies. In lectures on the ideas of discovery and invention delivered in Illinois in the 1850s, Lincoln had linked those important qualities of innovation to Anglo-Saxons (and noted their apparent absence in Mexicans and Indians) but he had said nothing by way of a grand theory of superior and inferior races and destinies. Lincoln was forced into the company of such dangerously impractical men as Mitchell, with whom he did not necessarily agree, because colonization did not really have any political future. One must assume that Lincoln had to use the material at hand. Lincoln's surviving correspondence reveals Mitchell to have been the only applicant for a position to head up the colonization effort made possible by the congressional appropriations in the D.C. emancipation bill and elsewhere.[72] Few offices lacked for suitors in the nineteenth century.[73]

James Mitchell was interested in race, not freedom. By contrast with Mitchell, it must be noted, at least one genuine antislavery activist allowed himself to be compromised by Lincoln's colonization enterprise.

Lincoln somehow managed to get Senator Samuel Pomeroy of Kansas, a Republican with sound antislavery bona fides, to head up the proposed colonization experiment after the address to the delegation in the White House. Pomeroy was not a colonization advocate before this event, and the president knew it, but, according to Pomeroy, in a conversation with Lincoln the Kansas senator gained the impression that the president would be slow to move to emancipation if he did not have a realistic hope that colonization was possible. Pomeroy thus agreed to head the expedition meant to prove it so—for the sake of the cause of freedom.[74] The subsequent attempt to organize a voyage failed in very short order. Thus Pomeroy's reputation was yet another casualty of the colonization address in the White House.

EMPHASIS ON COLONIZATION has obscured the real argument used by Republicans to anticipate or meet racist criticism of the Emancipation Proclamation: they embraced isothermalism. That is, Republicans insisted that because of climate, African Americans were suited only to tropical climes and would never come north. In fact, Republicans argued, the only reason African Americans came north now was to escape slavery. Abolish slavery and no more would leave the South, and those in the North would depart for the South. Even the radical Republican nominee for governor in New York, Gen. James Wadsworth, in his letter accepting his party's nomination on October 14, 1862, stated the typical Republican position: "The emancipation, once effected, the Northern States would be forever relieved, as it is right that they should be, from the fears of a great influx of African laborers. . . . This done, and the whole African population will drift to the South, where it will find a congenial climate, and vast tracts of land never yet cultivated." Commenting on Wadsworth's idea, the newspaper in Oneida, New York, observed: "This is truth and common sense. . . . Were the institutions of the South rendered tolerant to the black man, not a person of African blood would remain in our northern climate. . . . The way to clear the North of blacks is to guarantee freedom to them at the South."[75]

President Lincoln eventually embraced the isothermal argument himself, but he did not lead in devising it. In his annual message to Congress of December 1, 1862, Lincoln began to hop on the political bandwagon of soothing racism invented by other Republicans while still blending it with his old favorite, colonization. "It is dreaded," he said, "that the freed people will swarm forth, and cover the whole land? Are they not already in the land? Will liberation make them any more numerous?" He went on to offer an important caveat:

> But why should emancipation south, send the free people north? People, of any color, seldom run, unless there is something to run from. *Heretofore* colored people, to some extent, have fled north from bondage; and *now*, perhaps, from both bondage and destitution. But if gradual emancipation and deportation be adopted, they will have neither to flee from. Their old masters will give them wages at least until new laborers can be procured; and the freed men, in turn, will gladly give their labor for the wages, till new homes can be found for them, in congenial climes, and with people of their own blood and race. . . . And, in any event, cannot the north decide for itself, whether to receive them?[76]

The embrace of isothermalism constituted the greatest reverse of principle in the history of the Republican Party to date. It had been founded back in the mid-1850s on the premise that only Congressional law could keep slavery out of unsettled territories. The northern Democrats had argued that isothermalism would keep slavery and, with it, African Americans, out of the territories, and there was therefore no need to pass laws obnoxious to proud white southerners; the climate simply did not suit. Lincoln himself had once strained to answer that argument. In his Peoria speech of October 16, 1854, Lincoln had laid the ground carefully for rejection of isothermalism: "It is argued that slavery will not go to Kansas and Nebraska, *in any event*. This is a *palliation*—a *lullaby*. . . . As to climate, a glance at the map shows that there are five slave States—Delaware, Maryland, Virginia, Kentucky, and Missouri—and also the District of Columbia, all north of the Missouri compromise line. . . . It is not climate, then, that will keep slavery out of these territories."[77] "It takes . . . law . . . to keep it out," he insisted in his famous debates with Douglas in 1858.[78]

LINCOLN HAD NO elaborate or systematic political plan for easing fears about emancipation. Only one of the events of the period between July 22 and September 22, 1862, bears the trademark characteristics of a political public relations campaign initiated by Abraham Lincoln as president: the justifiably famous letter to Horace Greeley of August 22, 1862. Lincoln wrote that text carefully himself and sent it to the press himself. He did not leave it to a newspaper reporter to write down his statements and transmit them to the people as the reporter understood them (as was the case, apparently, with the address to the African American delegation to the White House). The letter to Greeley did still rely on Lincoln's favorite strategy of misdirection: it did not sound as though he had already decided to free the slaves: "My paramount object in this struggle *is* to save the Union, and is *not* either to save or to destroy slavery. If I could save the union without freeing *any* slaves I would do it, and if I could save it by freeing *all* the slaves I would do it; and if I could save it by freeing some and leaving others alone I would also do that. What I do about slavery, and the colored race, I do because I believe it helps to save the Union; and what I forbear, I forbear because I do *not* believe it would help to save the Union."[79] It did make clear to anyone who read carefully that Lincoln no longer had any doubts about the constitutional power to act. The decision lay purely in the realm of expediency.

Moreover, close students of Lincoln's writing habits and texts assert that the president had the carefully prepared letter already written, awaiting the suitable opportunity to release it.[80] The close attention to timing that characterizes that argument should be even further applied to understand the famous document fully.

Lincoln's letter to Greeley, dated August 22, answered a public letter that Greeley wrote in the *Tribune* called "The Prayer of Twenty Millions," asking the president to emancipate the slaves. Lincoln released his answer to the *Washington Intelligencer* on August 23. Afterward numerous newspapers across the country reprinted Lincoln's letter. The *New York Tribune*, for example, did so on the 25th.

Something else of interest occurred in the same period. On August 22, the day Lincoln's letter was dated in manuscript, but before it appeared in any newspaper, the *New York Tribune* released a story based on a leak from Lincoln's cabinet:

> In justice to all parties, it seems proper to state the following, which we learn from so many sources that it can no longer be considered a state secret. Two or three weeks ago the President laid before his Cabinet a proclamation of Emancipation abolishing Slavery wherever on the first of next December the Rebellion should not be crushed, and asked the opinion of his Ministers touching the propriety of issuing it. All but two, Secretary Smith, we believe, being

absent, approved. Secretary Seward and Post-master General Blair, however, opposed it with all their might, and the result was that it did not appear.[81]

The source provided the wrong date, December 1 rather than January 1, for the deadline, and was in error about Caleb Blood Smith, who was present at the meeting and ardently opposed to the measure. Otherwise the story was uncannily accurate: the proclamation would abolish slavery only in areas in rebellion on a future date, and the cabinet members who opposed it with long and articulate arguments were Blair and Seward.

It seems possible that the leak prompted Lincoln's release of the letter to Greeley. The president's letter appeared on the 23rd, after the leak, and not on the 21st, after Greeley's "Prayer" had appeared. At any rate, Lincoln thought he needed to make clear that the decision to abolish slavery was constitutional and not a product of fanaticism. So he released the carefully wrought letter on the 23rd.[82] The Greeley letter did not deal with race.

The importance of understanding the trigger for the release of Lincoln's explanatory letter lies in its further destruction of the myth of careful political planning for the Emancipation Proclamation. True, Lincoln apparently had at the ready a carefully drafted and politic letter explaining the motivation for any future move against slavery. But his control of the political operation in the White House was poor. A leak might force his hand. Thus the only carefully honed political explanation of the impulse to emancipate in fact had to be rushed into the public well before any possible military victory was in sight.

NOTHING IN THIS mysterious period matches the myth we are being asked to believe, that Lincoln was a "pragmatist" who "recognized" that his principles "could only be achieved in gradual, step-by-step fashion through compromise and negotiation, in pace with progressive changes in public opinion and political realities."[83] In such a conception of the period between July 22 and September 22, 1862, the next step in the practical political plan after the address to the African Americans in the White House was the address to the Chicago delegation of Christians. In that, Lincoln scorned a paper proclamation against slavery as being like "the Pope's bull against the comet."[84] Lincoln made these remarks on September 17 in the White House. But they did not appear in the

"President Lincoln and his cabinet: in council, Sept. 22nd 1862 adopting the Emancipation Proclamation, issued Jany. 1st 1863." Published by Currier & Ives (c. 1876). A much latter print of the first reading of the Emancipation Proclamation, published nearly fifteen years after Lincoln issued the Proclamation. Courtesy of the Library of Congress.

newspapers until the Chicagoans went home, prepared their own reply, and released the president's remarks, along with their own, to the press— on the 23rd of September 1862. So Lincoln was quoted all over the North, on the day *after* the preliminary Emancipation Proclamation was announced, as himself believing that such proclamations were useless and akin to "the Pope's bull against the comet." This is not political legerdemain, it is political comedy!

But, of course, it is not funny, not really. It is serious commentary on Lincoln and on the times. To the degree that history takes away any subtle political motive for the statements Lincoln made about emancipation in the mysterious period of July 22 to September 22, 1862, then what Lincoln said in that period was not calculated but spontaneous and, very possibly, sincere, though politically irrational.[85] Such a view has serious implications for judging Lincoln's racial views. It is bound to remind historians of the luck of archival survival. If Lincoln's two addresses to the Illinois Colonization Society had survived—along with the report of the meeting with the African American delegation of August 14, 1862—it is difficult to believe that Lincoln's reputation on race would not have been significantly altered by historians reading a record on the subject triple the size of what exists now.

More important, the idea that emancipation was palatable to northern white people only if accompanied by soothing promises of colonization is a misrepresentation of the masses of American people. The eagerness with which historians accept such a myth is an eagerness rooted partly in despising those people as hopelessly steeped in an ineradicable racism. But as the history of emancipation from 1863 through 1865 shows, northern racism was not so powerful that many of the American people could not, for a brief time at least, accommodate emancipation, celebrate it as the greatest act of the age, understand that the future of African Americans lay *inside* the United States, go on fighting the Civil War beside them in the ranks, and praise as courageous heroes the freed men who served their country rather than leaving it.

Notes

I want to thank Eric Foner for reading an early version of this essay and offering useful criticism and for allowing me to read an early draft of his essay on "Lincoln and Colonization," which was helpful to me particularly for seeing the larger background of the colonization movement. I also want to thank Thomas Schwartz, of the Abraham

Lincoln Presidential Library and Museum, for help with materials related to James Mitchell.

1. Michael Vorenberg, "Abraham Lincoln and the Politics of Black Colonization," *Journal of the Abraham Lincoln Association* 14 (Summer 1993): 44.

2. David Herbert Donald, *Lincoln* (New York: Simon & Schuster, 1995), 368.

3. James M. McPherson, "What Did He Really Think about Race?" Review of James Oakes, *The Radical and the Republican: Frederick Douglass, Abraham Lincoln, and the Triumph of Antislavery Politics* (New York: W. W. Norton, 2007), in the *New York Review of Books*, March 29, 2007, 18–19. Oakes's discussion of the colonization meeting appears on pages 191–94.

4. William H. Herndon and Jesse W. Weik, *Herndon's Lincoln*, ed. Douglas L. Wilson and Rodney O. Davis (Urbana: University of Illinois Press, 2006), 60.

5. John G. Nicolay and John Hay, *Abraham Lincoln: A History*, 10 vols. (New York: Century, 1890), 1:72.

6. Roy P. Basler, ed., *The Collected Works of Abraham Lincoln*, 9 vols. (New Brunswick, N.J.: Rutgers University Press, 1953–55), 4:64 (hereafter cited as *CW*).

7. *CW*, 7:281, 282. David Herbert Donald takes Lincoln's confession of being controlled by events as the theme of his biography of Lincoln, but on the events preceding the issuance of the proclamation he takes the view that the speech on colonization was a matter of political preparation.

8. T. Harry Williams, *Lincoln and the Radicals* (Madison: University of Wisconsin Press, 1965), 18; on the proclamation itself see pp. 168–70.

9. See for example Barbara J. Fields's essay in *The Civil War: An Illustrated History*, ed. Geoffrey C. Ward, Ric Burns, and Ken Burns (New York: Alfred A. Knopf, 1990), 179–81.

10. *CW*, 5:371–74.

11. *Philadelphia Inquirer*, September 4, 1862.

12. V. Jacque Voegeli, *Free but Not Equal: The Midwest and the Negro during the Civil War* (Chicago: University of Chicago Press, 1967), 34–35. The anti–African American riots were more than a midwestern phenomenon, however.

13. *Chicago Tribune*, August 10, 1862.

14. Ibid., July 15 and 17, 1862.

15. Ibid., July 11 and 14, 1862.

16. *New York Herald*, July 19, 1862; *Cleveland Plain Dealer*, July 9, 11, and 18, 1862. Black and white dock hands cooperated in a strike at the end of July; see ibid., July 30, 1862.

17. *Chicago Tribune*, August 14, 1862.

18. In New Orleans, white police fought with a group of slaves who had freed themselves from nearby plantations and had come into the occupied town armed with sugarcane knives. One of the slaves was killed; nine were wounded; and six were taken prisoner. The press noted that the policemen would not likely have been so forceful had there not been a local law rewarding policemen with $25 for capturing runaway slaves. *New York Herald*, August 17, 1862.

19. Philip S. Foner and Yuval Taylor, eds., *Frederick Douglass: Selected Speeches and Writings* (Chicago: Lawrence Hill Books, 1999), 511.

20. Ibid. See also "A Trip to Haiti," 439–42. For the idea of comparing Lincoln and Douglass as nationalists. I am indebted to the work of Melinda Lawson in *Patriot Fires: Forging a New Nationalism in the Civil War North* (Lawrence: University Press of Kansas, 2002), 144.

21. For a solid description of the response see Benjamin Quarles, *Lincoln and the Negro* (New York: Oxford University Press, 1962), 115–23.

22. *Chicago Tribune*, August 10, 1862.

23. Robert Purvis to S. C. Pomeroy, August 28, 1862, printed in the *New York Tribune*, September 18, 1862.

24. *An Appeal from the Colored Men of Philadelphia to the President of the United States* (Philadelphia: 1862), accessed at <http://www.learner.org/channel/workshops/primarysources> (July 26, 2007).

25. *New York Tribune*, September 3, 1863.

26. *Chicago Tribune*, September 2, 1862. For the statement by a "small assemblage" of African Americans in Washington rejecting the delegation's acceptance of Lincoln's message, see the *Washington National Intelligencer*, August 29, 1862.

27. Douglass's letter commending his sons to the organizer of the expedition does not appear in Foner and Taylor's selection of Douglass's works, but it is referred to in the *Philadelphia Inquirer*, September 4, 1862. See also the letter by one John Sampson quoted from the *Cincinnati Enquirer* of August 15, 1862, before the news of Lincoln's meeting with the delegation reached the West, in *Harrisburg Patriot and Union*, August 21, 1862.

28. *Chicago Tribune*, August 22, 1862.

29. *Philadelphia Inquirer*, August 29, 1862. It did present an "opportunity" for the African American population "to nationalize themselves such as has seldom been presented to any people."

30. *Philadelphia Evening Bulletin*, August 29, 1862. The *Roman Citizen* of Rome, New York, an antiradical New York paper, commended the plan. The *Pittsburgh Daily Dispatch* of August 19, 1862, denounced it. The *Oneida Weekly Herald* was silent.

31. *New York Times*, August 26, 1862.

32. *New York Herald*, August 16, 1862.

33. Ibid., August 29, 1862.

34. Quoted in the *Harrisburg Patriot and Union*, August 22, 1862.

35. See the *McKean County (Pa.) Democrat* of September 20, 1862, quoting the *Harrisburg Patriot and Union*.

36. *Washington National Intelligencer*, September 9, 1862. Forrest G. Wood in *Black Scare: The Racist Response to Emancipation and Reconstruction* (Berkeley: University of California Press, 1970), 23, regards Cox as a "more strident" political racist than the notorious Copperhead Clement Laird Vallandigham.

37. The *Springfield Illinois State Register* said nothing about colonization after the president's address on the subject and before the appearance of the proclamation. The

Pittsburgh Post reprinted Orpheus C. Kerr's satirical piece on the proposal, discussed later in this essay, on September 3, 1862. See also issues of August 21 and September 12. The *Bellefonte (Pa.) Democratic Watchman* said nothing about colonization from late July to November.

38. *Cleveland Plain Dealer*, August 16 and 20, 1862.

39. *Harrisburg Patriot and Union*, August 22, 1862. It eventually ridiculed the idea.

40. I borrow the term "partisan imperative" from Joel Silbey, *The Partisan Imperative: The Dynamics of American Politics before the Civil War* (New York: Oxford University Press, 1985).

41. For a survey of newspaper positions identified by party see *Washington National Intelligencer*, October 8, 1862, describing ten Democratic newspapers outside the border states.

42. Quoted in the *Washington National Intelligencer*, October 8, 1862.

43. *York Gazette*, September 30, 1862. On October 7 the paper expressed the usual skepticism about the practicality of colonization plans.

44. See for example editorials in the *Harrisburg Patriot and Union*, which had expressed a mild skepticism about colonization before the announcement of the proclamation and which described the "present context . . . [as] a contest between the white and black races for supremacy" after the issuance of the proclamation (see their editorial of September 25, 1862).

45. *Chicago Tribune*, September 21, 1862. On Garnet see Edwin G. Burrows and Mike Wallace, *Gotham: A History of New York City to 1898* (New York: Oxford University Press, 1999), 855, 857, 858.

46. Foner and Taylor, *Frederick Douglass*, 510.

47. *New York Evening Post*, August 19, 1862. It was also reproduced in the abolitionist *Liberator* and numerous other newspapers. For an example of a Democratic paper, see the *Pittsburgh Post*, September 3, 1862.

48. Eric Foner, *Free Soil, Free Labor, Free Men: The Ideology of the Republican Party before the Civil War* (New York: Oxford University Press, 1970), 267–76.

49. Gwendolyn Crenshaw, "'Bury Me in a Free Land': The Abolitionist Movement in Indiana, 1816–1865," 8–9, Indiana Historical Bureau, accessed at <http://www.in .gov/history/3123.htm> (July 21, 2007).

50. I am assuming that he was paid for reports he made to the legislature. At the least, he saw the state circulate his message on colonization.

51. Indianapolis: J. P. Chapman, 1852.

52. *Illinois State Register*, January 1, 1855.

53. Springfield, Ill.: Lanphier & Walker, 1851.

54. Springfield, Ill.: 1853 (broadside).

55. Earl Schenck Miers, ed., *Lincoln Day by Day: A Chronology, 1809–1865*, 3 vols. in 1 (Dayton, Ohio: Morningside, 1991), 1:104–5.

56. *Illinois State Register*, January 16, 1854.

57. Springfield, Ill.: Lanphier & Walker, 1855.

58. Miers, *Lincoln Day by Day*, 1:114.

59. Ibid., 1:136.

60. *CW*, 2:255–56.

61. Miers, *Lincoln Day by Day*, 1:188.

62. *Illinois State Register*, February 5, 1858.

63. See Lincoln to William H. Seward, October 3, 1861, in *CW*, 4:547 and n. and the editors' note at 5:370n.

64. They are worth looking at also because they have been substantially ignored to date. Two standard works ignore Mitchell completely, despite his obvious relevance to their subject: George M. Fredrickson, *The Black Image in the White Mind: The Debate on Afro-American Character and Destiny, 1817–1914* (New York: Harper & Row, 1971); and Voegeli, *Free but Not Equal*. Benjamin Quarles examined his ideas briefly in *Lincoln and the Negro*, 115.

65. James Mitchell to Abraham Lincoln, December 13, 1861, reel 30, Abraham Lincoln Papers, Library of Congress, Washington, D.C. (hereafter cited as Lincoln Papers).

66. James Mitchell, *Letter on the Relation of the White and African Races* (Washington: GPO, 1862), 3, 5, 7.

67. Ibid., 10, 13, 14.

68. Ibid., 13, 26.

69. James Mitchell to Abraham Lincoln, July 1, 1862, reel 37, Lincoln Papers.

70. James Mitchell to Abraham Lincoln, July 3, 1862, ibid.

71. *CW*, 7:55.

72. See Caleb Blood Smith to Abraham Lincoln, May 5, 1862, and Robert Dale Owen to Lincoln, May 6, 1862, reel 35, Lincoln Papers. Both Smith and Owen were from Indiana.

73. After Lincoln's death Mitchell characterized the Emancipation Proclamation as "a colonization document." See Mitchell's *Brief on Emancipation and Colonization and Report in Answer to a Resolution of the Senate* (Washington, D.C.: H. Polkinhorn & Son, 1865).

74. *Chicago Tribune*, August 28, 1862.

75. *Oneida Weekly Herald*, October 14, 1862. The best treatment of the idea appears in Fredrickson, *The Black Image*.

76. *CW*, 5:535–36.

77. *CW*, 2:262.

78. *CW*, 3:130.

79. *CW*, 5:388. Lincoln was careful to add, at the end of the letter, the statement, "I have here stated my purpose according to my view of *official* duty; and I intend no modification of my oft-expressed *personal* wish that all men every where could be free" (p. 389).

80. Douglas L. Wilson, *Lincoln's Sword: The Presidency and the Power of Words* (New York: Alfred A. Knopf, 2006), 149–55.

81. *New York Tribune*, August 22, 1862.

82. The leak was particularly damaging to Seward's reputation among the anti-slavery rank-and-file of the Republican Party. Writing from Brooklyn on the 22nd

itself, one Albert G. Allen asked Seward, "Is it possible that Mr Seward has turned his back upon Freedom?" William Henry Seward Papers, microfilm edition, reel 71, Rush Rhees Library, Dept. of Rare Books, Manuscripts and Archives, University of Rochester, N.Y.

83. McPherson, "What Did He Really Think?," 18.

84. *CW*, 5:420.

85. Thus the best theory remains that of Gabor Boritt, who explores the psychological rather than rational sources of Lincoln's interest in colonization in "Did He Dream of a Lily-White America? The Voyage to Linconia," in Boritt, ed., *The Lincoln Enigma: The Changing Faces of an American Icon* (New York: Oxford University Press, 2001), 1–19. The psychological was more stressed in an earlier version of this, "The Voyage to the Colony of Linconia: The Sixteenth President, Black Colonization, and the Defense Mechanism of Avoidance," *Historian* 37 (1975): 619–33.

Whatever Shall Appear to Be God's Will, I Will Do

The Chicago Initiative and Lincoln's Proclamation

Shortly after the Union's military disaster at the second battle of Bull Run in late summer 1862, Confederate troops crossed the Potomac just twenty-five miles northwest of Washington. Commanding some forty thousand men, Robert E. Lee euphorically urged Maryland slaveholders to throw off their "foreign yoke."[1] If hindsight reveals that the Union capital faced no real threat of capture and that Marylanders were not going to rise en masse, it remains the case that Lee's invasion acted as a hammer blow to northern morale after a summer of desperate military failure. On the day Lee invaded Maryland—September 4—several hundred Chicago Christians gathered in the city's largest meeting place, Bryan Hall. A Methodist reporter emphasized the gathering's social and political mix: "men from the bench, . . . from the counter, . . . from hard daily toil, . . . from the pulpit"; Democrats "who had stood beside [Stephen] Douglas . . . , men of old whig associations, men of the old free-soil party, men who voted the republican ticket." But, he purred, "party was out of sight" as all united to declare "that in this struggle God had been too much forgotten[,] . . . that a great sin stood up against us, and that we must put it away or God's anger must burn against us."[2]

Although the military reversal at Bull Run cast its shadow over the Bryan Hall meeting, it was the cumulative setbacks of the summer that had prompted an appeal to "Christians of all denominations, who believe that the country is now suffering under divine judgments . . . , and who favor the adoption of a memorial to the President of the United States urging him to issue a decree of Emancipation as a sign of national repentance, as well as military necessity."[3] The appeal's hundred or so signatories included laymen from Protestant churches across Chicago, together with all the Congregational clergy and almost all the Baptist and Methodist ministers. (Presbyterian ministers, notoriously conservative, considered the call at their weekly meeting and voted not to sign it.)[4]

This initiative would result nine days later in a meeting between the president and a ministerial deputation from Chicago. That White House encounter commonly features in the historical narrative of the events that began with the cabinet meeting of July 22, 1862, where Lincoln declared his intention of issuing an emancipation edict, and culminated on September 22 in the preliminary proclamation of freedom. As recounted, that narrative takes two conflicting forms. One, set out forcefully and at length by John Nicolay and John Hay in their ten-volume history of Lincoln and his administration, holds that the president maintained a "fixed purpose" throughout this period.[5] Lincoln made an irrevocable decision in July, but he kept the draft proclamation in his desk drawer, waiting—on William Henry Seward's advice—for a battlefield victory that would deny his proclamation any appearance of weakness. This is the interpretative burden of several landmark biographies, including those by Lord Charnwood, James Randall, Benjamin Thomas, Mark Neely, and Allen Guelzo.[6] In this context the visit of the Chicago ministers—along with Horace Greeley's editorial imprecation a month earlier[7]—is remarkable only for putting Lincoln in a position where he had to conceal his intentions, creating a mental strain that, according to Nicolay and Hay, made him "sensitive and even irritable" in his dealings with well-meaning petitioners.[8] On this reading, the simple—if harsh—truth is that the Chicago clergymen's visit was an irrelevant and distracting sideshow, while the wartime reflection of Illinois governor Richard Yates that their memorial "must have had great influence upon the President" prompts a patronizing smile.[9]

A contrasting argument holds that during these two summer months the die was not cast. Rather, the president continued to tussle with the issue. Ida M. Tarbell judged that "an incessant struggle against . . . emancipation went on in his mind through the whole period."[10] A century later, David Herbert Donald is equally clear that the direction of events in August and September, including the Bull Run disaster and Lincoln's recall of George McClellan to command, invited a retreat from emancipation to a more limited war and forced Lincoln to reconsider his policy: "Always hesitant to assume positions from which there could be no retreat, Lincoln deliberated long before making a hard choice."[11] On this reading, the president's discussions with the Chicago visitors indicate a

"The first reading of the Emancipation Proclamation before the cabinet." Painted by
F. B. Carpenter; engraved by A. H. Ritchie (c. 1866). The print shows Abraham Lincoln,
seated at left, with members of his Cabinet on July 22, 1862, on the occasion of Lincoln
reading his preliminary Emancipation Proclamation. Courtesy of the Library of Congress.

man still tussling with a fundamental decision yet to be taken. Indeed, the
case has been made—most forcefully by Lerone Bennett—that Lincoln's
overriding ambition throughout the summer of 1862 was to end the war
with slavery still in place: having changed his mind about emancipation
after the July cabinet meeting, he was waiting for a Union victory, which,
in destroying Lee's army, would eliminate the need for a proclamation.[12]

The matter is not open to a definitive conclusion. Lincoln's account, as
told to the painter Francis Bicknell Carpenter some eighteen months or
so after the event and later corroborated by Nicolay and Hay, underpins
the interpretation of a president who had set an irreversible course.[13] It is
possible that in conversation with the artist—then painting his celebratory portrayal of the first reading of the emancipation edict—Lincoln was
either burnishing his reputation or succumbing to self-deception, but
there is no compelling evidence that he had abandoned the policy that he

Rev. William Weston
Patton, portrait pho-
tograph. Photograph
by Charles Delevan
Mosher. By permis-
sion of the Chicago
Historical Society
Research Center.

had earlier declared. In fact, the case for emancipation was daily growing
stronger: the Confederacy was resilient; Union recruitment had stalled;
foreign recognition of southern independence seemed increasingly likely.

On balance, Lincoln's account is more credible than the alternatives.
But to accept it does not mean having to dismiss as an irrelevance his
meeting with the Chicago deputation. By exploring the particulars of the
occasion, and placing it in the context of Lincoln's broader dialogue with
church communities, it becomes clear that the encounter had a larger, if
often unappreciated, significance.

THE DRIVING FORCE behind the Chicago initiative was a forty-year-old
Congregationalist minister, William Weston Patton. The son of an emi-
nent Presbyterian and trained at New York's Union Theological Seminary,
Patton had accepted calls from Congregational churches in Boston and
later Hartford, Connecticut. These pastorates gave him rein to preach the
Oberlin doctrine of sanctification and champion the antislavery radical-

ism that it inspired. An admirer of the preeminent evangelist Charles G. Finney, Patton won a reputation as a successful revivalist and organizer. His achievements prompted a summons at the age of thirty-five to Chicago's First Congregational Church, a base from which he aimed to strengthen the hold of New England progressive theology and benevolent social action amongst the rapidly growing Yankee population of the Northwest. He quickly won admirers as an able and single-minded antislavery advocate.[14]

Patton is a largely forgotten figure, but he merits attention. With the coming of war his antislavery radicalism translated into a principled Unionism. He encouraged enlistments and drilled new recruits. As the elected vice president of the Sanitary Commission of the Northwest, he inspected camps and hospitals in the western theater. Above all, he was concerned with the bearing of the war upon emancipation. Unhesitating in his admiration for John Brown, whose execution he had honored in the pulpit, he turned his hand to writing new, Christian lyrics to the song "John Brown's Body." In these, Brown emerges as a prophetic figure:

> John Brown was John the Baptist of the Christ we are to see—
> Christ who of the bondmen shall the Liberator be;
> And soon throughout the sunny South the slaves shall all be free,
> For his soul is marching on!

Patton characterized the Union forces as a Christian army of liberation, vindicators of what he deemed Brown's valor in Kansas and Virginia:

> The conflict that he heralded he looks from heaven to view,
> On the army of the Union with its flag red, white and blue.
> And heaven shall ring with anthems o'er the deed they mean to do,
> For his soul is marching on.

These words—widely circulated and predating Julia Ward Howe's version by several months—soon echoed from the mouths of the Union's fighting men.[15]

DURING THE SUMMER of 1862 Patton made an extended visit to the eastern theater of war. Within mainstream religious circles he found strong support for emancipation, but he regretted that it was not being effectively mobilized. Returning home, he set about organizing the Christian sentiment of the Northwest to lobby the Lincoln administration and drew up the call for the Bryan Hall event of Thursday, September 4.[16] He prompted that meeting to set up a committee to draft a memorial to the president and to issue a call for a further mass meeting three days later.

A "mighty gathering" of professing Christians—their regular services cancelled—met that Sunday evening. It was but the latest in a series of meetings of Union loyalists that swelled the hall during the summer, each addressed by the city's combined political, business, and religious leaders.[17] The participants' overblown accounts of this most recent event reveal an occasion buoyed by a sense of "sublime" historic purpose. After preliminaries that included prayer and a rousing rendition of "America," a rapt audience listened as Patton read out his memorial. Subsequent speakers included Thomas M. Eddy, the Methodist editor of the region's leading religious newspaper, and the Congregationalist Joseph Sturtevant —the president of Illinois College and a personal friend of Lincoln— whose address elicited "outbursts of applause, which not even the sanctity of a Sabbath evening could repress." After a collection, and a rousing solo of the "Star Spangled Banner," the assembly rose as one to adopt the memorial and endorsed a set of resolutions prepared by the Baptist minister William Evarts. Patton closed the meeting with the benediction.[18]

Of the ecumenical committee of four appointed to take the memorial to Washington, only two made the journey: Patton himself, as chairman, and John Dempster, a sixty-eight-year-old professor at Evanston's Garrett Biblical Institute.[19] As a young man Dempster had been a stalwart of the Methodist itinerancy in his native New York. Never in robust health, he had withdrawn from the traveling ministry to pioneer ministerial education in New England and, more recently, in the Northwest. Dempster's passionate belief in the future of the United States and its capacity for progress made him a steely opponent of what he deemed slaveholding Methodists' "vicious" reinterpretation of the antislavery tenets of their denomination's founding generation. As a delegate to the Methodist Episcopal Church's General Conference of 1856, he had helped lead the fight to stiffen the rule on slavery in the face of the "anathemas of border State men."[20]

The two ministers set out on the grueling rail journey to Washington in some concern over the direction of military events. But reaching Baltimore "in safty & fateague," as he put it, Dempster took up his pen to reassure his wife. "We hear nothing new of the position or purpose of the Rebbles," he explained, though a major battle was undoubtedly imminent.[21] Arriving at the federal capital early on Thursday, they had no immediate access to the president. A sleepless Lincoln remained preoccupied for the next two days with issues of military command and troop movements. But Patton asked a sympathetic Gideon Welles to effect an introduction. "The President assented cheerfully," Welles recorded, and agreed to meet them on Saturday morning. Riding to the White House from the Soldiers' Home early in the day, Lincoln sprained his wrist trying to restrain his runaway horse, but he received his two visitors affably enough, motioning them to seats near the end of his desk while he took the armchair behind it. The meeting opened with some formality as Patton spent ten minutes reading out the Chicagoans' memorial and presented Evarts's resolutions and a petition from the city's German citizens.[22]

The memorial began with a claim of legitimacy: it was the voice of "all Christian denominations" in Chicago.[23] The key to Patton's document, however, and the premise on which he built its argument, was the interrelationship of the nation and its rulers with "the government and providence of Almighty God." The war was a "terrible visitation" explicable only as a just God's retribution on the land "for its manifold sins, and especially for the crime of oppression." Hearing the cry of the slave, a God of justice had acted, as Thomas Jefferson had warned that He would, with "exterminating thunder." War was also a just punishment for the political rebellion of the slave oligarchy—"the most unnatural, perfidious, and formidable rebellion known to history"—which had set up "an independent government on the avowed basis of slavery," even while conceding that the "Union was constituted to conserve and promote liberty."[24]

Because God could not be expected "to save a nation that clings to its sin," there could be "no deliverance from Divine judgments *till slavery ceases in the land*." The war was becoming daily more destructive, despite the Union's superior resources. Time was running out: "National existence is in peril: our sons and brothers are falling by tens of thousands on the battle-field. . . . While we speak the enemy thunders at the gates of the capital." A lesson lay in the divine judgments visited on Old Testament Egypt and "God's stern command—'LET MY PEOPLE GO!'" Measures already taken—abolishing slavery in the District of Columbia, prohibiting it in the territories, and offering inducements to border-state loyalists to emancipate their slaves—were welcome but inadequate signals of national repentance.

In these circumstances the president—"as the head of this Christian nation"—had the awesome duty to proclaim national emancipation without delay. Addressing the issue of constitutional power, Patton pressed the line of argument implied in Lincoln's public letter to Horace Greeley a few weeks earlier: "However void of authority in this respect you might have been in time of peace, you are well aware . . . that the exigencies of . . . a war to preserve the very life of the nation . . . include all measures that may most readily and thoroughly subdue the enemy." But the case for presidential action went beyond the military. The rebels' bringing of slavery within warrantable attack had created a *moral* as well as political necessity, "and now God . . . demand[s] that the opportunity be used." That the rebels had "placed in our power a system which, while it exposes them, is itself the grossest wickedness, adds infinitely to the obligation to strike the blow."

Developing this argument, Patton rebuked presidential action driven by political and military expediency alone. The change in executive authority over slavery occasioned by the war demanded "an equal change in duty." Yet "gloom" had descended at each sign that the administration treated the war "as simply an issue between the federal authorities and the rebel states; and that therefore slavery was to be touched only to the extent that the pressure of rebel success might absolutely necessitate." Pointedly he asked: "Have we not reason to *expect* rebel success on that policy? . . . Has the fact no moral force, that the war has suddenly placed within the power of the President, the system that has provoked God's wrath? Is there not danger that while we are waiting till the last terrible exigency shall force us to liberate the slave, God may decide the contest against us . . . ?" One conclusion alone was admissible: "We claim that justice, here as everywhere, is the highest expediency."

Patton's memorial closed by invoking the scriptural example of Queen Esther, who had hesitated before intervening to protect the Jews in a time of "national peril," and had acted only after the solemn warning of her adoptive father Mordecai that she and her family would perish through inaction. The episode was the prelude to the dramatic story of Haman, hanged on the high gallows he himself had erected for Mordecai. Lincoln's deep knowledge of scripture—as well as the fact that Mordecai was, along with Abraham, the commonest name in his father's family—made it a story he knew well and had used more than once for political effect.[25] Esther's was a cautionary tale but one also designed to remind Lincoln of the inspiring truth that rulers worked under a God who gave them wide fields of opportunity. The memorialists declared, "in Divine Providence you have been called to the Presidency to speak the word of justice and authority which shall free the bondmen and save the nation." Their prayer was that Lincoln would go down to posterity as George Washington's true heir, "the second SAVIOR OF OUR COUNTRY."

Patton then extemporized, anxious to remove any idea that, at a time of rebel invasion, they were attempting to dictate to the president, who, Patton noted, "had his own responsibility to God, to the nation, and to the world." Rather, they were moved by "the fear, that our reverses might be made needful . . . to learn the moral lessons of the war." The president would surely see that "if military success was thought to render emancipation unnecessary, and defeat to make it unavailing, duty would become an idle word, and God's providence unmeaning."[26]

The three men talked freely for about an hour. Lincoln left no record of the occasion, so we must rely on his visitors' accounts.[27] The president, Patton recalled, spoke "quite deliberately" and solemnly, though often "letting fall a half-humorous observation." As they talked, he "warmed up towards us personally, as if we were true friends." Sitting stiffly at first, he gradually unbent, throwing a leg over the arm of his chair, "gesticulating freely, and looking us intently in the face." Such easy informality, Patton reflected, "would have shocked European ideas of official propriety," but it impressed on his visitors "the simplicity, frankness and sturdy honesty of his nature." Whatever signs of impatience might be read into Lincoln's reported words, the two Chicagoans felt they had been talking with a man who, mixing earnestness and lightness of touch, had given them a respectful, sympathetic hearing.

The discussion revolved around three issues: how to uncover the right answer to the question of emancipation; the practical difficulties standing in the way of emancipation; and the possible benefits that it might yield. Lincoln raised the first of these at the outset. For months he had wrestled with the question. "I am approached with the most opposite opinions and advice, and that by religious men, who are equally certain that they represent the Divine will." But one or the other set of beliefs must be mistaken, possibly both. When the visitors remarked that "nevertheless *the truth was somewhere*," and that they "appealed to the intelligence of the President and to his faith in Divine Providence," Lincoln replied: "Unless I am more deceived in myself than I often am, it is my earnest desire to know the will of Providence in this matter. *And if I can learn what it is I will do it!"* But, he continued, "I hope it will not be irreverent for me to say that if it is probable that God would reveal his will to others, on a point so connected with my duty, it might be supposed he would reveal it directly to me."[28] Since these were no longer "the days of miracles . . . I suppose it will be granted that I am not to expect a direct revelation." Only "the plain physical facts of the case" would reveal "what appears to be wise and right." Patton and Dempster agreed that God worked by means, not miraculous revelation, and that this meant He might use "such humble instrumentalities as ourselves," representative of Christian sentiment in the Northwest and beyond, "to make the way of duty more plain than it might otherwise be." When Lincoln pointed to religious disagreement ("the rebel soldiers are praying with a great deal more earnestness, I fear, than our own troops, and expecting God to favor their side"), his visitors acknowledged this as a historical truism, but one that should not obstruct duty: "It was so in the war of our Revolution, and in the religious wars of Europe. Nevertheless, there was a right side, in each case. And we must pray, and must act, according to our own convictions of righteousness."

Lincoln then moved to ponder the danger that an emancipation edict would remain toothless and unenforceable. "I do not," he remarked with rueful humor, "want to issue a document that the whole world will see must necessarily be inoperative, like the Pope's bull against the comet! Would *my word* free the slaves, when I cannot even enforce the Constitution in the rebel States?" The second Confiscation Act, which he had signed earlier that summer, offered freedom to the slaves of rebel masters crossing into Union lines. "Yet I cannot learn that that law has caused a single slave to come over to us." When the delegation proposed that the advance of the Union armies would spread news of an emancipation decree to the slaves, so prompting their flight, Lincoln asked, "*What should we do with them?* How can we feed and care for such a multitude?" That was exactly the headache then afflicting Ben Butler, commander of Union forces in New Orleans. And what of the consequences when federal troops had to shift ground and leave blacks, free and slave, exposed to imprisonment by rebels, as had occurred recently in an incident on the Tennessee River?[29] Patton replied that Butler's difficulties were the result of half measures and timidity, adding, "It is folly merely to receive and feed the slaves. Paul's sound doctrine was, that those who eat must work." Slaves should be freed, made to labor, enlisted, and drilled "to fight for their own liberty and for the Union which is to protect it." This was what the rebels most feared.

The two parties next discussed the likely benefits of a proclamation. If they were not of one mind, they reached a certain accord. Lincoln conceded that slavery was "the root of the rebellion, or at least its *sine qua non.*" He accepted the delegation's argument that emancipation would be a help in foreign relations, by convincing the European powers "that we are incited by something more than ambition." When Patton and Dempster argued that a proclamation would inspire a more potent patriotism, Lincoln granted "that it would help *somewhat* at the North, though not so much, I fear, as you . . . imagine," adding, "I think you should admit that we already have an important principle to rally and unite the people in the fact that constitutional government is at stake. This is a fundamental idea, going down about as deep as any thing." Weighing once more the visitors' argument that the advance of Union armies would attract refugee slaves who could be deployed in the front line, the president conceded that this would weaken the enemy but doubted "we could do much with the blacks. If we were to arm them, I fear that in a few weeks the arms would be in the hands of the rebels; and indeed thus far we have not had arms enough to equip our white troops." The two visitors demurred: given the scarcity of weapons, "it might be wise to place a part of the supply in the hands of those nearest the seat of the rebellion, having most at stake, and able to strike the heaviest blow."

In setting out the case against an emancipation edict Lincoln raised a concern ("though it meet only your scorn and contempt") that had shaped his approach to slavery and freedom since the first summer of the war: the reaction of the loyal and Union-controlled areas of the Upper South: "There are fifty thousand bayonets in the Union armies from the Border Slave States. It would be a serious matter if, in consequence of a proclamation such as you desire, they should go over to the rebels." Lincoln judged that not all of them would, "not so many indeed as a year ago, or as six months ago—not so many to-day as yesterday." But the concern was real. For their part, Patton and Dempster—no political innocents, and fully alert to the issue's chronic influence on administration policy—seized on the president's admission that the danger was now much reduced. And whatever desertions might result would be more than offset by the animating effect of emancipation on the patriotic majority, who knew that "*nothing else has put constitutional government in danger but slavery.*" They restated their view that a proclamation of free-dom would make "Union and Liberty" the inspirational watchwords of the war, "appealing alike to conscience, sentiment, and hope," and fan-ning nationalist ardor to a new intensity. When the visitors declared, "No one can tell the power of the right word from the right man to develop the latent fire and enthusiasm of the masses," Lincoln exclaimed with some earnestness, "I know it!"

The meeting drew to a close with what Patton described as expressions of mutual cordiality and respect. The Chicagoans commended the presi-dent "to the gracious guidance of the All-Wise God" and left the White House buoyed by Lincoln's parting remarks. According to Patton, Lincoln alluded to the issue of timing. "Matters look dark just now. I fear that a proclamation, on the heels of defeat, would be interpreted as a cry of despair. It would come better, if at all, immediately after a victory."[30] He continued: "Do not misunderstand me, because I have mentioned these objections. . . . I have not decided against a proclamation of liberty to the slaves, but hold the matter under advisement. And I can assure you that the subject is on my mind, by day and night, more than any other." Then, more or less repeating what he had declared earlier, he added, "Whatever shall appear to be God's will, I will do." Comparing impressions after-ward, Patton and Dempster took heart from their interview, convinced that Lincoln's rehearsing of "old and outworn" objections indicated "they had lost to his mind most of the force which they might once have had," that he was in earnest in his scrutiny of divine Providence, and that a proclamation might be expected to follow a battlefield victory.[31]

RETURNING TO CHICAGO, Patton and Dempster presented a written report to an immense meeting at Bryan Hall on September 19, two days after Federal forces had claimed a strategic victory at Antietam, driving Lee out of Maryland. The ministers' report appeared in the press on September 23, printed alongside the preliminary Emancipation Procla-mation that Lincoln had issued the previous day.[32] This sequence of events prompted opponents of the measure to charge the Chicagoans with malign influence, just as emancipationist Christians rejoiced at the lobbyists' success.[33] If, as we have noted, the balance of evidence indicates that Lincoln's course had been fixed since July, then the White House encounter should merit no more than a modest mention in the narrative of wartime emancipation. That meeting, however, takes on greater significance when placed in a larger context, that of the continuing interaction between the White House and the churched community of loyal and progressive Unionists.

Lincoln's meeting with the Chicago deputation was just one, albeit unusually high-profile, instance of his readiness to engage directly with those religious constituencies that lobbied him throughout the war. During the first eighteen months of the conflict the president played host to meetings with committees and individual ministers across the Protestant institutional spectrum: Methodists, Old and New School Presbyterians, Reformed Presbyterians, Baptists, Congregationalists, Evangelical Lutherans, and Progressive Friends. Beyond these, he had conversations with Catholics and Jews.[34] Several of these visitors presented memorials. These, however, represented only a fraction of the petitions with which religious bodies peppered the White House. A definitive total is beyond calculation, but the Abraham Lincoln Papers contain over a hundred memorials and petitions. Lincoln took them seriously and discussed some of the resolutions with his cabinet.

The petitions and memorials that reached the president served two important functions. First, they provided one of the means by which Lincoln was able to read opinion amongst key constituencies and identify significant shifts in public attitudes; second, many of these documents, in reflecting on the role of providence in wartime, worked with the grain of Lincoln's own ruminations on the theological meaning of the conflict, doing so in ways that served his own Calvinistic framework of thought.

First, the president's reading of the religious public. Lincoln would later say that getting the timing of the Emancipation Proclamation right had been one of his chief concerns. "Many of my strongest supporters urged Emancipation before I thought it indispensable, and, I may say, before I thought the country ready for it," he told Francis Carpenter. "It is my conviction that, had the proclamation been issued even six months earlier than it was, public sentiment would not have sustained it."[35] The president took every opportunity to take the public pulse: it was this that kept his door open to visitors of every kind and station. The political importance of the mainstream denominations was not lost on him; rather, he did much to stay accessible to representatives of the churches, especially those that commanded large and influential memberships. It is not necessary to assert—implausibly—that Lincoln pored over every word of the resolutions directed to him to conclude that he noted enough of them to get a feel for shifts in opinion.

The memorials and visitors represented a broad range of denominations and opinion. Between April 1861 and September 1862 at least fifty-three sets of resolutions reached the White House. They included submissions from bodies of Congregationalists (15), Methodists (13), Baptists (8), New School, Reformed and United Presbyterians (8), Wesleyans (2), Lutherans (2), Old School Presbyterians (1), Episcopalians (1), and Quakers (1). As well as offering denominational diversity, they emanated from across the North and were by no means skewed toward the antislavery heartland of New England. Almost half—twenty-three—were the work of church bodies in the mid-Atlantic states of New York, Pennsylvania, and New Jersey. Another twenty emanated from the Northwest: Ohio, Indiana, Illinois, Iowa, Michigan, and Wisconsin.

During the spring and summer of 1861 the chief feature of these patriotic memorials was their uncomplicated loyalty in the face of "iniquitous rebellion" against the flag and the federal constitution. National integrity and reverence for the Union's founders provided the key themes. New York Methodists promised "to use all means legitimate to our calling to sustain the Government . . . in its defence and support of the Constitution and of the nation's welfare"; their Indiana brethren similarly endorsed "defensive war" against "national anarchy and ruin," while New School Presbyterians in their General Assembly styled themselves champions of constitutional liberty against despotism. The rebels, however, were judged not just politically mad: they were unholy. As Connecticut Congregationalists put it: "the right of violent revolution can exist only when a government . . . [has] become intolerably oppressive, . . . the Divine Word in all other cases recognising obedience to human government as to the ordinance of God." This was a rebellion against "the common interests of evangelical religion & civil liberty," an insurgency that threatened "a system of government far in advance of all its contemporaries, and which has so long secured to millions inestimable privileges," one that commanded "the highest regard of the lovers of liberty everywhere, as the model government of the world." Since the Confederate masses were "under the satanic influence of a few leading spirits," Unionists must turn to "the God of our Washington" to "defend the right against the wrong."[36]

Abolitionist sentiment, earnest though it was, formed only a minor stream within this early flood of patriotism. Within a few weeks of the firing on Fort Sumter, Illinois Congregationalists told Lincoln there was "no hope of permanent peace except with the utter eradication of [slavery's] system of iniquity." Shortly afterward, the radical petitioners of the Church Anti-Slavery Society, gathered in Boston, called for government-directed emancipation, quoting John Quincy Adams on the use of presidential war power to abolish slavery: "the guiding star through the war into which we have been forced, is the purpose of God in regard to slavery . . . ; and if our government is still claiming that this struggle can be successful, while the laws of Jehovah are ignored, and His command, 'Let the oppressed go free,' is disregarded, then there is preparing for us a terrible awakening." On the same logic, New York Freewill Baptists called for "the severest penalties" against slavery, including confiscation and the repeal of the fugitive slave law.[37]

From the first, however, ministers who would previously have resisted the label "abolitionist" identified slavery as the cause of the war, not only because it was the slaveholding class that had prompted secession and headed the Confederacy, but also more profoundly because, in the words of New School Presbyterians, "present national difficulties" had to be seen as a just God's chastisement of the country's sins, "both social & political," and above all of slavery. Philadelphia Baptists, in a typical analysis, saw in the war "the judgment of Heaven upon our National sins, among which, as not the least, we confess the sin of human slavery, and earnestly pray for the time when, in some wise and just way, the last vestige of this evil shall be banished from our land."[38] The wickedness of slavery and the heaven-directed cries of enslaved millions had prompted a wise God in His mysterious providence to humble a beloved country with the violence of rebellion: this would remain the steady drumbeat of the vast majority of the messages Lincoln received throughout the period that culminated in his emancipation edict.

Increasingly the circumstances of war turned into ardent emancipationists those whose antebellum loathing of slavery had been checked politically by respect for slaveholders' constitutional rights.[39] The Union's military setback at First Bull Run and the lack of progress across the slaveholding border region led ever more church voices to declare that the war must lead to emancipation. Lincoln's overturning of John C. Frémont's proclamation freeing the slaves of rebel masters in Missouri prompted cross-denominational protests. "Why should that which is the *cause* of all our present calamities & the chief strength of the rebellion, be treated so delicately & guarded so cautiously?" asked a group of Illinois Congregational, Baptist, and Methodist ministers who urged Lincoln to use his war power to rescind his order and press on to abolish slavery. "We greatly fear that the God of justice will *take no part* with us in our present fearful conflict so long as the inhuman relation of human chattel-hood is thus recognized & sacredly protected by our national govern-ment." New Jersey Baptists likewise told Lincoln: "If the rebels raise the issue between slavery and the Constitution . . . we will support the Government in sweeping from the Country that infamous outrage on the rights of man."[40]

Lincoln had powerful strategic reasons for rescinding Frémont's proc-lamation, but the expressions of emancipation sentiment from within mainstream Protestantism during September and October 1861 could hardly have been lost on him. Nor would the words of support from a variety of denominational bodies for his emancipation initiatives during the spring of 1862: a special message recommending congressional finan-cial support for any loyal state adopting gradual, compensated abolition; and signing the bill for abolition in the District of Columbia.[41] Then, during the summer of 1862, as Lincoln pondered the timing of an eman-cipation proclamation, the ecclesiastical chorus of encouragement grew louder still. A new surge of church petitions, the vast majority calling specifically for emancipation and further rights for African Americans, and a few simply hoping the war would bring about slavery's demise, reached the White House before the president issued his edict: they numbered four in June, three in August, and ten in September.[42]

We cannot be sure how much attention Lincoln paid to individual petitions that summer, but his anxiety over whether and when to imple-ment a radical emancipation policy meant he had every reason to take note of reliable weathervanes of opinion. He needed to know how far politically moderate and conservative loyalists—war Democrats and old style Whigs—were ready to swallow a dramatic initiative of this kind. And just a cursory examination of the memorials' contents would have shown him that even among more conservative Unionists opinion was shifting. In August, the Clarion Baptist Association of Pennsylvania ap-proached Lincoln through the state's governor, Andrew Curtin, to proffer resolutions of some ambivalence: although slavery was the cause of the war, "we see not how our Government can interfere directly with the system . . . in the revolted, more than in the Loyal Slave States . . . [and] are glad of its uniform and steadfast refusal so to do"; yet—tellingly—they "rejoice[d] in the indications that God in his Providence, is about to make . . . a great step" to effect its removal.[43] A rare discordant voice was that of the Old School Presbyterian minister and editor of the conservative *New York Observer*, Samuel Irenaeus Prime, who warned Lincoln not to submit to the pressure of Wendell Phillips and other abolitionists to "pervert the war of self defence and national safety, into a revolutionary struggle in which the CONSTITUTION will perish, and republican institutions will be blotted out from this continent." The guileless Prime did his cause no favors, however, by seeking to impress Lincoln with the burgeoning strength of the abolitionist menace: "Countless political and religious newspapers advocate a policy of war by which the constitution is virtually subverted, and REVOLUTION indirectly encouraged."[44] Lincoln responded noncommittally, with a short, polite note of thanks.[45] Prime himself addressed further letters to the president in which, significantly, he made plain that "ultra-conservatives" would accept an emancipation measure as long as a constitutional justification could be found. He conceded that the desire to see slavery eradicated was universal in the North, that few believed that the Union could be restored while the antagonism between free and slave labor persisted, and that the answer lay in a scheme of gradual emancipation and colonization.[46]

Patton and Dempster's visit to the White House thus coincided with an upsurge of petitions, several of them inspired by that month's events in Chicago.[47] When he met the deputation Lincoln knew that since the outbreak of war the vast majority of religious petitioners had blamed the conflict on slavery. He would also have been aware that many went beyond this, calling explicitly for emancipation (in fact, almost half of the submissions during the first eighteen months of the war demanded action to free the slaves).[48] The Chicago initiative confirmed the impressionistic evidence of the petitions and memorials, that emancipationist voices had moved from the antebellum margins to command the wartime Protestant mainstream. Massachusetts Republican George S. Boutwell—against the evidence—remarked of the White House meeting that Lincoln "stated the reasons against emancipation . . . so forcibly that the clergy were not prepared to answer them."[49] More plausibly, however, we should see Patton and Dempster's polite but firm responses to Lincoln's routine arguments acting to confirm the president's sense that mainstream opinion in the Union now stood reassuringly behind emancipation as a war measure.

The memorials addressed to Lincoln served a further purpose. Just one part of his broader dialogue with religious men and women, they collectively expressed an understanding of the war's meaning that complemented his own search to comprehend the workings of providence. The petitioners' God was as an all-seeing, active force in history, ready to dispense retributive justice on a sinful people and delinquent nation, but equally ready to sustain human efforts when directed toward a righteous end. The American Union enjoyed a special purpose in world history as a latter-day Israel. It was the responsibility of the president, "under God," to rescue the nation—a moral being—from its complicity in covenant breaking and sin.

Lincoln did not share the evangelical faith that most of his pious correspondents and visitors proclaimed, but his wartime experience and the responsibilities of office encouraged in him a new religious understanding, closer to the historic Calvinism that had shaped so much of northern Protestantism. Lincoln thought much about the operations of providence throughout his life. Before the war, he regarded providence as a superintending but remote force, working predictably within the rules of the universe that He had created. During the war, however, Lincoln's "providence" became a more personal God: intrusive, active, judgmental, mysterious, and less predictable.[50]

Lincoln himself explained that "from the beginning" he had seen that "the issues of our great struggle depended on the Divine interposition and favor. If we had that, all would be well." In his proclamation for a national day of fasting and prayer, after the defeat at First Bull Run, he confessed private and national sins, acknowledged a justly vengeful God, and prayed for His intervention in support of Union arms. If the Calvinist language here suggests formulaic convention, this was not the case with his private words to Orville Browning during the summer or fall of 1861. When his friend opined that "we can't hope for the blessing of God on the efforts of our armies, until we strike a decisive blow at the institution of slavery," Lincoln replied: "Browning, suppose God is against us in our view on the subject of slavery in this country, and our method of dealing with it?" Browning, impressed, reflected that this "indicated to me for the first time that he was thinking deeply of what a higher power than man sought to bring about by the great events then transpiring."[51] An unfathomable God, actively but mysteriously shaping events, appeared in Lincoln's remarks during the summer of 1862, when a visiting delegation of Progressive Friends urged him to proclaim the slaves free. "Perhaps," he replied, "God's way of accomplishing the end which the memorialists have in view may be different from theirs." These words suggest a man whose changing ideas on divine intervention indicated some movement toward the Protestant mainstream, but whose hesitancy over equating the Union cause with God's will set him apart from it.

Thus, when Lincoln told the Chicago deputation, "Whatever shall appear to be God's will, I will do," he spoke not simply as a leader burdened by secular duty but as one attuned to acknowledging his responsibilities to an Almighty who ruled human actions. According to Lincoln's old Springfield neighbor, the Baptist minister Noyes Miner, who visited Washington in the spring of 1862, the president told him: "It has pleased Almighty God to put me in my present position, and looking up to him for divine guidance, I must work out my destiny as best I can." At other times during this year Lincoln spoke of his "firm reliance upon the Divine arm," of "seeking light from above," and of being "a humble instrument in the hands of our Heavenly Father."[52] Alexander K. Mc-Clure, the Pennsylvania Republican political organizer, was sure that—whatever the disputed particulars of the president's religious views—his declaration to the Chicago ministers that he would seek and do God's will "tells the whole story of Lincoln's action in the abolition of slavery," reflecting as it did his "profound belief in God and in God's immutable justice": "he was one of the last men to believe in miracles . . . but he did believe that God overruled all human actions; that all individuals charged with grave responsibility were but the means in the hands of the Great Ruler to accomplish the fulfillment of justice."[53]

As his discussion with Dempster and Patton revealed, Lincoln's search to discover God's purposes was inextricably entwined with his developing emancipation policy during 1862. It reached its culmination on September 22 when, according to Gideon Welles, Lincoln explained to his cabinet secretaries that "he had made a vow, a covenant, that if God gave us the victory in the approaching battle, he would consider it an indication of the Divine will, and that it was his duty to move forward in the cause of emancipation." Not he, but "God had decided this question in favor of the slaves." Now he would keep "the promise to myself, and"—here Salmon P. Chase spotted a hesitation—"to my Maker." This does not mean that Lincoln's theological reflection in itself explained the change in policy toward emancipation. Military need, political pressure, and the slaves' own pursuit of freedom were the key considerations. But his evolving religious perspective provided new sources of philosophical and psychological support at a time when the old constitutionalism was losing its power. And unlike the majority of evangelical Protestants, who could comfortably embrace emancipation within their familiar millennial doctrine, Lincoln fashioned his own personal theological framework, albeit one with recognizable elements of Calvinism.[54]

FOR SOME OBSERVERS, Lincoln's encounter with the Chicago ministers revealed his idiosyncratic method of reaching and sustaining political conclusions. According to Schuyler Colfax, the president put his searching questions and counterarguments to Patton and Dempster not because he was uncertain about the course he should take, but in order to elicit further arguments to sustain and refine an emancipationist position already inflexibly held.[55] Whether or not the meeting successfully served that purpose, it is surely the case that it had its benefits in reassuring the president that the time was ripe for action and that he could rely on the mainstream Protestant churches as political engines of progressive Unionism. In any event the Chicagoans' insistence on the inspirational effect of an emancipation edict on Unionist sentiment proved accurate enough, not least as denoted in the subsequent flow to Washington of exultant church petitions and memorials extolling a proclamation that, in purifying the war and the nation, opened the way to victory. The edict, Pittsburgh Presbyterians told the president, "inspires the friends of the government and the country with new hope and courage. . . . It is a rainbow upon the political clouds. . . . In the rays of its holy light there is the dawn of a new era. . . . It is the proclamation of the first jubilee America has ever enjoyed." Lincoln's action "evinced a high spirit of devotion to the cause of truth and righteousness, unparalleled Executive courage, and a principle of the purest and most disinterested patriotism."[56]

As Patton and Dempster predicted, the endorsement and widespread celebration by the Protestant mainstream of the preliminary and final Emancipation Proclamations colored the wider political response among loyalists. It encouraged secular Republican-Unionist presses to present what was technically a weapon of war and an administration measure as a

"President Lincoln, writing the Proclamation of Freedom. January 1st, 1863."
Painted by David Gilmour Blythe. Printed in colors by Ehrgott, Forbriger & Co.
Cincinnati. Published by M. Depuy (Pittsburgh, 1863). The proclamation was issued
in 1862 and went into effect in January 1863. The print shows Lincoln at work on the
document in a cluttered study. His left hand rests on a Bible that sits atop a copy of
the Constitution. Some of the many symbolic details and meaningful references in
the print include the bust of the strongly Unionist former president Andrew Jackson
near the window. The bust of Lincoln's predecessor, James Buchanan, widely viewed
as ineffectual against secessionism, hangs by a rope from a bookcase behind Lincoln.
The scales of justice appear to Lincoln's left, and a rail-splitter's maul lies on the
floor at his feet. Courtesy of the Library of Congress.

moral initiative and evidence of the Union's righteousness. Appropriately, there was no more explicit blending of the secular and the religious than in the city of Chicago itself, where the *Tribune* exulted that the New Year's Day proclamation of freedom delivered a tighter bond of Union and an assurance "that until the last soldier of the righteous cause has offered up his life for the unity and indivisibility of the Republic . . . the grand effort for the preservation of national life and honor will not be given up." What gave the edict its "fearful potency" was its closing substantive sentence, in which the president—accommodating Salmon P. Chase's last-minute suggestion—had invoked "the gracious favor of Almighty God" upon an "act of justice, warranted by the Constitution, upon military necessity," and in so doing had proceeded to turn a legal document that could be defended under his war powers into one that also acknowledged his private faith. The *Tribune* cheered this welcome if tardy "recognition of the finger of God in the affairs of nations," an acknowledgment that "the cause which wins an enduring victory must be that which has set upon it the seal of the everlasting Right." Success was inevitable when efforts were based "not upon entities of political growth, but upon the eternal verities acknowledged of God and men." The president, the newspaper declared, "may hereafter claim a proud place among the benefactors of the human kind."[57] Whatever pleasure Lincoln took from such personal accolades, he knew that the tough work of making emancipation a reality lay ahead. But he also knew that his proclamation, in fusing Christian emancipationist sentiment with loyalty to republican freedom, gave him a fighting chance of success.

Notes

I am especially grateful to Nichola Clayton for the excellence of her research assistance in preparing this essay, and to Professor Robert Cook and Dr. Linda Kirk for their shrewd comments on a draft.

1. James M. McPherson, *Battle Cry of Freedom: The Civil War Era* (New York: Oxford University Press, 1988), 536.

2. Thomas Eddy, "Righteous Men and the War," *Northwestern Christian Advocate*, September 10, 1862, 292.

3. "Appeal to the President by the Christian Community of Chicago," Joseph E. Roy Papers, Chicago Historical Society, Ill. See also *Chicago Tribune*, September 4, 1862.

4. William W. Patton, *President Lincoln and the Chicago Memorial of Emancipation, a paper read before the Maryland Historical Society December 12th, 1887* (Baltimore: J. Murphy, 1888), 9–10.

5. John G. Nicolay and John Hay, *Abraham Lincoln: A History*, 10 vols. (New York: Century, 1890), 6:147–58. For an early statement of this narrative, see J. G. Holland, *The Life of Abraham Lincoln* (Springfield, Mass.: Gurdon Bill, 1866), 391–95.

6. Lord Charnwood, *Abraham Lincoln* (London: Constable, 1916), 321–22; James G. Randall, *Lincoln the President*, 4 vols. (New York: Dodd, Mead, 1945–55), 2:156–57; Benjamin P. Thomas, *Abraham Lincoln: A Biography* (New York: Alfred A. Knopf, 1952), 342; Mark E. Neely Jr., *The Last Best Hope of Earth: Abraham Lincoln and the Promise of America* (Cambridge, Mass.: Harvard University Press, 1993), 109–12; Allen C. Guelzo, *Abraham Lincoln: Redeemer President* (Grand Rapids, Mich.: William B. Eerdmans, 1999), 338–42; Allen C. Guelzo, *Lincoln's Emancipation Proclamation: The End of Slavery in America* (New York: Simon & Schuster, 2004), 160–61 (for Lincoln's irreversibility). See also Phillip Shaw Paludan, *The Presidency of Abraham Lincoln* (Lawrence: University Press of Kansas, 1994), 149–52.

7. "The Prayer of Twenty Millions," *New York Tribune*, August 20, 1862.

8. Nicolay and Hay, *Abraham Lincoln*, 6:154.

9. Randall, *Lincoln the President*, 2:157n.

10. Ida M. Tarbell, *The Life of Abraham Lincoln*, 4 vols. (New York: Lincoln Memorial Association, 1895–99), 3:118–19.

11. David Herbert Donald, *Lincoln* (New York: Simon and Schuster, 1995), 374.

12. Lerone Bennett Jr., *Forced into Glory: Abraham Lincoln's White Dream* (Chicago: Johnson Publishing Co., 2000), 468–508. The argument that Lincoln issued the proclamation for essentially political reasons, to wrong-foot Republican radicals and delay emancipation, is set out (though not endorsed) in Richard N. Current, *The Lincoln Nobody Knows* (New York: McGraw-Hill, 1958), 226–28.

13. F. B. Carpenter, *Six Months in the White House with Abraham Lincoln* (New York: Hurd and Houghton, 1866), 20–23.

14. Cornelius H. Patton, *Honour Thy Father. A sermon in memory of William Weston Patton by his son, Rev. Cornelius H. Patton. Congregational church of Christ, Westfield, N.J., April 13, MDCCCXC*. (n.p., 1890), 14–23, 42–43.

15. Ibid., 23–25.

16. Patton, *President Lincoln and the Chicago Memorial*, 9; "The Christian War Meeting," *Chicago Tribune*, September 5, 1862. Almost a year earlier Patton had prompted his First Congregational Church to direct a series of antislavery resolutions to the president. William W. Patton to Abraham Lincoln (AL), October 12, 1861, Abraham Lincoln Papers, Library of Congress, Washington, D.C. (hereafter cited as Lincoln Papers). The concept of a combined political initiative by churches in Chicago and the Northwest was by no means new. For the protest against Stephen A. Douglas's Nebraska Bill in 1854, see Richard J. Carwardine, *Evangelicals and Politics in Antebellum America* (New Haven, Conn.: Yale University Press, 1993), 236.

17. *Chicago Tribune*, July 7, 21, 28. August 7, 1862.

18. "Religious War Meeting at Bryan Hall," September 8, 1862, ibid.; and "The Christian War Meeting," September 9, 1862, ibid.; *Northwestern Christian Advocate*, September 10, 1862. In a letter to Charles Francis Adams, Lincoln called Sturtevant "one of my most highly valued personal friends." We need not doubt that they were

reasonably close, even though Lincoln referred to him as "John" not "Julian." AL to Charles Francis Adams, April 3, 1863, Lincoln Papers. Cf. J. Sturtevant to AL, December 2, 1860, Lincoln Papers.

19. Two of Chicago's leading citizens had been chosen to accompany the ministerial pair. Judge Mark Skinner, a Presbyterian and leading Republican as well as the first chairman of the U.S. Sanitary Commission in the Northwest, had built his civic reputation through the law and real estate. Charles H. Walker, grain merchant, railroad developer, and sometime president of the Chicago Board of Trade, enjoyed a similar reputation for energetic philanthropy and business enterprise. As a Democrat and leading Baptist he extended the denominational reach of the four-man deputation and gave it a cross-party mien. *Chicago Tribune*, June 30 and July 1, 1868; ibid., December 14, 1887.

20. Otis H. Tiffany, "Dr. Dempster as a Man of Progress," in John Dempster, *Lectures and Addresses*, ed. D. W. Clark (Cincinnati: Poe & Hitchcock, 1864), 11–20, 63–70.

21. John Dempster to Lydia Dempster, September 10, 1862, John Dempster Papers, Garrett Evangelical Theological Seminary, Evanston, Ill. Dempster's unorthodox spelling was the mark of an autodidact, an educationalist who—in Otis Tiffany's words— was "unblessed with early culture." Dempster, *Lectures and Addresses*, 66.

22. Earl Schenck Miers, ed., *Lincoln Day by Day: A Chronology 1809–1865*, 3 vols. (Washington, D.C.: Lincoln Sesquicentennial Commission, 1960), 3:138–39; Patton, *President Lincoln and the Chicago Memorial*, 11; Gideon Welles, *Diary of Gideon Welles*, 3 vols. (Boston: Houghton Mifflin, 1911), 1:130; Patton, *Honour Thy Father*, 25.

23. Although there was no roll call of those who thronged Bryan Hall when the memorial was adopted, it is clear that the great majority were mainstream evangelical Protestant churchgoers: Baptists, Congregationalists, Methodists, and Presbyterians.

24. For the full text of the memorial see *Chicago Tribune*, September 9, 1862, reprinted in Patton, *President Lincoln and the Chicago Memorial*, 11–16.

25. "It may do no harm to say that 'Abraham' and 'Mordecai' are common names in our family." AL to Solomon Lincoln, March 6, 1848, in *The Collected Works of Abraham Lincoln*, 9 vols., ed. Roy P. Basler (New Brunswick, N.J.: Rutgers University Press, 1953–55), 1:456 (hereafter cited as *CW*); cf. 1:459–60. Lincoln's Uncle Mordecai was the eldest of three brothers, his father Thomas being the youngest. As a boy of fourteen, Mordecai killed one of the Indians at whose hand Lincoln's grandfather, Abraham, died. Ibid., 2:217. Referring to the Democratic administration of President James K. Polk and the conflict with Mexico, Lincoln told William H. Herndon: "The war is now to them, the gallows of Haman, which they built for us, and on which they are doomed to be hanged themselves." Ibid., 1:477. Cf. AL to Joshua Speed, August 24, 1855, ibid., 2:321.

26. Patton, *President Lincoln and the Chicago Memorial*, 17.

27. After the meeting Patton and Dempster promptly recorded their account. *CW*, 5:421–25. This purports both to quote Lincoln verbatim and to summarize their discussion. Patton's later account, as delivered to the Maryland Historical Society in 1887, better captures the give-and-take of the occasion while mostly retaining the

phraseology of the earlier version. Patton, *President Lincoln and the Chicago Memorial*, 17–33. The next four paragraphs draw on both accounts.

28. This elegant formulation is more dryly humorous than the vulgarized version reported by Schuyler Colfax: "if it [the call for emancipation] is, as you say, a message from your Divine Master, is it not odd that the only channel he could send it by was that roundabout route by that awfully wicked city of Chicago?" Allen Thorndike Rice, ed., *Reminiscences of Abraham Lincoln by Distinguished Men of His Time* (New York: North American Publishing Company, 1886), 335.

29. On August 31, 1862, Confederates captured the U.S. transport steamer *W. B. Terry*, which had run aground at Duck River Shoals. On September 5 the vessel's master reported to Gen. Henry W. Halleck in Washington that his "deck and cabin crew numbered 17 (all negroes), . . . some of whom were free, [but they] were all sent back in the country immediately after capture." *The War of the Rebellion: A Compilation of the Official Records of the Union and Confederate Armies*, 128 vols. (Washington: GPO, 1880–1901), ser. 1, 17(1):52–53. The question of how to deal with "contrabands"—Ben Butler's coinage for runaways who crossed into Union lines—had prompted a variety of responses from federal civilian officials and military commanders since the early weeks of the war: that there was no single, clear-cut policy reflected both military realities and political need.

30. Patton, *President Lincoln and the Chicago Memorial*, 32. This particular passage is not in the contemporary newspaper report. It appears only in Patton's account of 1887, which must raise the question of its authenticity.

31. Ibid., 32–33.

32. *Chicago Tribune*, September 23, 1862. The report appeared in the *National Intelligencer* on September 26.

33. Dempster, *Lectures and Addresses*, 68.

34. *The Lincoln Log: A Daily Chronology of the Life of Abraham Lincoln* (an electronic publication of the Papers of Abraham Lincoln: a project of the Illinois Historic Preservation Agency and the Abraham Lincoln Presidential Library and Museum), <http://www.thelincolnlog.org>. See entries for June 11, October 29, November 26 and 27, December 11, 1861; January 10 and 12, March 17, April 8, May 13, June 20, July 17, and August 22, 1862.

35. Carpenter, *Six Months in the White House*, 77.

36. George W. Woodruff to AL, Thursday, April 18, 1861 (resolutions of the New York East Conference of the Methodist Episcopal Church); T. B. Gary to AL, April 18, 1861 (Greensburg District, South Eastern Indiana Conference, Methodist Episcopal Church); Edwin F. Hatfield to AL, May 21, 1861 (Presbyterian General Assembly); G. B. Willcox to AL, June 30, 1861 (General Association of the Congregational Ministers of Connecticut); Presbytery of Oregon, United Presbyterian Church (Linn County, Oregon) to AL, September 18, 1861, Lincoln Papers.

37. Congregational Union of Fox River to AL, May 6, 1861; Henry T. Cheever to Department of State, June 6, 1861; George H. Ball to AL, June 22, 1861, Lincoln Papers.

38. Edwin F. Hatfield to AL, May 21, 1861 (Presbyterian General Assembly); Philadelphia Baptist Association to AL, October 8, 1861, Lincoln Papers.

39. James H. Moorhead, *American Apocalypse: Yankee Protestants and the Civil War, 1860–69* (New Haven, Conn.: Yale University Press, 1978), 96–112; Victor B. Howard, *Religion and the Radical Republican Movement, 1860–1870* (Lexington: University Press of Kentucky, 1990), 11–67; John R. McKivigan, *The War against Proslavery Religion: Abolitionism and the Northern Churches, 1830–1865* (Ithaca: Cornell University Press, 1984), 183–201.

40. Hamilton, Ill., ministers to AL, October 1, 1861; Central New Jersey Baptist Association (resolutions), October 16, 1861, Lincoln Papers. Cf. Branch County, Michigan, Baptists, September 28, 1861, Lincoln Papers.

41. Cleveland Congregational Conference to AL, April 18, 1862; H. H. Van Dyck (General Synod of the Evangelical Lutheran Church of the United States) to William H. Seward, May 9, 1862, Lincoln Papers.

42. Religious Society of Progressive Friends to AL, June 7; Albert Church to AL, June 9 (East Maine Annual Conference of the Methodist Episcopal Church); H. G. Woodworth to AL, June 20 (Wisconsin Free Will Baptists); Emerson Davis to AL, June 28 (General Association of Congregational Ministers in Massachusetts); Clarion Association of Baptist Churches to A. G. Curtin, August 23; Benjamin H. West to AL, August 27 (Boston Park Street Church); New Hampshire Association of Presbyterian and Congregational Ministers, August 28; Milwaukee Wisconsin Congregational Church Resolutions, September 5; J. W. Chaffin and William Froth to AL, September 6 (Miami Conference of Wesleyan Methodist Connection); Cincinnati, Ohio, Methodist Church Conference to AL, September 8; Indiana Methodist Convention to AL, September 12; J. W. Wellman to AL, September 12 (Massachusetts Congregational Churches); Millburn, Illinois, Congregation to AL, September 14; North Illinois Conference of the Methodist Church to AL, September 14; J. Durbin to AL, September 15 (North Ohio Annual Methodist Conference); W. C. McCarthy and Thomas Pert to AL, September 16 (churches of Waverley, N.Y.); J. Lester Williams et al. to AL, September 18 (West Wisconsin Methodist Church Annual Conference); Timothy Stillman to AL, September 18 (Genesee, N.Y., Presbyterian Synod), Lincoln Papers (all 1862).

43. Clarion Baptist Association, Pennsylvania, August 23, 1862, Lincoln Papers.

44. Samuel I. Prime to AL, August 21, 1862, Lincoln Papers.

45. The letter is in John Hay's hand, but signed by Lincoln. AL to Samuel I. Prime, August 23, 1862, *CW*, 5:391.

46. *New York Observer*, August 28, 1862. See also ibid., September 4, 1862. Neither letter is in Lincoln Papers.

47. See, for example, Millburn, Illinois, Congregation to AL, September 14, 1862; North Illinois Conference of the Methodist Church to AL, September 14, 1862, Lincoln Papers; Howard, *Religion and the Radical Republican Movement*, 34–35.

48. Twenty-five out of the fifty-three petitions submitted from April 1861 to the end of September 1862 called for emancipation (or approved the preliminary proclamation, once issued).

49. Rice, *Reminiscences of Abraham Lincoln*, 125.

50. For a fuller discussion of the points of convergence between Lincoln's Calvinism and antislavery evangelicalism see Richard Carwardine, *Lincoln: A Life of Purpose and Power* (New York: Alfred A. Knopf, 2006), 221–28. See also Guelzo, *Abraham Lincoln*, 325–29.

51. *CW*, 4:482–83, 5:279, 6:244–45; Michael Burlingame, ed., *An Oral History of Abraham Lincoln: John G. Nicolay's Interviews and Essays* (Carbondale: Southern Illinois University Press, 1996), 5. Similar sentiments, but more fully developed, can be found in Lincoln's "Meditation on the Divine Will," which Nicolay and Hay, and Basler, believe to have been composed in September 1862. Douglas L. Wilson, *Lincoln's Sword: The Presidency and the Power of Words* (New York: Alfred A. Knopf, 2006), 254–56, persuasively places it in or nearer the year 1864.

52. "Remarks to a Delegation of Progressive Friends," June 20, 1862, *CW*, 5:279; "Reply to Eliza P. Gurney," October 26, 1862, *CW*, 5:478.

53. A. K. McClure, *Abraham Lincoln and Men of War Times* (Philadelphia: Times Publishing Co., 1892), 90.

54. *Diary of Gideon Welles*, 1:143; John Niven, ed., *The Salmon P. Chase Papers*, vol. 1: *Journals, 1829–1872* (Kent, Ohio: Kent State University Press, 1993), 1:394; Douglas L. Wilson and Rodney O. Davis, eds., *Herndon's Informants: Letters, Interviews, and Statements about Abraham Lincoln* (Urbana: University of Illinois Press, 1998), 167–68.

55. Rice, *Reminiscences of Abraham Lincoln*, 334–35.

56. Pittsburgh [Reformed] Presbyterian Church to AL, October 1, 1862, Lincoln Papers. Cf. Lynn, Massachusetts, Congregationalists to AL, 1862 [September–December]; New York Association of Congregational Churches to AL, September 25, 1862; Marcellus Barman and E. W. Stevens to AL, September 25, 1862 (Wisconsin Conference of Wesleyan Methodist Connection); A. C. Hand and W. W. Satterlee to AL, October 11, 1862 (West Wisconsin Annual Conference of the Wesleyan Methodist Connection); Robert Patterson to AL, October 13, 1862 (Chicago Reformed Presbytery); Chester County, Pennsylvania, Society of Progressive Friends to AL, October 1862; Samuel Hersey, E. G. Brooks, and Abel C. Thomas to AL, November 3, 1862 (General Convention of the Universalist Church); J. K. W. Levane and A. M. Milligan to AL, [September–December] 1862 (Reformed Presbyterians); Caleb Russell and Sallie A. Fenton to AL, December 27, 1862 (Iowa Quakers); W. B. Raber to AL, January 29, 1863 (Pennsylvania Annual Conference of the United Brethren), Lincoln Papers.

57. *Chicago Tribune*, January 3, 1863; *CW*, 6:28–30; Guelzo, *Lincoln's Emancipation Proclamation*, 179–80.

STEVEN HAHN

But What Did the Slaves
Think of Lincoln?

During the months surrounding the presidential election campaign of 1860, and especially during the late winter and spring of 1861, reports circulated across the southern states of political attentiveness and restlessness among the slaves. Observers noted the slaves' attraction to "every political speech" and their disposition "to linger around" the hustings or courthouse square "and hear what the orators say." But even more significantly, witnesses told of elevated hopes and expectations among the slaves that Lincoln intended "to set them all free." Indeed, once Lincoln assumed office and fighting erupted between the Union and Confederacy, hopes and expectations seemed to inspire actions. On a plantation near Petersburg, Virginia, a group of slaves celebrated Lincoln's inauguration by proclaiming that they were free and marching off their owner's estate. In northern Alabama slaves had apparently come to believe that "Lincoln is soon going to free them all" and had begun "making preparations to aid him when he makes his appearance." A runaway slave in Bossier Parish, Louisiana, told his captors in late May 1861 that "the North was fighting for the Negroes now and that he was as free as his master." Shortly thereafter, Louisiana planter Kate Stone breathed a sigh of relief when the Fourth of July, when Lincoln called Congress into special session, "passed without any trouble with the Negroes." "In some way," she confided to her diary, "they have gotten a confused idea of Lincoln's Congress meeting and of the war; they think it is all to help them and they expected for 'something to turn up.' "[1]

Historians have, for the most part, treated reports such as these as evidence of the generally unsettled state of affairs in the slave South of this period, and particularly of the fears and stresses that secession and the outbreak of hostilities placed on the minds of slaveholders and other white southerners. But the very geographical breadth of the reports, and their alignment with the appropriate moments of political salience, should encourage us to think more deeply about their meanings. They appeared to emanate from all over the slave states: from the Chesapeake to Texas, from the Lowcountry to the Lower Mississippi Valley, from plantation and nonplantation districts alike. "During the campaign when Lincoln was first a candidate for the Presidency," Booker T. Washington, who grew up in western Virginia, later remembered, "the slaves on our far-off plantation, miles from any railroad or large city or daily newspaper, knew what the issues involved were." And "when the war was begun . . . every slave on our plantation felt and knew that, though other issues were discussed, the primal one was that of slavery."[2]

Washington's recollections as to what western Virginia slaves thought about Lincoln's election and the goals of the Civil War bear close resemblance to what slaves seemed to imagine elsewhere, and together they suggest both networks of communication able to stretch into remote areas of the rural South and the circulation of political ideas and discourses—indeed, the development of what might be called political narratives—that framed and drew into relation events near and far.[3] These narratives helped place episodic rumors, or truth claims, in an unfolding interpretive context and gave slaves the opportunity to engage in political conversations with each other and to build individual and collective political knowledge. They must, in short, be regarded as a central way in which slaves practiced politics, and they offer a new perspective on what slaves did and did not do at a variety of conjunctures, and for our purposes, especially during the Civil War. In a sense, that is, it might be useful for us to devote a bit less time to the question of what Lincoln thought about slavery and slaves and a bit more time to the question of what slaves thought about Lincoln—about who he was, what he represented, what he intended to accomplish—and what they did as a result.

EVIDENCE OF THE slaves' political narratives comes to us in a number of forms. It comes to us in the accounts of slaves who fled to the North during the antebellum era or of former slaves who spoke or wrote at some point in the postemancipation period. It comes to us in testimonies presented at federal or state hearings during the Civil War and Reconstruction. It comes to us in speeches commemorating emancipations

"The effects of the Proclamation—freed Negroes coming into our
lines at New Bern, North Carolina." Illustration in *Harper's Weekly*,
February 21, 1863. Courtesy of the Library of Congress.

before and after the Civil War—including emancipation in the West
Indies—or perhaps commemorating the independence of Liberia. And it
comes to us in confessions rendered, often under duress, by those accused
of plotting, abetting, or participating in acts of rebellion.[4] More often, the
evidence comes to us in fragments, in the papers and diaries of slaveholders or in reports printed in local newspapers, and thus in the words of
white observers speculating as to the causes of slave unrest. Few historians have uncovered more of these fragments, over greater temporal and
geographical space, than has the late Herbert Aptheker in his book, *American Negro Slave Revolts*, a work that deserves new reading, not so much
for its arguments about the incidence of slave rebellion as for the world of
political discourse it makes available to us.[5]

The fragments very much suggest discursive and interpretive dynamics by which slaves assimilated information about the social and political
world around them to their own specific concerns and aspirations. They
indicate that slaves could become aware of conflicts that erupted between

groups of white people and nations ruled by whites; that slaves often imagined a host of possible allies as well as enemies; that slaves could learn about the national and international struggle over slavery and the slave trade, and, depending on where they resided, about momentous emancipations; that slaves often became acquainted with institutions and issues of local and national politics, and might develop sophisticated understandings of how the American political system operated; and that slaves fashioned interpretations of what seemed to be afoot, sometimes in ways that moved well beyond the intentions of the political actors.

The most arresting evidence of the slaves' political interpretations joined news of some event or the appearance of some official with potentially far-reaching changes in their circumstances. Thus, as early as 1730, the arrival in Virginia of Governor Alexander Spotswood provoked "unlawful Meetings" and "loose Discourses" among the slaves, who speculated that he carried an order from the king "to sett all those slaves free that were Christians." Such speculation might also accompany news of shifting military balances among warring European nations at other points in the eighteenth century—as during the Seven Years' War—not to mention incite flight and rebellion, as in Stono, South Carolina, in 1739 or during the American Revolution.[6] But the pulse of political discussion and assessment—of political expectation—among slaves appeared to quicken in the nineteenth century, as slavery came under growing international attack and as American politics was increasingly rent by the slavery question.

It often required little more than signs of political tension or division among white leaders to generate intense speculation among the slaves, all the more so if there was any possible association with the fate of slavery. Small wonder that black preachers in eastern North Carolina attempted to convince their congregations in the early 1820s—apparently with some success—that "the national government had set them free . . . and that they were being unjustly held in servitude." This was, after all, the very time when the debate over Missouri's admission to the Union embroiled the country and rang a "firebell in the night" perhaps even louder than Thomas Jefferson may have feared. Could the slaves not have imagined—given the frets of their owners and reports of the votes in Congress—that opponents of Missouri's admission as a slave state had greater designs and had carried the day, only to see their victory blocked on the ground in the South? Slaves in Charleston, South Carolina, may have reached a similar conclusion in 1822 after learning that the state legislature had taken up the question, not of emancipation but of private manumission.[7]

Hotly contested presidential elections, even with no obvious connection to the slavery issue, could also stir expectations. The bitter election of 1800 between John Adams and Thomas Jefferson, Federalists and Republicans, when many free Americans worried that the nation teetered on the brink of dissolution or civil war—together with the more than decade-long revolution in St. Domingue—provided the context for Gabriel's massive conspiracy in the vicinity of Richmond, Virginia. Years later, according to the recollections of a fugitive slave, "there came a report from a neighboring plantation," just before the election of 1836, "that if Van Buren was elected, he was going to give all the slaves their freedom." Indeed, the rumor "spread rapidly among the slaves," prompting great "rejoicing" and identifications with "the children of Israel." In Georgia in 1840, William Henry Harrison's campaign led some slaves to assert boldly that if Harrison "became President of the United States, they should have their freedom."[8]

It is difficult to know whether slaves had some sense of Adams's and Jefferson's different views on the Haitian Revolution, or whether they had heard about Van Buren's stand on Texas annexation, or whether they made something of Harrison's Whig affiliation and Ohio residence. But what they seemed to glimpse was that their owners might have committed enemies and themselves potential allies. This was what Georgia politician Howell Cobb surmised during the national election of 1844, when the Liberty Party chose a presidential candidate. The "negroes," he recorded, "are already saying to each other that great men are trying to set them free and will succeed." By the fall of 1856, as the Republican Party fielded its first contestant for presidential office, rumors that liberation might be at hand flew so vigorously among the slaves that they, in turn, sent rumors of slave insurrection circulating among the whites. William Webb, who spent his years in bondage moving between Kentucky and Mississippi, dated the slaves' awareness of "another Nation wishing for [us] to be free" to Frémont's campaign and went on to describe secret meetings and discussions over an extended territory.[9]

When Frémont suffered defeat, the slaves, according to Webb, spoke "among themselves about what steps to take." Some, he claimed, talked of "rebelling and killing"; others were prepared to "wait four more years," feeling that "the next President would set the colored people free." The idea of waiting "four more years" not only suggests a familiarity with the cycles of formal American politics but also conveys a sense of growing, if not impending, possibility. Lincoln thus quickly came to embody the greatest hopes and expectations, in good measure because slaveholders made such dire predictions as to what his presidency would bring: warning of abolition, the destruction or confiscation of plantations, racial "amalgamation," a veritable world turned upside down at the hands of "Black Republicans." In the view of a worried Kentucky slaveholder, the slaves "know too much about [Lincoln], there has been so much talk about the matter all through the State, . . . [they] know as much about it as we do . . . and too much for our own safety and peace of mind." The historian Winthrop Jordan was certain that by early 1861 slaves in Adams County, Mississippi, "knew the name of Lincoln and that he was an enemy of those who claimed to own them," and it is likely that there and elsewhere such knowledge had come at least several months before.[10]

The hopes and expectations, the rumors of imminent freedom, the narratives of impending change carried forth by an agent with great power are compelling for many reasons, not least because they are common to the history of slave and peasant societies more generally and have hastened crises of servile orders in Europe, Asia, and the Americas. From at least the 1790s onward—and likely well before that—many plots and rebellions were surrounded by rumors that amelioration (improvement of material conditions, shortening of the work day or week, the end to whipping) or emancipation had been decreed by the king, the imperial parliament, or the colonial office only to be withheld by planters, lords, or representatives of the local regime. As news of the French Revolution began to circulate in the colonies, slaves in St. Domingue, Martinique, and Guadeloupe imagined that the king and the National Assembly had either abolished the use of the whip and provided slaves with more free time or abolished slavery entirely; before long what would become the Haitian Revolution exploded among the sugar plantations of St. Domingue's northern plain. Word that the British parliament had discussed a motion in early 1823 for gradual emancipation and the extension to slaves of the protection of British law was interpreted by slaves in Demerara to mean that they had been granted freedom and were being unjustly held in bondage. Several months later, more than 10,000 slaves from sixty plantations rose in rebellion, hoping to force the colonial governor to give them freedom or, at minimum, some free days each week.[11]

The great Jamaican revolt of 1831–32, known as the "Baptist War," was similarly accompanied by rumors that the king had intervened on the slaves' behalf but that their freedom papers were being withheld by the masters. Ninety years later and half a world away, peasants in colonial India spread what were deemed to be "fantastic rumors" that Mohandas Gandhi, who traveled among the villages to mobilize nationalist sentiment, was in fact being sent by the British viceroy or king to redress their grievances and that his mandate superseded that of all local officials and courts.[12]

Some scholars have come to call rumors and narratives such as these "naive monarchism": an ill-placed belief on the part of peasants, slaves, or other subaltern groups that the king, the czar, or some other powerful leader favored their interests but was being thwarted in his efforts by unfaithful subordinates. "If the czar only knew!" But, in truth, the rumors and narratives displayed more sophistication than naiveté. By invoking the will and authority of the monarch or the president or even some presidential candidate whose power to effect change was generally acknowledged, peasants or slaves who had no standing in the formal arenas of politics were nonetheless able to project themselves and their aspirations onto the terrain of political struggle. Indeed, by imagining a distant and all-powerful ally who shared their goals, they simultaneously gave the lie to their master's or lord's haughty claims and lent confidence to their followers who otherwise would have been reluctant to risk defeat.[13]

Now, it may well be said that by misunderstanding and misrepresenting the will and intentions of the sovereign, peasants and slaves were only exposing their followers to brutal repression in what would likely be an utterly lost cause. And in many instances this was surely what happened. Their imaginations failed them, and the consequences were disastrous. No sovereign came to their aid, and they were left to face the onslaughts of militias and paramilitaries with few weapons or other means of defense. Their leaders were cut down in battle or executed and mutilated after being captured, and their communities suffered further vengeance. Yet there were significant occasions when peasants or slaves—acting on incorrect interpretations—managed to shift the political balances and create circumstances in which what they imagined might in fact be achieved. There probably were no other ways in which what they imagined and hoped for could be achieved.

THE SLAVES IN the American South who came to believe in 1860 and 1861 that Abraham Lincoln intended to abolish slavery and that he waged war against the Confederacy from the first to achieve that purpose for the most part got it wrong. Lincoln's policy, as is well known, was to restrict the expansion of slavery into the federal territories of the West but also to recognize that slavery in the states was a local institution, beyond the reach of the federal government. And he went to great lengths to assure southern slaveholders that he would uphold the Constitution, even as to the Fugitive Slave Law, and make no moves against them and their property. At the very moment when slaves in the vicinity of Kate Stone's Louisiana plantation imagined that the meeting of "Lincoln's Congress" would produce something beneficial for them, Lincoln's Congress was in fact promising to respect "established institutions" when federal armies marched south.[14]

The slaves, of course, were not entirely misguided. "You think slavery is *right* and ought to be extended," Lincoln could observe to his friend Alexander Stephens in December 1860, "while we think it is *wrong* and ought to be restricted. That I suppose is the rub." More important, the slaves' interpretations comported, in many respects, with those of their owners, and especially with the secessionist sentiment coursing throughout the South. Many slaves undoubtedly learned about the political stakes in 1860–61 from overhearing their owners' discussions and debates, or had their own assessments validated in that way. At all events, they appeared to develop their interpretations in consultation with each other, perhaps, as William Webb suggested, at clandestine meetings where they may well have conducted their own debates, and then they appeared to act upon those interpretations. Which is to say that the slaves' understandings of local and national events composed an important part of their political consciousness; that they could stimulate forms of organization on and between plantations and farms; and that they could result in action.[15]

Consider the case of Harry Jarvis. Born a slave in Northampton County, on the eastern shore of Virginia, around 1830, Jarvis labored under a particularly harsh master who became even tougher and more brutal once the Civil War began. After being shot at, Jarvis took to the woods for several weeks where he survived owing to fellow slaves who kept him informed and brought him food. Then, when an opportunity presented itself, Jarvis hustled down to the shore, found a canoe and a sail, and headed to Fortress Monroe, thirty-five miles across the bay, where Union troops under the command of Gen. Benjamin F. Butler were stationed. "That was before General Butler had allowed we was contraband," Jarvis remembered, though certainly not before Jarvis had determined to his satisfaction what the war was about. "I went to Butler and asked him to let me enlist," Jarvis claimed, "but he said it *wasn't a black man's war*." Jarvis held his ground: "I told him it *would* be a black man's war before they got through."[16]

Jarvis had fled to the woods and then to Fortress Monroe in the spring of 1861. It seems clear that he did so with understandings as to what was going on and what he might find. It seems clear, too, that he relied heavily on the intelligence and support provided by other slaves, and that he took flight at great personal risk from his gun-toting owner. At this stage in the war, slaves like Jarvis seemed to be testing their expectations. They tended to head to Union lines as individuals or in small groups, over-whelmingly young and male, assisted by other slaves, but also in the face of great danger and uncertainty. Jarvis himself was set to work and, by his lights, "was getting on very well, till one day I see a man given up to his master that come for him." Concluding that Fortress Monroe was no place for him, Jarvis hired onto a ship bound for Cuba and what turned out to be a two-year absence from the United States.[17]

Yet, in testing their expectations, the slaves began to reshape Union policy. By the time of the first battle of Bull Run, General Butler had declared fugitives like Jarvis to be "contrabands of war," and nearly one thousand slaves had made their way to Union lines. Before too much longer, northern armies moved into the densely populated slave planta-tion districts of coastal South Carolina (November 1861) and the lower Mississippi Valley (spring 1862), and the volume and character of the slaves' flight changed rather dramatically. Now the slaves often came in large groups, often linked by kinship, encompassing much of the labor force of entire plantations and farms.[18]

By the middle of 1864, nearly 400,000 of them had reached Union lines—about 10 percent of the entire slave population of the South—and, as if to ratify Harry Jarvis's prediction, it had become something of a *black man's war*. Congress had passed confiscation acts in the summers of 1861 and 1862, which validated Butler's contraband policy and then granted freedom to slaves owned by rebel masters once they made it to Union

"Seated African American soldier, wearing uniform and gloves." This unidentified figure was one of nearly 200,000 African American men who fought for their freedom during the Civil War. Courtesy of the Library of Congress.

lines. It prohibited slavery in the western territories, overturning the Supreme Court's ruling in the *Dred Scott* case of 1857, and abolished slavery in the District of Columbia, although with monetary compensation for the slave owners. Lincoln had issued both the preliminary Emancipation Proclamation (which still held out the prospects of compensation for slaveholders and colonization for slaves) and then the Emancipation Proclamation (which jettisoned both compensation and colonization), and, based in part on its directives, African American men—the great majority of whom had been slaves when the war began—were being enrolled in the Union armed forces.[19]

The flight of the slaves and its role in transforming federal policy on the slavery question is very well known. However one might choose to interpret Lincoln's views on slavery and the future status of slaves, it is very difficult to conceive of him embracing uncompensated emancipation when he did had it not been for the ways in which slaves simultaneously disrupted slavery in the Confederate states and made themselves available for military service to the Union. Yet scholars have effectively presented the slaves' actions as little more than a spontaneous *response* to the invasion of the Union army, almost entirely disconnected from the slaves' many struggles of the prewar era, even though documentary evidence close at hand suggests a range of deliberations in which slaves engaged, some ending in decisions to stay put.

THE QUESTION OF what the slaves thought of Lincoln offers us an opportunity to look at the slaves' activities during the Civil War in a new and different light. It allows us to recognize slaves as the political actors they surely were, participating in a complex universe of politics with interconnecting arenas, influencing the dynamics and understandings of sectional conflict and then war itself: that is to say, it enables us to see plantations, farms, and the liminal terrain in between, much as polls, hustings, courthouses, conventions, and legislatures, as important political sites. It also permits us to think about how the slaves themselves may have imagined the coming of emancipation, about what was and was not interpretively transformed by the wartime process, and about how understandings of emancipation shaped their perspectives on the projects and struggles of postemancipation society.

If the question of what the slaves thought of Lincoln suggests a world of politics among them—a world of communication, conversation, debate, organization, expectation—then it might also encourage us to consider the possibility that the Civil War involved two rebellions: a rebellion of slaveholders against the authority of the federal government (secession and the formation of the Confederacy); followed by a rebellion of slaves against the authority of their masters. With the exception of W. E. B. Du Bois, there has been a great reluctance—indeed an outright refusal—on the part of scholars to regard what thousands of slaves did during the war as a rebellion. But one wonders why. After all, this is precisely how slaveholders and Confederate officials regarded what many slaves did in fleeing their plantations and joining the Union army. They spoke of "disturbances," "contagions," "symptoms of revolt," "terrible stirs," "stampedes," "mutinies," "strikes," "turn outs," and "states of insurrection." Georgia slaveholding evangelist and one-time reformer Reverend Charles Colcock Jones had no confusion about how to characterize "Negro slaves absconding to the enemy." "Can such Negroes be summarily dealt with under any acts of the state?" he asked his son, who was serving as an officer in the Confederate army. "Could they be taken up under the head of insurrection? Could their overt rebellion in the way of casting off the authority of their masters be made by construction insurrection."[20]

The slaves' rebellion—if we may call it that—in the Civil War South shared important features with slave rebellions that occurred at various times and places in the Americas. It erupted at a moment of bitter division and conflict between the society's white rulers, exposing fissures in the ranks of the dominant elites. It utilized networks of communication, intelligence, and interpretation that had been built over years, if not decades, among the slaves. It imagined powerful allies, including those who wore the badges of government authority, coming to their aid, whose goals and objectives were thought to coincide with theirs. It witnessed individual and collective acts of flight, not as efforts to settle scores or protest specific grievances, but as a means of leaving enslavement behind and embracing a newly available or imagined freedom. And it ultimately saw slaves seize arms and battle against the slaveholders in an attempt to defeat them and destroy the institution of slavery. In these regards, there are powerful resonances with the Stono Rebellion (1739) in South Carolina, with marronage in the Caribbean and Latin America, with Gabriel's conspiracy in Virginia (1800) and the rising in St. John the Baptist Parish, Louisiana (1811), with nineteenth-century rebellions in Barbados, Demerara, and Jamaica, and with the flight of thousands of American slaves to British lines during the Revolutionary War that Gary Nash has termed "the greatest slave rebellion in the history of Great Britain's New World colonies."[21]

The slaves' rebellion during the Civil War, in its dynamics and outcome, may in fact bear closest resemblance to what has long been regarded as the greatest and only successful slave revolt in modern history: the one that erupted in St. Domingue during the 1790s. Although such an association may appear odd if not counterintuitive, there is, on examination, a compelling case to be made. The sugar-growing Caribbean, unlike the American South, is generally seen to have been a hotbed of slave rebelliousness. Yet St. Domingue, like the American South, did not have much of a tradition of slave revolt before the late eighteenth century. Marronage was endemic, and a slave plot of some significance was hatched in 1757 only to be crushed brutally before it could be carried out; otherwise skirmishes on the plantations percolated, and St. Domingue emerged as the leading producer of sugar and coffee in the eighteenth-century world (just as the American South emerged as the leading producer of cotton in the nineteenth). The sparks leading to rebellion, moreover, flew out of a massive struggle between whites that initially had nothing to do with them—in this instance, the French Revolution of 1789—while many slaves in St. Domingue had accordingly come to believe that the King of France had granted them freedom or relief from the worst of slavery's exploitation, only to be thwarted by their oppressors in the colony (as many slaves in the American South had come to believe that Lincoln had granted them freedom or intended to do so when his armies conquered the Confederates).[22]

To be sure, the uprising in St. Domingue had many distinctive features compared to what transpired in the Confederate South or in any other slave society of the Americas. Still, in both St. Domingue and the Confederate South, flight from the plantations—marronage—was integral to the rebellions. In both places complex and shifting alliances with and struggles against large standing armies proved decisive to the rebellions' outcome. And in both places, the rebellions became social and political revolutions: resulting in the abolition of slavery, the military defeat of the slave owners, and the effective birth of new nations.[23]

There is indeed an argument to be made that the revolution made by slave rebellion was even more far-reaching in the Confederate South than it was in St. Domingue. Thousands of slaves took part in the revolution in St. Domingue, many more than took part in the great rebellions in Jamaica and Demerara. But St. Domingue had a slave population of about half a million—about the same number of slaves who rebelled against their masters and found their way to Union lines during the Civil War. The slaves' rebellion in the South, that is, was by far the largest of them all, and it took place and helped transform a slave society that was by far the largest and most stable in the Americas.

On the eve of the Civil War, few free people in the United States would have imagined that slavery would come to such a convulsive and decisive end by a combination of military action, executive order, and constitutional amendment. Most everywhere else in the Atlantic world slavery was abolished gradually, with compensation to slave owners, and even after the Civil War began Lincoln envisioned a lengthy emancipation process, replete with compensation and, perhaps, with colonization (features of which were still to be found in the preliminary Emancipation

"Beaufort, South Carolina. Group of negroes on J.J. Smith's plantation." Photograph by Timothy O'Sullivan. A group of approximately thirty African Americans are gathered around a large slave cabin in 1862. Courtesy of the Library of Congress.

Proclamation). The slaves alone seemed to imagine something different, and in organizing and acting upon what they imagined, they helped bring history in line with their expectations. It was a rare, stunning, and immensely courageous historical feat, and our nation has yet to acknowledge it adequately.

Notes

1. *Macon (Ga.) Daily Telegraph*, September 8, 1860, quoted in Clarence Mohr, *On the Threshold of Freedom: Masters and Slaves in Civil War Georgia* (Athens: University of Georgia Press, 1986), 37; John J. Cheatham to Hon. L. P. Walker, May 4, 1861, and Wm. H. Lee to J. Davis, May 4, 1861, both in Ira Berlin et al., eds., *Free At Last: A Documentary History of Slavery, Freedom, and the Civil War* (New York: New Press, 1992), 4–5; Merton Dillon, *Slavery Attacked: Southern Slaves and Their Allies, 1619–1865* (Baton Rouge: Louisiana State University Press, 1990), 240–42; Armstead Robinson, *Bitter Fruits of Bondage: The Demise of Slavery and the Collapse of the Confederacy, 1861–1865* (Charlottesville: University of Virginia Press, 2005), 44; John Q. Anderson, ed., *Brokenburn: The Journal of Kate Stone, 1861–1868* (Baton Rouge: Louisiana State University Press, 1955), 37. See also Anthony E. Kaye, *Joining Places: Slave Neighborhoods in the Old South* (Chapel Hill: University of North Carolina Press, 2007), 177–87.

2. Booker T. Washington, *Up from Slavery*, ed. William L. Andrews (1901; reprint, New York: Norton, 1996), 10.

3. Our understanding of the development and workings of these networks is being advanced in important work by Anthony Kaye, *Joining Places*, and Susan O'Donovan, "Trunk Lines, Land Lines, and Local Exchanges: Operationalizing the Grapevine Telegraph" (unpublished manuscript, 2007). I have discussed slave communication networks at length in *A Nation under Our Feet: Black Political Struggles in the Rural South from Slavery to the Great Migration* (Cambridge, Mass.: Harvard University Press, 2003), especially in Chapters 1–3.

4. These would include the WPA ex-slave narratives, edited and published by George Rawick, *The American Slave: A Composite Autobiography* (Westport, Conn.: Greenwood Publishing Company, 1972), as well as a number of other collections of WPA narratives for specific states, such as Charles L. Perdue et al., eds., *Weevils in the Wheat: Interviews with Virginia Ex-Slaves* (Bloomington: Indiana University Press, 1976); the narratives of fugitives from slavery published in the first half of the nineteenth century, as well as a variety of narratives, autobiographies, and interviews published after the Civil War, some of which are collected in John W. Blassingame, ed., *Slave Testimony: Two Centuries of Letters, Speeches, Interviews, and Autobiographies* (Baton Rouge: Louisiana State University Press, 1977); investigations by the American Freedmen's Inquiry Commission in 1863 (Record Group 94, National Archives, Washington, D.C.), the Joint Congressional Committee on Reconstruction (*Report of the Joint Committee on Reconstruction*, 39th Cong., 1st sess. [Washington: GPO, 1866]); and the *Testimony Taken by the Joint Select Committee to Inquire into the Affairs of the Late Insurrectionary States*, 42nd

Cong., 2nd sess., 13 vols. (Washington: GPO, 1872); studies of emancipation celebrations by Jeff Kerr-Ritchie, *Rites of August First: Emancipation Day in the Black Atlantic World* (Baton Rouge: Louisiana State University Press, 2007), Kathleen Ann Clark, *Defining Moments: African American Commemoration and Political Culture in the South, 1863–1913* (Chapel Hill: University of North Carolina Press, 2005), William H. Wiggins Jr., *O Freedom!: Afro-American Emancipation Celebrations* (Knoxville: University of Tennessee Press, 1987), and David Blight, *Race and Reunion: The Civil War in American Memory* (Cambridge, Mass.: Belknap Press of Harvard University Press, 2001); and confessions and testimonies by accused slaves, handled in a particularly interesting way by Winthrop D. Jordan, *Tumult and Silence at Second Creek: An Inquiry into a Civil War Slave Conspiracy* (Baton Rouge: Louisiana State University Press, 1993).

5. Herbert Aptheker, *American Negro Slave Revolts* (New York: Columbia University Press, 1943).

6. Ibid., 179–80; Peter Wood, *Black Majority: Negroes in Colonial South Carolina from 1670 to the Stono Rebellion* (New York: Knopf, 1974); Mark Smith, ed., *Stono: Documenting and Interpreting a Southern Slave Revolt* (Columbia: University of South Carolina Press, 2005), 4, 9, 14, 16–17; Gary Nash, *The Forgotten Fifth: African Americans in the Age of Revolution* (Cambridge, Mass.: Harvard University Press, 2006), 1–67; Sylvia Frey, *Water from the Rock: Black Resistance in a Revolutionary Age* (Princeton, N.J.: Princeton University Press, 1991).

7. Merton L. Dillon, *Slavery Attacked: Southern Slaves and Their Allies, 1619–1865* (Baton Rouge: Louisiana State University Press, 1990); Michael P. Johnson, "Denmark Vesey and His Co-Conspirators," *William and Mary Quarterly* 58 (October 2001): 960–71.

8. See, for example, Douglas R. Egerton, *Gabriel's Rebellion: The Virginia Slave Conspiracies of 1800 and 1802* (Chapel Hill: University of North Carolina Press, 1993); James Sidbury, *Ploughshares into Swords: Race, Rebellion, and Identity in Gabriel's Virginia, 1730–1810* (New York: Cambridge University Press, 1997); Gerald W. Mullin, *Flight and Rebellion: Slave Resistance in Eighteenth-Century Virginia* (New York: Oxford University Press, 1972), 140–63; Dillon, *Slavery Attacked*, 187–88.

9. William Webb, *The History of William Webb, Composed by Himself* (Detroit: E. Hoekstra, 1873), 14, 23, 26; Wendell Addington, "Slave Insurrections in Texas," *Journal of Negro History* 35 (October 1950): 414–17; Eugene D. Genovese, *From Rebellion to Revolution: Afro-American Slave Revolts in the Making of the Modern World* (Baton Rouge: Louisiana State University Press, 1979), 128–29.

10. Webb, *History of William Webb*, 13; Jordan, *Tumult and Silence*, 5; Robinson, *Bitter Fruits of Bondage*, 41–42.

11. See, for example, David P. Geggus, *Haitian Revolutionary Studies* (Bloomington: Indiana University Press, 2002), 12; Laurent Dubois, *Avengers of the New World: The Story of the Haitian Revolution* (Cambridge, Mass.: Belknap Press of Harvard University Press, 2004), 97–98; Laurent Dubois, *A Colony of Citizens: Revolution and Slave Emancipation in the French Caribbean, 1787–1804* (Chapel Hill: University of North Carolina Press, 2004), 85–123; Emilia Viotti da Costa, *Crowns of Glory, Tears of Blood: The Demerara Slave Rebellion of 1823* (New York: Oxford University Press, 1994), 169–206.

12. Mary Turner, *Slaves and Missionaries: The Disintegration of Jamaican Slave Society, 1787–1834* (Urbana: University of Illinois Press, 1982), 150–51; Michael Craton, *Testing the Chains: Resistance to Slavery in the British West Indies* (Ithaca: Cornell University Press, 1982), 300–301; Shahid Amin, "Gandhi as Mahatma: Gorakhpur District, Eastern UP, 1921–1922," in *Selected Subaltern Studies*, ed. Ranajit Guha and Gayatri Chakravorty Spivak (New York: Oxford University Press, 1988), 292–93.

13. For a pioneering consideration of "naive monarchism," see Daniel Field, *Rebels in the Name of the Tsar* (1975; reprint, Boston: Unwin Hyman, 1989), 1–29. For important treatments of how peasants, slaves, and other subaltern groups practiced politics in these ways, see James C. Scott, *Domination and the Arts of Resistance: Hidden Transcripts* (New Haven, Conn.: Yale University Press, 1990); Jerome Blum, *The End of the Old Order in Rural Europe* (Princeton, N.J.: Princeton University Press, 1978), 332–76; Ranajit Guha, *Elementary Aspects of Peasant Insurgency in Colonial India* (1983; reprint, Durham, N.C.: Duke University Press, 1999).

14. When, for example, Gen. Benjamin Butler led his Massachusetts troops toward Fort Monroe, Virginia, in April 1861, he offered to "co-operate" with Governor Thomas Hicks of Maryland in "suppressing" any slave "insurrection" that might break out, and other Union officials ordered their officers and troops on the ground elsewhere to do the same. See Gen. B. F. Butler to Gov. Thomas H. Hicks, April 23, 1861; Maj.-Gen. George B. McClellan to Col. Irvine, May 26, 1861; F. J. Porter to U.S. Troops of This Department, June 3, 1861, all in *The War of the Rebellion: A Compilation of the Official Records of the Union and Confederate Armies*, 128 vols. (Washington: GPO, 1880–1901), ser. 1, 2:47–48, 593, 661–62. On Lincoln's views, see "First Inaugural Address," March 4, 1861, "Proclamation Calling Militia and Convening Congress," April 15, 1861, both in Abraham Lincoln, *Selected Speeches and Writings* (New York: Vintage Books, 1992), 284–93, 296–97. On Congressional pledges, see Edward McPherson, *The Political History of the United States of America during the Great Rebellion* (New York: Philp & Solomons, 1864), 286.

15. Lincoln to Alexander H. Stephens, December 22, 1860, in *Selected Speeches and Writings*, 275–76. On the circulation of political ideas and interpretations during this period in the Natchez District of Mississippi, see Kaye, *Joining Places*, 177–87.

16. Harry Jarvis in Blassingame, *Slave Testimony*, 607–8.

17. Ibid., 608–9.

18. Louis Gerteis, *From Contraband to Freedman: Federal Policy Toward Southern Blacks, 1861–1865* (Westport, Conn.: Greenwood Publishing Company, 1973); Robert F. Engs, *Freedom's First Generation: Black Hampton, Virginia, 1861–1890* (Philadelphia: University of Pennsylvania Press, 1979), 25–28; Joel Williamson, *After Slavery: The Negro in South Carolina during Reconstruction, 1861–1867* (Chapel Hill: University of North Carolina Press, 1965), 4–5; Ira Berlin et al., eds., *The Destruction of Slavery*, ser. 1, vol. 1 of *Freedom: A Documentary History of Emancipation, 1861–1877* (New York: Cambridge University Press, 1985), 22–27, 103–7, 187–99, 249–56; John Eaton, *Lincoln, Grant, and the Freedmen: Reminiscences of the Civil War* (1907; reprint, New York: Negro Universities Press, 1969), 1–2; Robinson, *Bitter Fruits of Bondage*, 138–45.

19. McPherson, *Political History*, 197–98, 237–38; Ira Berlin et al., *The Wartime*

Genesis of Free Labor: The Lower South, ser. 1, vol. 3 of *Freedom: A Documentary History of Emancipation, 1861–1877* (New York: Cambridge University Press, 1990), 77–80.

20. Rev. C. C. Jones to Lt. Charles C. Jones Jr., July 21, 1862, in Robert Manson Myers, ed., *The Children of Pride: A True Story of Georgia and the Civil War* (New Haven, Conn.: Yale University Press, 1972), 935. Also see Anderson, *Brokenburn,* 28; Alexander F. Pugh Plantation Diary, July 3, 1863, Alexander F. Pugh Family Papers, Louisiana State University Archives, Baton Rouge, La.; Anonymous to Friend, January 3, 1863, Department of the Gulf, Record Group 393, Part I, Letters Received, Series 1756, National Archives, Washington, D.C.; C. Peter Ripley, *Slaves and Freedmen in Civil War Louisiana* (Baton Rouge: Louisiana State University Press, 1976), 97; Bell I. Wiley, *Southern Negroes, 1861–1865* (New Haven, Conn.: Yale University Press, 1938), 74–75. In his enormously important book on Reconstruction, W. E. B. Du Bois described the slaves' flight from their plantations and farms to Union lines as a "general strike." See *Black Reconstruction in America, 1860–1880* (New York: Atheneum, 1935), 55–83.

21. See Smith, *Stono;* Craton, *Testing the Chains;* Stuart Schwartz, *Slaves, Peasants, and Rebels: Reconsidering Brazilian Slavery* (Urbana: University of Illinois Press, 1992), 103–36; Egerton, *Gabriel's Rebellion;* Adam Rothman, *Slave Country: American Expansion and the Origins of the Deep South* (Cambridge, Mass.: Harvard University Press, 2005); Viotti da Costa, *Crowns of Glory;* Nash, *The Forgotten Fifth,* 30–31 and passim.

22. For recent and influential treatments of the rebellion in St. Domingue, see Dubois, *Avengers of the New World;* Madison Smartt Bell, *Toussaint Louverture: A Biography* (New York: Pantheon Books, 2007); Geggus, *Haitian Revolutionary Studies;* Carolyn Fick, *The Making of Haiti: The Saint Domingue Revolution from Below* (Knoxville: University of Tennessee Press, 1990); Laurent Dubois and John Garrigus, eds., *Slave Revolution in the Caribbean, 1789–1804: A Brief History with Documents* (Boston: Bedford/St. Martins, 2006). Also see the still powerful C. L. R. James, *The Black Jacobins: Toussaint L'Ouverture and the San Domingo Revolution* (New York: Dial Press, 1938).

23. The rebellion-turned-revolution in St. Domingue lasted for more than a decade (1791–1804). Slavery was initially abolished at the behest of French commissioners on the ground in 1793 and then ratified by the revolutionary government in France in 1794. The slave rebels succeeded in defeating the armies of Spain and Britain and finally of France when Napoleon sent his forces to his Caribbean colonies to reimpose slavery. In 1804 the newly independent republic of Haiti was proclaimed.

STEPHANIE MCCURRY

War, Gender, and Emancipation
in the Civil War South

There is an important pattern in the history of slave emancipation in the western hemisphere, one insufficiently specified in the historical literature and of considerable significance for the history of slave and freed women—the intimate association of war and emancipation in the modern period. From the American War of Independence to which the "first" U.S. emancipation was tied, to the Brazilian, surrender of slavery in the aftermath of the Paraguayan War, to virtually everything in between—St. Domingue, the Spanish-American Wars of Independence, the U.S. Civil War, the Ten Years War in Cuba—in every major case except the British colonies slaves fought for and won their independence in the context of war.[1] It was in the context of war that slave men became particular objects of state interest, "able bodied men of military age," the focus of intense competition between warring states for political loyalty and military service. In this respect the American Civil War was hardly unique: In those two warring states, the United States of America and the Confederate States of America, as in so many others, military service and emancipation were linked temporally and causationally, as manhood and citizenship would be when they followed with Union victory.

But if that pattern of war and emancipation emerges so strikingly from the record, historians have not accorded it much significance. Robin Blackburn, whose magisterial survey, *The Overthrow of Colonial Slavery*, affords him a bird's eye view of the comparative landscape (he misses only Cuba), repeatedly references the context of war in the destruction of colonial slave regimes, but declines to identify it as a causational factor. "The rise of antislavery reflected pressures at every level of the social formation," Blackburn insists, "and significant advances were only to be made in the context of crises gripping the whole system." In another context he explains, "Social revolutionary overturns are more important than the simple disruption associated with war." While Blackburn is surely correct that it is not war itself that precipitates emancipation— "that no element of antislavery should be considered in isolation"—it is also surely the case that there is no such thing as the simple disruption of war, especially for modern slave regimes.[2] Indeed, Blackburn's own combined emphasis on crises of state, the slaves' antislavery, and the necessity of widening the conception of citizen all point to one crucial condition of war: The reaching into, and claiming of, the male slave population by various states in the competition for soldiers. The relationship of war, slave enlistment, and emancipation is a significant and underappreciated one in the history of emancipation.

There is, moreover, one compelling reason to focus on war itself, even if, in a larger sense, Blackburn is right: Because it isolates for purposes of analysis a particular relationship between military service and the gender patterns of emancipation, fundamental—emphatically not incidental— to the way the process unfolded in the United States, as in so many other times and places before and after. What, it is fair to ask, are the implications for women of an emancipation accomplished during war? It is something of a pressing question, I would argue, given that we now so commonly think of "slaves" (a gender neutral term) as earning emancipation by military service. It is worth noting that the question has not really been posed, not in the now massive literature on emancipation in the United States or in newer literatures on gender and emancipation and on the history of arming slaves. The literature on the gender history of emancipation, which is now considerable and broadly comparative, is focused decidedly on *post*emancipation societies, on the differences in the meanings of freedom, rights, and citizenship that men and women were able to claim as free people. My immediate interest, however, is not on what happened after (a critical problem for sure) but more narrowly on the process by which slavery was destroyed and emancipation accomplished, changes fired all too often in the crucible of war.[3]

The idea that emancipation ought to be understood as a process— protracted, regionally uneven, and highly contingent—is now well understood. In the U.S. literature, especially under the influence of the editors of the Freedmen and Southern Society Project, historians have been led away, interpretively speaking, from "the apparent certitude and finality of the great documents that announced the end of chattel bondage" to an appreciation of the complex process so long obscured and the ways in which slaves "became the prime movers in securing their own liberty."[4] But the elemental contingency of a process drawn out over five years of war was, for enslaved men and women, not only a matter of administrative reluctance, regional circumstance, proximity to Union troops, or any number of other random circumstances as the literature emphasizes but, everywhere, also of gender itself. For where military service emerged as a critical route to emancipation, as it did in the United States, enslaved men's and women's opportunities to lay claim to the status of free people—and the means by which they did so—differed fundamentally, such that we might think of them as taking particular gendered routes to emancipation and to the citizenship that service allegedly secured.

This chapter begins to trace out those routes and their gender patterns, focusing on the relation of war and emancipation as it shaped the historical process for enslaved women. In that respect, the essay is intended as a corrective to a history of emancipation now overly focused on the figure of the slave soldier and on the way slaves earned emancipation and citizenship through military service. Whatever the merits of that story, and they are considerable, its simplifications distort. For if "slaves" can be said to have come to freedom and citizenship by military service clearly only some (male ones) could do so, which thus implies a related story about how slave women were liberated by their men. Sometimes the argument is explicit, as in the emphasis on slave men's flight to Union lines, their enlistment in the Union army or navy, and their daring raids back into Confederate territory to "liberate their wives and children." More often it is just grammatically implicit in the heroic narrative of those slaves (who could only be men) who fled to Union lines, demonstrated the value of their military labor or service, and made emancipation a matter of military necessity.[5] In that now standard account, slave men took the martial route to emancipation, and slave women, apparently, the marital one, which is to say that women got freedom at second hand, by way of marriage and in relation to their husbands' rights.

There was a distinct gender logic and design to Union and (less well-known) Confederate policies intently focused on the military recruitment of slave men, something this essay attempts to lay out. But wartime military policies hardly provide a reliable description of, or good basis for, a full history of slave emancipation, especially not of slave women's

"Cumberland Landing, Va. Group of 'contrabands' at Foller's House."
Photograph by James F. Gibson. The African Americans shown in the
picture—mostly women and children—are sitting in front of a cabin during the
Peninsula Campaign in May 1862. Courtesy of the Library of Congress.

experience in the Civil War, their part in the destruction of slavery, or their political self-perception. Freed women, it is true, could not be thought of as fighting for their freedom. But neither, of course, could most freed men. After all, only about 150,000 slave men fought in the Union armed services.[6] Rather, like the rest of the slaves,—the 3.5 million trapped within Confederate lines—women waged their own kind of war against the slaveholders' state. As many freed women would say for the record, on the rare occasion they had to tell their story, freedom was no gift or attribute of marriage but something they had earned for themselves no less than had the men in their political community.

Although the essay is concerned primarily with the United States, it begins with the quintessential case of St. Domingue, where slave emancipation emerged as French Republican policy in the context of a revolutionary and imperial war that consumed the island and the whole Caribbean for more than fifteen years. It then turns to a consideration of the policies of the Union and Confederate states in the American Civil War with respect to arming slaves.

THE AMERICAN CIVIL War was a late development in the history of slave emancipation in the Americas and hardly the first emancipation to unfold in the vortex of war. The pattern emerged early and dramatically in the French colony of St. Domingue in the revolutionary struggle initiated by free colored colonists and transformed decisively in 1791 by a massive revolt of slaves on plantations in the northern part of the island. The onrushing course of events quickly yielded a many-sided struggle—between free colored men, insurgent slaves, and planters and, after 1793, when Britain declared war, between France, Spain, and Britain, all of whom moved to arm slaves in a war of imperial competition and land grab that played out across the whole Caribbean for more than a decade.[7] A full accounting of the arming of slave men in St. Domingue's revolutionary war would be a lengthy affair, but a few key moments, all following the slave revolt in the North in 1791, are suggestive of the central and, as it turns out, perseverant patterns involved.

As early as 1790, some parties in the revolutionary struggle in St. Domingue had moved to arm and train their own slaves, notably the wealthy *gens de couleur* emboldened in their demands for equal citizenship by events in Paris and especially by the decrees of the Constitutional Assembly in 1791 extending voting rights to qualified mulattoes. From the outset factional conflict had led to the arming of some (still modest numbers of) slaves.[8] But the real competition for slave soldiers was set in motion by the massive self-arming of slaves in the North in August 1791, in the historic revolt of enslaved men and women against the planters, against slavery and the French Republican state still intent on preserving it. By the end of 1791 black leaders had built substantial slave armies that continued to grow in numbers in part from alliance with already existing maroon bands. And it was from that position of strength that the self-proclaimed black generals proceeded with a war begun in 1793 to negotiate the terms of their service between contending European powers, first with the Spanish forces invading St. Domingue, and then with the beleaguered and overmatched French Republican forces scrambling to repulse and defeat the Spanish.

In the early years of the Haitian Revolution, as we now call it, universal emancipation was an unthinkable goal, liberty an issue only in the most militarily delimited way, available only to men directly under arms—and not even to all of them.[9] In early negotiations with French Republican civil commissioners in late 1791, for example, the black generals demanded freedom for themselves and 400 of their followers.[10] The deal would have obligated them to force the remainder of their own insurgents —men and women both, presumably—back into plantation labor. Even that limited deal was refused. By late 1792, facing French Republican forces allied with *gens de couleur* in the project of restoring slavery on the island, leaders of the biggest slave armies in the North had cut deals with the Spanish in exchange for supplies and official recognition of the freedom of the black soldiers. If there were any terms negotiated for women and other members of their families and kin groups historians have not noted them. A full two years after the slave insurrection in the North, then, there were massive numbers of slave men under arms (Biassou had at least 6,000, and Jean François almost as many).[11] But many more men and women were still on the plantations, in maroon bands in the hills, or trapped in the British occupied zone, and the only new route to emancipation—military service—was one that could only be taken by men. It was entirely closed to women.

In this highly militarized context, the terms on which slave women, including insurgent ones, would be able to negotiate freedom were soon announced. On June 21, 1793, Léger Félicité Sonthonax, one of the civil commissioners sent by the French Republic, facing a coup by the governor-general of the colony, made a desperate bid for the loyalty and military service of the mass of slave men, offering liberty to all slave insurgents who would fight for the Republic. Only the timely arrival of reinforcements under the control of two black generals (Macaya and Pierrot) and the sack of Le Cap (the principal city) turned the tide. Emboldened, Sonthonax extended the offer, two weeks later issuing a proclamation in Creole and French promising freedom "to the women-folk of black warriors *as long* as they were prepared to go through a Republican *marriage ceremony.*"[12]

Although mentioned only in a footnote in Blackburn's otherwise de-tailed account, this emancipation policy was, as historian Elizabeth Col-will has remarked, a critical reflection of the centrality of marriage and patriarchal authority in French Republican policy, as it would be fifty years later in the American Civil War. Indeed, as Colwill notes, because owners were to be compensated by the state for slave soldiers freed, the emancipation of women (such as could claim it) "took the form of a purchase (indemnity) that transferred women slaves from the hands of their masters to those of their husbands thorough the intervention of the Republic." The difficulties of access to that provision—not least because slave women did not possess the right to enter contracts, and notaries often refused to register the marriages—was only one of its limitations, although one that would come up again in the United States. Not only did whites and colored men across the political spectrum thus construct the slaves in insurrection as male, they also forged a new model of the re-publican citizen-soldier that would long constrain the meanings of free-dom and access to it for women.[13]

For French radicals, especially Sonthonax, emancipation was a prin-cipled and not purely instrumental act, but it was the conditions of war and, crucially, slave insurrection that necessitated it in 1794. Shaped irreducibly by war, emancipation touched men directly and women only indirectly, by virtue of their marriage to the republic's soldiers. So when Toussaint L'Ouverture took his army over to the French following the general emancipation decree of February 1794, he preceded it with a call to his "brothers" to unite with him in the fight for liberty and equality in St. Domingue.[14] It could seem sometimes as if the nation itself, born in war, was male. The differences were not short lived. Even after Sontho-nax, backed by legislators in Paris, declared *all slaves* free, the reach of that administrative decree depended entirely (as would the Emancipation

Proclamation in the U.S. Civil War) on military victory. For years women in the British occupied zone had no route (not even marriage) to emancipation, and women in the North would struggle to document their own and their children's freedom through marriage and baptismal records, so tenuous was their hold on it.[15]

Notwithstanding the great document—the first universal emancipation decree in history—there was nothing final about emancipation in 1794. Until 1803, when Napoleon and the French were defeated by the black armies of St. Domingue, the restoration of slavery still threatened (indeed it was accomplished in the other French islands); emancipation was not secured; and the military service of formerly and still potentially enslaved men was required in the extended process by which St. Domingue slaves finally could call themselves free.[16]

As elsewhere where emancipation was secured in war—which is to say in most places in the late eighteenth and nineteenth centuries, including the United States of America in 1861–65—emancipation in St. Domingue came in stages and was tied first to the freedom of those willing to perform military service in defense of the republic. The gendering of freedom thus was no abstraction; its meanings for women were concrete and real, although in St. Domingue, as in the United States, this has not much been recognized.[17] In St. Domingue and Haiti, the militarization of society meant that for years men were siphoned off to the army and women forcibly returned to the plantations as part, first of the colonial, and then of the national project of resurrecting the plantation sector of the export economy. It comes, then, as a sharp reminder of women's alternate conception of the new citizenship when, in 1796, women workers (scheduled to receive two-thirds of a male worker's share of the crop), went on strike during the harvests until promised equal pay.[18] Whatever else this action means, it suggests the limits of a state view of slave women as recipients of freedom through marriage, dependent parties, or minors in the historic project of slave emancipation.

WHEN, MORE THAN half a century later, American slaves made their bid for emancipation in the context of a war that exceeded in scale even that which had convulsed the Caribbean in the 1790s, many of the same conditions and conceptions of republican freedom pertained. In the United States, despite the apparent certitude and finality of the Emancipation Proclamation, the process by which slaves reached freedom was dangerous, uncertain, usually protracted, and, as in St. Domingue, had to be negotiated differently by men and women. For in the U.S. Civil War, southern slaves' insurrection against both slavery and the Confederate state alerted Union military men to the potential utility of their labor, loyalty, and military service and put emancipation on the agenda (as Lincoln put it in his economical way in the Emancipation Proclamation) as a "fit and necessary war measure."[19] In that respect the text of the great document inscribed the process that had necessitated it.

The slave insurgency on the plantations in the Confederate South was the work of men and women both. But as in St. Domingue, the Union government and army's instrumental interest in the military-age men among them immediately construed "the slaves of persons . . . engaged in rebellion" as if they were all male. The women fugitives among them thus emerged immediately as a problem in policy terms.[20] The implications for women were lived in historical time and have lingering effect even in the most progressive accounts of slave emancipation written in our own time.

Four particular moments in the tangled course of emancipation in the Civil War South begin to elucidate the scale of the argument: the formulation of contraband policy at Fort Monroe, Virginia, in May 1861; the federal policy that evolved in the Union-occupied Mississippi Valley starting in mid-1862; the belated arrangement to recruit and emancipate slaves in the Union border states, and especially in Kentucky, all of which were exempt from the terms of the Emancipation Proclamation; and finally, and most surprisingly perhaps, the terms of the Confederate plan to enlist slaves in the second half of the war.

Union general Benjamin Butler had no sooner taken command of Fortress Monroe, a federal fort near Hampton Roads in coastal Virginia, when slaves began to "deliver themselves up" to his picket guards, first three men, then, three days later, a group ("squad") of men "bringing," as Butler put it, "their women and children." The "contraband policy" Butler forged justified holding those slaves on the grounds that it deprived the Confederate government of the military use of labor in support of the rebellion.[21] From the outset, then, federal policy focused on precisely those military-age male slaves impressed from their owners by Confederate authorities to build batteries and other fortifications. But the gender problematic of that policy—"the most difficult with which we have to deal" (as another official later put it)—was immediately apparent. As Butler acknowledged, it provided no rationale for holding women and children. For despite the obvious value of their labor, Confederate authorities never impressed women slaves. "As a military question it would seem to be a measure of necessity to deprive the masters of their services." But how, Butler asked his superiors, "can this be done? As a military question and a question of humanity can I receive the services of a Father and a Mother and not take the children?" Unwanted, still the women and children came. As late as March 1863 one federal commander in the Mississippi Valley complained about the thousands of useless negroes within his command, "two thirds to three fourths of whom are women and children incapable of army labor, a weight and incumbrance." One census of "contraband" with the Union lines at Yorktown and in Elizabeth City and Warwick Counties, Virginia, in August 1863 reported 24,000 black men and women, 15,000 of them slaves of Confederate owners; fully 11,949 were women.[22]

If the problem of women in contraband policy emerged first at Fort Monroe, so too did the outlines of the solution resorted to repeatedly throughout the war: to transmute women fugitives into (contrabands') wives. Edward Pierce, the young Boston attorney who had been stationed at Fort Monroe when the first contraband arrived, took upon himself the task of publicly vindicating the policy haphazardly arrived at there, explaining in *Atlantic Monthly* in November 1861 that the Union public ought to embrace the contrabands as part of the American people. Each negro who served the cause of Union, he wrote, "had vindicated beyond all future question, for *himself, his* wife, and their issue, a title to citizenship and become heir to all the immunities of Magna Charta, the Declaration of Independence, and the Constitution of the United States."[23] From the earliest moments of the war, advocates of slave emancipation in the United States imagined the contraband—those fugitives subtracted from the enemy and added to the Union war effort—as male, and the women as their wives; they proposed that male slaves would earn citizenship with service to the Union (military service, that is) and pass on its benefits to their wives and children. No matter that marriage was illegal for slaves or, more immediately, that many of the women who made it to Union lines or contraband camps had come on their own or as heads of families themselves. The "woman who came through 200 Miles in men's clothes" to Fortress Monroe had no husband, or at least none with her when she arrived.[24] Marriage was part of the basic template of federal emancipation policy from its earliest imaginings in the American Civil War.

The recourse to marriage, at Fort Monroe and everywhere else it cropped up, reflected deep-seated assumptions about adult women's dependency and normative position as wives. But these were also ideas animated by a host of pressing concerns, chief among them male responsibility for dependents. Worries about self-support and the specter of massive public welfare hung over all of the discussions about how to administer an ever-growing population of fugitive slaves under Union control. Would slave men assume responsibility for the support of their dependents? The very question opened up Pandora's box, and the problem of marriage (of *slaves' marriages*) was one of the first things to pop out. The problem was not new. Indeed, the idea of male "self-possession" and of slave marriage as a *condition* of emancipation—as evidence of the male slaves' willingness to embrace subjection to the patriarchal ethos—had been central to emancipation schemes from their earliest eighteenth-century versions, as Christopher Brown has recently pointed out. And it had, obviously, assumed a significant place in radical republican emancipation plans in late eighteenth-century St. Domingue. In the mid-nineteenth-century United States, too, the willingness to embrace marriage and its attendant responsibilities was always part of the assessment of slave men's fitness for freedom and citizenship. That was why slaves' sense of the marriage relation was one of such public interest. It was one of the first questions asked at the hearings conducted in March 1863 by the congressional committee appointed by Secretary of War Stanton to investigate the condition of former slaves and make recommendations about their employment and welfare. And it was why regularizing slave marriages was a sometime preoccupation of Union occupying forces, commanders of contraband camps, missionary teachers, and army chaplains. In the South Carolina Sea Islands, where Union occupation dated from November 1861 and the massive flight of planters left thousands of slaves under federal jurisdiction, Parson French took it as one of his chief tasks to get slaves to marry. In that effort he was eventually supported by an order issued by Gen. Rufus Saxton in the summer of 1862 requiring that "Negroes having more than one 'wife' were now obliged to make a choice." Marriage and monogamy were official policy.[25]

Whatever the complications, and they were many, as the quotation marks around "wife" suggest, marriage and the administration of slave women as wives was the solution to the problem of contraband women and of dependency most often reached for in federal policy. From the earliest moments of the war, when contraband first emerged as a population under Union governance, policy makers immediately sought to render male slaves to the jurisdiction of the state and the army, and women slaves to the jurisdiction of marriage. That instinct, so socially ingrained it appeared natural (to historians in our own time, as well), would resurface virtually everywhere the Union army came into control of large populations of slaves of rebel owners.

From its earliest formulations in coastal Virginia, Union policy touching slave property took shape as a competition with the Confederate States of America for the bodies of slave men, first for military labor and, later, military service. That position was formalized in the First Confiscation Act of August 1861, which provided access to freedom only for slaves of rebel owners who had been forced to take up arms against the United States or, as was more likely, employed at work on any "fort, navy yard, dock, armory, ship, entrenchment, or in any military or naval service whatsoever." That narrow calculation about whose labor counted meant, as historians have noted, that the First Confiscation Act provided "slight access to freedom" for any slaves, and virtually none (I would add) for women.[26]

Early and defeated proposals to arm slaves (by Secretary of War Cameron, Union general David Hunter, and others after the occupation of the densely black South Carolina Lowcountry in the fall of 1861) only deepened the gender divide in Union military emancipation policy. As late as July 1862 the Second Confiscation Act which (in admirably expansive, gender-neutral language) declared "forever free of their servitude" *all* slaves of rebel owners now under the control of the government of the United States, also empowered the president to employ "as many persons of African descent as he shall deem necessary" in any capacity to suppress the rebellion. The military logic of confiscation, its gendered terms, and the implications for women were all spelled out the same day in the Militia Act. That provided for the employment of "persons of African descent" in military service and granted freedom to those so employed who were slaves, as well as their families, so long as they belonged to rebel owners. But clearly it was not all "persons of African descent" who federals intended to employ; some specificity was thus in order, and the meanings for women slaves were spelled out in brutally concrete fashion: "And be if further enacted, That when any man or boy of African descent [belonging to a rebel owner] shall render any such service as is provided for in this act, *he, his mother and his wife and children*, shall forever thereafter be free." Words to make the heart sing, even if they did construe women and children as entitled to freedom only as the dependents of particular soldiers. But that was not the only limiting condition of gender. For the law carefully excluded from its purview any mothers, wives, or children of black men in military service who, unlike their sons, husbands, or fathers, were slaves of *loyal* owners.[27] Thus even as military emancipation policy reached increasingly large numbers of male slaves as soldiers, it left many women with no route to claim their freedom.

Much of what the authors of these acts meant or intended about family emancipation remains obscure, and the lack of interest in the literature about the gender parameters of the statutes has not helped. It is not clear, for example, with respect to the Militia Act or any other piece of federal policy that had similar provisions, whether marriage was *required* as a condition of slave women's freedom or what would constitute evidence of marriage to a soldier in the absence of a legal certificate. Much of this remains to be figured out. What was clear is that, at least as officials saw it, women's freedom (although which women no one quite said) followed, as it so often had before, from the military service of their men. If slaves put themselves on the wartime political agenda, as we now commonly acknowledge, then the women slaves who kept on coming into Union lines unbidden, unwelcome, and unmarried did so in direct contravention of a federal policy that construed them as a problem and a burden, at best as dependents of the slave men whose labor the army sought.

The military route to emancipation has carried tremendous political and interpretive weight, in the estimation of contemporaries and historians alike. Even before the passage of the Emancipation Proclamation, but on a far larger scale after, the Union military generated plans for the systematic recruitment of black soldiers. Nowhere did this policy work to greater effect than in the Mississippi Valley, where, starting in the winter of 1862, a string of Confederate military defeats left the upper and lower parts of the river and the rich plantation territories on each side of it increasingly subject to occupation by Union troops. As Confederates tried to run off their slaves to points west, Louisiana and Texas, huge numbers escaped their owners' control, either staying put on plantations as owners fled or running themselves into Union lines. The numbers of slaves under Union control in the Mississippi Valley reached unprecedented numbers. By the summer of 1863 when Vicksburg finally fell, the whole valley was in Union hands, and the richest plantation districts in the South were under federal occupation. Massive numbers of slaves remained on abandoned plantations; the numbers of men, women, and children in contraband camps swelled; and military recruiters went to work with a vengeance.[28]

In Mississippi, which was not (unlike southern Louisiana) exempt from the Emancipation Proclamation, Adjutant General Lorenzo Thomas was dispatched from Washington to head up a huge campaign amongst the now-freed slaves to recruit black soldiers *and* to reorganize the constantly growing number of plantations in occupied territory. Plans proceeded in tandem, with Thomas and his men aggressively routing (or impressing) black men of military age into the army while assigning women, children, and elderly or unfit men to plantation labor under northern lessees.[29] The similarity of that federal policy to the one of Sonthonax, Toussaint, and Jean-Jacques Dessalines more than fifty years before is frankly unnerving.

The scale of the recruitment was huge, and freedmen's consent often irrelevant. Thomas and his men would visit abandoned plantations, announcing the Emancipation Proclamation and ordering all young men ages eighteen to forty-five to march out with the army. They sent raiding parties into Confederate-held territory, taking all of the male slaves they could get their hands on. Whatever the circumstances, slaves were all subject to the same military process of "sorting." Men of military age were siphoned off to the army; women, children, the elderly, and the unfit to the plantations. Mary Jane Clear stuck close to her husband when Union troops recruited him off their Washington County plantation. But she did not get far. "All the women were put off the boat at Hawes Harris' landing," an army friend of her husband later recalled, "and the men were carried off to Lake Providence to enlist." Clear was immediately hired out to a lessee and remanded to a plantation to labor at a wage fixed by the government ($7 per month for the women, $10 for the men). In one three-month period in 1864, the superintendent of freedmen sent 12,700 freedpeople, the majority of them women, from contraband camps and shantytowns around Vicksburg to work on plantations.[30]

President Lincoln himself articulated the difference gender made even among people already ostensibly and equally free by the terms of the Emancipation Proclamation. It is surely not a good sign that, notwithstanding the proclamation, President Lincoln and Edwin Stanton, his secretary of war, persisted in referring to the freedpeople as "contrabands" and in making rigid distinctions between those capable of military labor or service and those of no use to the state, who presented a massive problem of dependency. Advising Stanton on how to respond to General Hurlbut's dilemma in the Mississippi Valley—it was Hurlbut who had complained about women as a "weight and encumbrance"—Lincoln put it bluntly: "The able bodied male contraband are already in the army. But the rest are in confusion and destitution. They had better be set to digging their subsistence out of the ground."[31] And so they were.

It was in the Mississippi Valley that the problem of contraband women, first glimpsed at Fortress Monroe, was confronted en masse. But with military recruitment came new and harder gender distinctions between fugitive slave men and women attempting to lay claim to freedom by sticking close to the U.S. army. As in St. Domingue, women did not simply submit to the official gender division of labor. In the South Carolina and Georgia Sea Islands, where the same policy was underway, field women on one plantation resisted the forcible drafting of the men, attacking "the black soldiers [sent to take them] with their hoes." The women were fired on. In the Mississippi Valley, women remanded to plantations often refused to work on the cotton crops, or simply left, following husbands and other family members to Union army camps, contraband camps, or the freedmen's villages that cropped up wherever the Union army and its growing numbers of black soldiers made camp.[32]

But the gender outlines of the policy were clear nonetheless. More than 17,000 black soldiers were recruited in Mississippi between 1862 and the end of the war, fully 20 percent of the military-age black male population and 18 percent of the black men recruited in the Confederate states. Only Louisiana and Tennessee raised more troops. But many more freedpeople —and virtually all of the women—made the transition to freedom not as soldiers of the republic but as laborers on Union-held plantations or as unwelcome dependents in contraband camps and freedmen's villages clinging to the authority and protection of the Union army.[33]

What the experience of freedpeople in the Mississippi Valley makes clear is that even when slave women had the same access to legal emancipation as men (by virtue of the Emancipation Proclamation) federal policies, especially the focus on the military recruitment of black men, established fundamentally distinct possibilities and conditions on men and women's attempts to claim and hold on to the status of freedpeople.

Some of the perseverant patterns involved in war and emancipation were evident to participants. Interestingly enough, Lorenzo Thomas cast the Union's Civil War as a black revolution in the Haitian mold. By that, he meant to direct attention to the obvious comparison—the federal government's willingness to link emancipation and black enlistment as a way to secure black men's loyalty to the Union state. In invoking Toussaint and Haiti he hardly meant to invoke the other comparison: the relegation of freed women to enforced plantation labor and the reliance on marriage to structure federal policies governing the transition of black men and women to freedom and citizenship. Yet as in Virginia in 1861 or the Sea Islands of South Carolina, federal officials in the Mississippi Valley, including Thomas, did just that, turning to marriage again and again to regulate the government's relations to, and especially their obligations to, the massive population of freedpeople they had to administer. When Thomas went down to Goodrich's Landing in southern Louisiana in 1863 and addressed the mixed group of freedpeople that gathered to hear him, welfare and the specter of dependency were foremost on his mind. And like so many others confronted with the same population— the American Freedmen's Inquiry Commission, for example—he urged marriage on the freedpeople as an integral part of the social contract they were making with the Union government. When he took up black soldiers' complaints about the conditions of their wives and the federal government's obligation to support them he did so out of a concern to secure the men's loyalty to the Union government.[34] Women's loyalty, as usual, was of no concern to the state.

What issued from federal officials in the Mississippi Valley for the remainder of the war were intermittent injunctions to black soldiers to legalize their marriages and a blizzard of directives and orders extending access, rights, and benefits to particular women as the wives of black soldiers. Here too, marriage and monogamy were official policy, although its workings were constantly thwarted by the complex forms black families and households had assumed under the regime of slavery and which they still took in 1863, 1864, and 1865. If some men and women simply followed orders and got married again, legally, by the Union chaplain and

"Alexandria, Virginia. Slave pen." An African American woman is standing outside a former slave pen during the Civil War. Slave pens were places slaves were held until being sold. Courtesy of the Library of Congress.

under the flag, so to speak, many others did not or could not. Women not recognized as wives but trying to reach male family members were repeatedly driven out of Union army camps, denied rations and benefits, and left in destitution.[35] If the Union model was that black soldiers would extend the benefits of loyalty, service, and citizenship to their wives, it proved both a bad fit and a very partial solution for the huge population of ex-slave women struggling to secure their freedom in the Mississippi Valley during the Civil War.

The problem of war, gender, and emancipation—the nexus of issues that everywhere proceeds from military emancipation policies—was posed nowhere with more clarity than in the Union border states, those four slave states in the Upper South that had thrown in their hand with the Union in 1861 and that remained exempt, as a result, from the reach of the Emancipation Proclamation. In those states, Maryland, Missouri, Kentucky, and tiny Delaware, and in the other Confederate areas exempted from the proclamation, the *only* route to emancipation was military service. It was not until October 1863 that the federal government laid the official basis of military recruiting of enslaved men of loyal owners, and even then the general order only pertained to Maryland, Missouri, Delaware, and Tennessee. In Kentucky, where loyal slave owners regarded emancipation as a betrayal of their political trust and where they fought it, with great success, to the bitter end, slavery was legal until December 1865, and slave men were not actively recruited into the army until the spring of 1864. With enlistment the only way to secure the title of freedman, it is little wonder that the Union border states and exempted Tennessee racked up the highest numbers of black soldiers contributed to the Union army. Kentucky, where conditions were worst and slave men crossed the mountains secretly to enlist in recruitment camps in Tennessee before official recruiting began in 1864, contributed more men proportionately than any other state, more than 23,000 slave men, fully 57 percent of the male slave population of military age enlisted.[36]

In Kentucky the modern relationship between enlistment and emancipation reached its purest form. For those in the Union border states or exempted states unable to offer military service to the Union army there simply was no way to lay claim to status as a free person. And for many who could claim no tie to particular black soldiers that would remain the case until the individual states enacted emancipation in late December 1864 (Louisiana) or January 1865 (Maryland, Missouri, Tennessee), or, as in Kentucky, until December 1865 when the Thirteenth Amendment was finally ratified. In the Union border states, and especially in Kentucky, even the usual recourse to marriage as a way to secure black men's loyalty and military service was slow to take effect. About the wives, elderly parents, and children of all of those border state recruits, still held as slaves by loyal owners, the general orders of October 1863 and 1864 said nothing. As late as March 1865, women whose spouses had enlisted in the Union army still had no legal claim to freedom, no route by which to exit slavery, none, that is, until Congress and the president finally adopted a joint resolution "liberating the wives and children of black soldiers regardless of their owners' loyalty."[37]

Until the ratification of the Thirteenth Amendment, military enlistment remained the only means to freedom for slaves in Kentucky. There, quite literally, slave men came to freedom (if they did so) by military service, slave women (if they did so) by marriage—if they had the patience to wait, if they could survive their masters' retribution, and if, presumably, they could prove marriage to a soldier and get officials to recognize it as legitimate. How "marriage," a right of contract denied slaves, could be grounds for freedom remains unclear, but for many enslaved women in the Civil War South that was the only official route open. The complicated and ambivalent responses with which freedmen and -women greeted injunctions to marry both during the war and in the immediate postwar period caution us against any facile use of federal policy as a historical blueprint for slaves' own strategies.

MOST OF THE literature on the process of emancipation in the Civil War South focuses on the North, the Union, and the federal army, which is reasonable enough given the origins of emancipation as a Union war goal and its final passage as a result of the decisive military defeat of the Confederacy. But the majority of slaves, men and women both—3.5 million by most estimates—ended the war as they had begun it, deep in Confederate territory, far from Union lines and their legions of record keepers. Ironically, perhaps the strongest measure of the relation of war and military service in the destruction of slavery comes there, in the Confederate States of America, where, against all imaginable odds, enslaved men and women forced an avowedly proslavery state to contend with their own political aspirations. For notwithstanding the foundational purpose of that new nation to extend the institution of slavery into the indefinite future, the Confederate States of America was nonetheless driven by "the stern logic of events" (as one congressman put it) along its own halting path to a slave enlistment and emancipation policy, as Confederates tried everything possible to make slaves "an element of strength in the war."[38]

In the Confederate States of America, where policies emerged out of purely instrumental considerations, the now-predictable gender patterns of military emancipations were, if anything, more starkly evident. For there the decision was always, in the first instance, about slave enlistment; and emancipation, if it was considered at all, was always incidental to the main issue. Indeed, the debate over slave emancipation (such as it was) did not begin de novo in 1864, as most historians assume, but was part of a much longer struggle, concurrent with the war itself, to make slaves material to the cause. From Confederates' voluntary impressment policies of 1861, to mandatory impressment imposed in 1863, to military orders permitting impressed slaves to do military labor, to the open debate over slave enlistment in 1864 and 1865, it was *slave men of military age* who were the relentless focus of state interest. Although planters did periodically try to send women slaves to fulfill their quotas, impressment orders invariably specified males: "one half of their male force of slaves to finish the works around Gloucester Point," was General Magruder's levy on citizens of three Virginia counties in July 1861. Even military orders for the forcible removal of slaves on approach of the enemy specified adult males, formalizing into policy again and again the Confederate state's view of slave "women's uselessness to the enemy."[39]

Private citizens floated the idea of using slave men as military laborers and as soldiers periodically from the beginning of the war as part of ongoing public debate about how to harness slaves' labor to the service of the state.[40] In that respect the constant innovations in impressment policy, and the endless struggles with planters to comply with them, were simply the prologue to what historians still mistakenly call "the Confederate debate over emancipation."[41] The enlistment debate, as it might better be called, emerged directly out of the exigencies of war in a slave republic and out of Confederate military men's constant calculus about how to field enough men. The CSA had access, in point of fact, to only 60 percent of its adult military-age population; the other 40 percent were enslaved and ineligible for service, as one assistant secretary of war put it. With enlistment rates among draft-age white men reaching saturation point (an estimated 75 to 85 percent) by 1864, and with the Union army putting under arms all black men they could get their hands on—including large numbers of Confederates' fugitive slaves—the competition for slave soldiers became overt and Confederate military calculations desperate.[42] Little wonder, then, that the most radical proposals for arming slave men came out of the military itself and, first, out of the beleaguered armies in the western theater.

In the Confederate States of America the usual terms of *military* emancipations were coldly exposed; even the most progressive version—subsequently rejected—rehearsed the manpower numbers in cold detail. And like the better known plans of Lincoln's government, both rejected plans and the Davis government's belated scheme to enlist slave men also figured slave women as marital recipients of freedom earned by men's military service, thus showing the perseverant pattern in the official view across time and national divisions.

The earliest and most expansive Confederate plan was Maj. Gen. Patrick Cleburne's, composed in December 1863 after the humiliating series of defeats suffered by the Army of Tennessee under the command of Gen. Braxton Bragg. Written while in winter quarters in northern Georgia, Cleburne's plan identified the "three great causes operating to destroy us": the numerical inferiority of southern armies, the poverty of their supply sources and "the fact that slavery . . . has now become, in a military point of view, one of our chief sources of weakness." His unflinching analysis of the military weakness of the slave state touched on every vulnerable point—the defection of slaveholders to save their property, the "scattering of forces to prevent slave escape," slave espionage and military service to the enemy—but Cleburne's core contention was that the Confederacy had to win slaves' loyalty with the promise of freedom.[43]

The logic was military, the goal more men in uniform, but the political vision was a radical one indeed for a slaveholding republic. For Cleburne, unlike his peers, looked slaves' anti-Confederate politics squarely in the face. It was the "chronic irritation of hope deferred," that alienated "the sympathies of his whole race" from the South, raised "insurrection in the rear," and filled the ranks of Union armies, he insisted. There was only one rational response in his view: the CSA had to harness "the slave's 'dream of freedom.'" "We must bind him to our cause by no doubtful bond," he declared, gendering slaves' emancipationist hopes and anti-Confederate politics male. "When we make soldiers of them we must make free men of them beyond all question," he said, and "thus enlist their sympathies also."[44]

Like republican commissioners in St. Domingue, and his counterparts in the Union proposing male enlistment and emancipation, Cleburne recognized the correlative gender imperative and, like them, he turned to marriage. To deliver a freedom more meaningful than that offered in the North, Cleburne said, we must be prepared to "give the negro not only his freedom but that of his wife and child." To that end, Cleburne proposed to make "his [the slave's] marriage and parental relations sacred in the eyes of the law" (something Confederate states had refused to do even under intense pressure from ministers), that is, to create marriage and then free women into it as a gift to their soldier husbands.[45] In his scheme, as in so many others, slave women would be delivered directly from the regime of property into the regime of coverture. For Cleburne, as later for Gen. Robert E. Lee, President Davis, and the Confederate War Department, the slave who dreamt of freedom was male, and it was the black man as husband and father who was to earn emancipation for his wife and children. Men would take the military route to emancipation; through the war and its devastation, slave women, somehow, the marital one.

Cleburne's proposal—brilliant but impolitic—was immediately suppressed by Davis.[46] But one can hardly help thinking about how its harsh truths and radical recommendations played on the Confederate president's mind between January (when he received it) and November 1864 when, facing the failure of impressment policy and an even more desperate manpower situation, he made his own proposal for the radical modification of slavery, as he put it. Virtually no one else, with the telling exception of Lee (who said little and wrote less) came as close as Cleburne to calling for general slave emancipation. A great many serious proposals to arm the slaves, including that of Davis, contemplated emancipation *only* of those who served, and there were many people in and outside the government who thought it possible to arm slaves *as slaves*. But sometime between November 1864 and February 1865 President Davis accepted the necessity of arming slave men, and accepted as well Lee's insistence that such men be emancipated. Davis abhorred the idea of arming slaves not least because of the political implications in a republic where the nexus of manhood, military service, and citizenship was inescapably tight.[47]

In March of 1865 Davis did the unthinkable. Backed by Lee, some of his cabinet, and a handful of governors, he pushed for legislation that would enlist and emancipate a potentially large number of slave men (Davis's first call was for 40,000). Congress, kicking and screaming the whole way, finally passed "An Act to Increase the Military forces of the Confederate States," a piece of legislation that made *no* provision for emancipation of the slave men in question. The Confederate Congress, that is to say, proposed to enlist still-enslaved men as soldiers. But Lee would have no part of that. For him, as for Cleburne, slave men's loyalty was the paramount concern and, as he knew, only emancipation could secure it. Davis and his War Department accepted Lee's stated assumption that "freedom" was the sine qua non of effective military service in a republic; what is not clear is whether they also accepted his assumption that such freedom had to be extended not just to soldiers but to their families and, gradually, as Lee had said quietly, to everyone else. With Congress refusing to take that step, it was left to the War Department to turn congressional enlistment into an emancipation policy. In General Orders, No. 14, officials in the department wrote the revolutionary clause that provided that "no slave will be accepted as a recruit *unless with his own consent and with the approbation of his master* by a written instrument conferring, as far as he may, the rights of a freedman."[48]

The Confederate States of America had been envisioned as the perfected republic of white men, a racial and patriarchal state for the modern age. Yet like so many other slave regimes in the late eighteenth and nineteenth centuries, it had been brought by war to bid for the political loyalty of slave men, to the necessity of a policy of slave enlistment, and with it the necessity of emancipating (begrudgingly, partially) some slaves. The historical significance of the Confederate experience lies not in the fact that what they undertook was so radical, for comparatively speaking it was not, but rather that they were forced to undertake it at all. Confederate military enlistment policy showed not only the instrumental logic of emancipations that emerged in the conditions of war, but also the gendered assumptions and patterns—including the figuring of women as problem dependents and the governance of women through marriage—that were such fundamental parts of those policies wherever they appeared.

BUT IF THAT was the view of state officials, Union and Confederate, it hardly serves as a description of the process, self-perception, or history of slave women and their struggle for freedom during the American Civil War. Indeed one of the seductions of the archives, and especially the rich federal records, appears to be the transference of an official story about the importance of male slaves as soldiers to the history of emancipation itself. Bringing that story up into the light, subjecting it to analysis, is to show it both as a formative dimension of slave women's experience of Civil War and emancipation (their bruising encounter with official policy), *and* as a specifically official story that bears only limited resemblance to slave men and women's struggle for emancipation in U.S. history.

The power of the heroic narrative of black soldiers and the struggle for freedom is difficult to gainsay. But that, I would argue, makes it all the more important to recognize that much of what constituted federal

emancipation policy during the Civil War were specifically *military* policies, and as such, carried a weight of assumptions about the differential
capacities of slave men and women: about their abilities to support and
advance the goals of the state and about the role and status that would
have to be extended to them as citizens of that state. To put it bluntly,
slave women's loyalty simply never assumed the strategic significance of
men's loyalty. In 1862 and 1863 when the issue was joined, and indeed for
a long time after, women's exclusion from the highest obligation of the
American citizen—to provide military service in defense of the state—
told decisively in estimations of their value and of their civil and political
rights. Itself tied up with marriage and the rights of husbands to the labor
and service of their wives, that exclusion fundamentally shaped slave
women's relationship to the Union state in the Civil War and thus shaped
the conditions and severely constrained the options open to them as they
struggled to lay claim to the status of free people. Military emancipations
and the policies they engendered powerfully shaped the terms of emancipation for slave women in the United States, as they had in other
places where enslaved men and women also made the treacherous passage through war to freedom.

The view from the state is only one vantage point, albeit a crucial one.
This essay, largely diagnostic as it is, thus serves only as an introduction
into a much fuller history of slave women and emancipation. That history unfolded in many places outside the purview of federal officials:
deep inside Confederate territory, most importantly, where the plantation emerged as a crucial site of local politics, where women figured
prominently among the rank and file and the leadership cadre of slaves in
plantation battles; and where, notwithstanding official views of women's
uselessness to the enemy, planters struggled constantly with the evidence
of slave women's betrayal and leadership in revolt. One could say planters
developed a ground zero view of slave women's capacity entirely at odds
with the official view. When Charles Manigault removed eighteen slaves
"beyond the reach of gunboats" in February 1862, the list included surprisingly large numbers of women slaves: "Bess and her infant," "Betty
and infant," "Catherine," "Betty," "Amey," etc., fully ten of the eighteen
identified as "rebels and leaders" were women, two with infant children.
"I can see a great deal of obstinacy in some of the people," one South
Carolina overseer reported, "Mostly among the Woman." In the long civil
war on Confederate plantations women proved to be formidable enemies,

and unlike officials, planters frankly acknowledged it.[49] If the state (Confederate and Union) could affect a studied disinterest in slave women's politics, that was a luxury planters could not afford.

Like the *cultivateurs* and *citoyennes* on plantations in St. Domingue after emancipation, slave and freedwomen in the Civil War and post-emancipation South hardly cast themselves as recipients of a gift of freedom as a boon of marriage. The struggles to survive slavery had been theirs, and so too, as they told it, were the struggles to destroy the institution and the planters' state during the Civil War. Their own rarely recorded accounts of their part in that revolutionary process are surely worth recovering if only because they would likely illuminate much that remains unclear about how freedwomen approached the struggles over the meaning of freedom in the post–Civil War South.[50]

Like the moment in St. Domingue in 1796 when women plantation workers went on strike for equal pay, one (probably often repeated) moment on a southern plantation at the end of the Civil War illuminates a great deal about freedwomen's sense of their own recent history and about what the future would require by way of further militancy. When the exiled Louis Manigault Jr. made a brief return visit to Gowrie, his old Savannah River plantation, in 1867, he found many of his former slaves still there. The slaves had outlasted the master. But Manigault's moment of truth came with the freedwomen, not the men. The men approached him, he reported, calling him "Mausa . . . still showing respect by taking off their capts." But the women would not even get to their feet. These were "young Women to whom I frequently presented Ear-rings . . . etc.," he recalled with bitterness, "formerly pleased to meet me but now not even lifting the head as I passed."

Finding themselves on plantations at the end of the war, sometimes in larger numbers than the men, freedwomen were on the front lines of the new labor struggles of the postwar world.[51] Like the women on the Manigault place, they were vigilant, making common cause with male kin and allies, but trusting, as in the past, to no one as much as themselves to protect and extend the freedom they had so recently earned. When interviewed by the commissioners of the Southern Claims Commission in the 1870s freedwomen told a strikingly consistent story about their role in the war and emancipation, one drawn from deep within the female slave experience. They had not fought for freedom, they said, they had worked for it. Nobody had bequeathed it to them, or given it to them as a gift. No, they said again and again. It was theirs. They had earned it.[52]

Notes

1. For an overview of most cases see Robin Blackburn, *The Overthrow of Colonial Slavery, 1776–1848* (London: Verso, 1988). On the American Revolution see Benjamin Quarles, *The Negro in the American Revolution* (Chapel Hill: University of North Carolina Press, 1961); Sylvia Frey, *Water from the Rock: Black Resistance in a Revolutionary Age* (Princeton, N.J.: Princeton University Press, 1991); Gary Nash, *Forgotten Fifth: African Americans in the Age of Revolution* (Cambridge, Mass.: Harvard University Press, 2006); Phillip D. Morgan and Andrew Jackson O'Shaughnessy, "Arming Slaves in the American Revolution," in *Arming Slaves From Classical Times to the Modern Age*, ed. Christopher Leslie Brown and Philip D. Morgan (New Haven, Conn.: Yale University Press, 2006), 180–208. On Haiti, see Carolyn Fick, *The Making of Haiti: The Saint Domingue Revolution from Below* (Knoxville: University of Tennessee Press, 1990); Laurent DuBois, *A Colony of Citizens: Revolution and Slave Emancipation in the French Caribbean, 1787–1804* (Chapel Hill: University of North Carolina Press, 2004); David Geggus, "The Arming of Slaves in the Haitian Revolution," in Brown and Morgan, *Arming Slaves*, 209–302. On Cuba, see Rebecca J. Scott, *Slave Emancipation in Cuba: The Transition to Free Labor, 1860–1899* (Princeton, N.J.: Princeton University Press, 1985); Ada Ferrer, *Insurgent Cuba: Race, Nation, and Revolution: 1868–1898* (Chapel Hill: University of North Carolina Press, 1999). On Brazil, see Hendrik Kraay, "Slavery, Citizenship and Military Service in Brazil's Mobilization for the Paraguayan War," *Slavery and Abolition* 18, no. 3 (December 1997): 228–56.

2. Blackburn, *Overthrow of Colonial Slavery*, 58; Robin Blackburn, "Explaining the Rise and Demise of Colonial Slavery in the Americas" (paper presented at the Center for the Humanities, Northwestern University, October 2, 2000), 28. Also see DuBois, *A Colony of Citizens*, 225.

3. That idea that slaves earned emancipation by military service is as old as Frederick Douglass and has taken hold in popular culture (one thinks immediately of the movie *Glory*), but for modern scholarly versions see B. Quarles, *The Negro in the Civil War* (Boston: Little, Brown, 1969). James M. McPherson, *The Negro's Civil War* (1965; new ed., New York: Ballantine Books, 1991); Ira Berlin et al., *Slaves No More: Three Essays on Emancipation and the Civil War* (New York: Cambridge University Press, 1992), 187–233. On gender and emancipation, one indication of the state of the field is the recent anthology, Pamela Scully and Diana Paton, eds., *Gender and Slave Emancipation in the Atlantic World* (Durham, N.C.: Duke University Press, 2005). Gendered histories of emancipation in the United States include Leslie A. Schwalm, *"A Hard Fight for We": Women's Transition from Slavery to Freedom in South Carolina* (Urbana: University of Illinois Press, 1998); Elsa Barkley Brown, "Negotiating and Transforming the Black Public Sphere: African American Political Life in the Transition from Slavery

to Freedom," in *The Black Public Sphere: A Public Culture Book*, ed. Black Public Sphere Collective (Chicago: University of Chicago Press, 1995), 111–50; Nora Lee Frankel, *Freedom's Women: Black Women and Families in Civil War Era Mississippi* (Bloomington: University of Indiana Press, 1999); Nancy Bercaw, *Gendered Freedoms: Race, Rights and the Politics of Household in the Delta, 1861–1875* (Gainesville: University of Florida Press, 2003); Susan E. O'Donovan, *Becoming Free in the Cotton South* (Cambridge, Mass.: Harvard University Press, 2007); Thavolia Glymph, *Out of the House of Bondage* (New York: Cambridge University Press, forthcoming).

4. Berlin et al., *Slaves No More*, 5–6.

5. See, for example, the chapter "A War for Freedom," in Ira Berlin et al., eds., *Free At Last: A Documentary History of Slavery, Freedom, and the Civil War* (New York: New Press, 1992), 95–166. For what, it is fair to say, is the standard view, see Eric Foner, *Reconstruction: America's Unfinished Revolution, 1863–1878* (New York: Harper & Row, 1988), 7–8.

6. The figures (of the number who served) are from Berlin et al., *Slaves No More*, 203. Estimates of the percentage of slaves who made it into Union lines are from McPherson, *The Negro's Civil War*, ix.

7. The still-classic account is C. L. R. James, *The Black Jacobins: Toussaint Louverture and the San Domingo Revolution* (1938; reprint, New York: Vintage Books, 1963); and more recently, Fick, *The Making of Haiti*, Blackburn, *Overthrow of Colonial Slavery*, David Geggus, *Slavery, War, and Revolution* (New York: Oxford University Press, 1982), and *Haitian Revolutionary Studies* (Bloomington: Indiana University Press, 2002); Laurent Dubois, *Avengers of the New World: The Story of the Haitian Revolution* (Cambridge, Mass.: Belknap Press of Harvard University Press, 2004); John D. Garrigus, *Before Haiti: Race and Citizenship in French San-Domingue* (New York: Palgrave Macmillan, 2006). My own thinking has been shaped most directly by Elizabeth Colwill, "'Fêtes de l'hymen, fêtes de la liberte': Marriage, Manhood and Emancipation in Revolutionary Saint-Domingue," in *The World of the Haitian Revolution*, ed. David Patrick Geggus and Norman Fiering (Bloomington: Indiana University Press, 2009), 125–55.

8. Geggus, *Haitian Revolutionary Studies*, 99–118, and "Arming of Slaves," 209–32.

9. Fick, *The Making of Haiti*, 115–16.

10. Blackburn, *Overthrow of Colonial Slavery*, 194.

11. For the numbers see Geggus, "Arming of Slaves," 222–23.

12. Blackburn, *Overthrow of Colonial Slavery*, 218; Colwill, "Fetes de l'hymen"; Fick, *The Making of Haiti*, 161.

13. Colwill, "Fetes de l'hymen," 12, 23.

14. Blackburn, *Overthrow of Colonial Slavery*, 218.

15. A process painstakingly reconstructed by Colwill, "Fetes de l'hymen"; and Dubois, *A Colony of Citizens*, 249–76.

16. See Fick, *The Making of Haiti*; Colwill, "Fetes de l'hymen"; Geggus, "Arming of Slaves"; and Dubois, *A Colony of Citizens*.

17. Elizabeth Colwill is the only one of the historians cited above to analyze directly

the role of marriage in republican emancipation policy in St. Domingue. But see also Fick, *The Making of Haiti*, 163.

18. Fick, *The Making of Haiti*, 170; Blackburn, *Overthrow of Colonial Slavery*, 235.

19. Emancipation Proclamation, January 1, 1863, accessed at <http://avalon.law.yale .edu/19th_century/emancipa.asp> (February 5, 2009).

20. Second Confiscation Act, July 17, 1862, *Statutes at Large, Treaties, and Proclamations of the United States of America*, vol. 12 (Boston: Little, Brown, 1863), 589–92.

21. Ira Berlin et al., eds., *The Destruction of Slavery*, ser. 1, vol. 1 of *Freedom: A Documentary History of Emancipation, 1861–1865* (New York: Cambridge University Press, 1985), 72, 70–72. See also testimony of Harry Jarvis in John Blassingame, ed., *Slave Testimony: Two Centuries of Letters, Speeches, Interviews and Autobiographies* (Baton Rouge: Louisiana State University Press, 1977), 606–11; Robert F. Engs, *Freedom's First Generation: Black Hampton, Virginia, 1861–1890* (Philadelphia: University of Pennsylvania Press, 1979).

22. Berlin et al., *The Destruction of Slavery*, 70–72, 304–6; numbers on p. 91. Leslie Schwalm was the first to notice the problem. See Schwalm, *A Hard Fight for We*, 90. Also see Thavolia Glymph, "'This Species of Property': Female Slave Contrabands in the Civil War," in *A Woman's War: Southern Women, Civil War, and the Confederate Legacy*, ed. Edward D. C. Campbell Jr. and Kym S. Rice (Richmond, Va.: Museum of the Confederacy, 1996), 55–71.

23. Willie Lee Rose, *Rehearsal for Reconstruction: The Port Royal Experiment* (1964; reprint, Athens: University of Georgia Press, 1999), 21–22 [emphasis mine].

24. Berlin et al., *The Destruction of Slavery*, 88–90.

25. Christopher Leslie Brown, *Moral Capital: Foundations of British Abolitionism* (Chapel Hill: University of North Carolina Press, 2007), 206, 236; American Freedmen's Inquiry Commission, Preliminary Report, *Senate Executive Document* No. 53, 38th Cong., 1st sess., 1–24; Rose, *Rehearsal for Reconstruction*, 236. On the problem of marriage and welfare in federal policy see especially Amy Stanley, *From Bondage to Contract: Wage Labor, Marriage and the Market in the Age of Slave Emancipation* (New York: Cambridge University Press, 1998). On the problem of freedwomen and dependency see Linda K. Kerber, *No Constitutional Right to Be Ladies: Women and the Obligations of Citizenship* (New York: Hill & Wang, 1998), 47–80. For a review essay that lays out my views of marriage and citizenship in the Civil War era, see *Signs: Journal of Women in Culture and Society* 30, no. 2 (Winter 2005): 1659–71.

26. *Statutes at Large*, 12:319; Berlin et al., *Slaves No More*, 23.

27. Second Confiscation Act, July 17, 1862; and Militia Act, July 17, 1862, *Statutes at Large*, 12:589–92, 597–600.

28. On military developments in the Mississippi Valley see Armstead L. Robinson, *Bitter Fruits of Bondage: The Demise of Slavery and the Collapse of the Confederacy, 1861–1865* (Charlottesville: University of Virginia Press, 2005); Berlin et al., *Slaves No More*; Bercaw, *Gendered Freedoms*.

29. Berlin et al., *Slaves No More*, 53. On the plantations under northern lessees, see Lawrence N. Powell, *New Masters: Northern Planters during the Civil War and Re-*

construction (New Haven, Conn.: Yale University Press, 1980); for military sorting, see Bercaw, *Gendered Freedoms*, 31–50; on Lorenzo Thomas and his policy see Erik Mathisen, "The Strange Career of Lorenzo Thomas" (Ph.D. diss., University of Pennsylvania, in progress), chap. 4.

30. Bercaw, *Gendered Freedoms*, 44, 36. Bercaw estimates that 69 percent of the laborers on leased plantations were women.

31. Berlin et al., *The Destruction of Slavery*, 304–6.

32. Rose, *Rehearsal for Reconstruction*, 247, 265–66; Bercaw, *Gendered Freedoms*, 36–47.

33. For the numbers see Berlin et al., *Slaves No More*, 203.

34. Mathisen, "The Strange Career of Lorenzo Thomas," chap. 4, 33.

35. On marriage and federal policy in the Civil War see Nancy F. Cott, *Public Vows: A History of Marriage and the Nation* (Cambridge, Mass.: Harvard University Press, 2000), 77–104, Bercaw, *Gendered Freedoms*; Mathisen, "Lorenzo Thomas." On the marriage of slaves and freedpeople during the war and for the debate over how common legal marriage was, see Herbert Gutman, *The Black Family in Slavery and Freedom, 1750–1925* (New York: Pantheon Books, 1976), 363–431; Noralee Frankel, *Freedom's Women: Black Women and Families in Civil War Era Mississippi* (Bloomington: Indiana University Press, 1999); Glymph, "This Species of Property"; Laura Edwards, "'The Marriage Covenant Is at the Foundation of All Our Rights': The Politics of Slave Marriages in North Carolina after Emancipation," *Law and History Review* 14 (Spring 1996): 81–124; Bercaw, *Gendered Freedoms*, 19–50.

36. Berlin et al., *Slaves No More*, numbers on p. 203; Aaron Astor, "Belated Confederates: The Union Border States in the Civil War" (Ph.D. diss., Northwestern University, 2006).

37. Berlin et al., *Slaves No More*, 70, 73.

38. Congressman Ethelbert Barksdale of Mississippi used the phrase in a speech reported in the *Richmond Sentinel*, March 6, 1865, and reprinted in Robert F. Durden, *The Gray and The Black: The Confederate Debate on Emancipation* (Baton Rouge: Louisiana State University Press, 1972), 242–49 (quotation on 248); *Richmond Dispatch*, April 12, 1861, quoted in Durden, *The Gray and the Black*, 14.

39. For Magruder's order see Berlin et al., *The Destruction of Slavery*, 686; for impressment of women slaves see Ervin L. Jordan Jr., *Black Confederates and Afro-Yankees in Civil War Virginia* (Charlottesville: University of Virginia Press, 1995), 63. The term "uselessness to the enemy" is from Louis Manigault, Marshland, December 29, 1864, Manigault Family Papers, ser. 1, folder 5, Southern Historical Collection, University of North Carolina, Chapel Hill. On Confederate impressment see, in addition to Jordan, Bernard H. Nelson, "Confederate Slave Impressment Legislation, 1861–1865," *Journal of Negro History* 31 (October 1946): 392–410. On exclusively male impressment see Schwalm, *A Hard Fight for We*, 81–82; and the explanation of how the quotas worked, counting in the women but taking only the men, by Alabama planters in Berlin et al., *The Destruction of Slavery*, 756–58.

40. For one early example see W. S. Turner to Honorable L. P. Walker, July 17, 1861, in *The War of the Rebellion: The Official Records of the Union and Confederate Armies*,

128 vols. (Washington: GPO, 1881–1901), ser. IV, 1:482; and Walker's response, 529 (hereafter cited as *OR*).

41. On the miscasting of the debate as "the Confederate debate on emancipation," see Durden, *The Gray and the Black*; Bruce Levine, *Confederate Emancipation: Southern Plans to Free and Arm Slaves during the Civil War* (New York: Oxford University Press, 2006). Phillip Dillard does not use the term in his title but he casts the debate as a binary choice for Confederates between independence and slavery, missing the primacy of the enlistment issue. See Phillip D. Dillard, "Independence or Slavery: The Confederate Debate Over Arming the Slaves" (Ph.D. diss., Rice University, 1999). One exception is N. W. Stephenson, "The Question of Arming the Slaves," *American Historical Review* 18 (January 1913): 295–308. The argument that enlistment ought to be understood in the context of Confederate impressment of slaves is developed more thoroughly in my book, "Confederate Crucible: The Political Transformation of the Civil War South" (Cambridge, Mass.: Harvard University Press, forthcoming), chapters 6 and 7.

42. For estimates of the percentage of the male population serving in the army see Gary W. Gallagher, *The Confederate War: How Popular Will, Nationalism, and Military Strategy Could Not Stave Off Defeat* (Cambridge, Mass.: Harvard University Press, 1997), 28–30. In the spring of 1864 the Bureau of Conscription reported to the secretary of war that no more men were to be had. Gallagher, *The Confederate War*, 35.

43. Major-General Patrick R. Cleburne et al. to Commanding General, the Corps, Division, Brigade, and Regimental Commanders of the Army of Tennessee, January 2, 1864, *OR*, ser. 1, 52(2):586–92 (quotations on 587).

44. Ibid., 590, 590–91.

45. Ibid., 591.

46. James A. Seddon to General Joseph E. Johnston, War Department, C.S.A., Richmond, Virginia, January 24, 1864, *OR*, ser. 1, 52(2):606–7; J. E. Johnston, General, Circular, Lieutenant-General Hardee, Major-Generals Cheatham, Hindman, Cleburne, Stewart, Walker, Brigadier-General Bates and P. Anderson, Dalton, Georgia, January 31, 1864, *OR*, ser. 1, 52(2):608; J. E. Johnston to Honorable James A. Seddon, Secretary of War, Dalton, Georgia, February 2, 1864, *OR*, series 1, 52(2): 608–9.

47. Jefferson Davis, "Address to the Senate and House of Representatives of the Confederate States of America," Richmond, November 7, 1864, *OR*, ser. 4, 3:790–800.

48. For the congressional act and the War Department legislation see General Orders, No. 14, Adjutant and Inspector General's Office, Richmond, Virginia, March 23, 1865, *OR*, series 4, 3:1161–62 (quotation on 1161). For Lee's position, see R. E. Lee to Hon. Andrew Hunter, Headquarters, Army of Northern Virginia, January 11, 1865, *OR*, ser. 4, 3:1012–13. Secretary of State Judah P. Benjamin proved a key ally, as did Governor William Smith of Virginia. [emphasis mine]

49. "List of Negroes who were sent from Gowrie to Silk Hope 21st February 1862 and are there to remain for the present," Louis Manigault Papers, "Slave List," Perkins Library, Duke University, Durham, N.C.; J. H. Easterby, ed., *The South Carolina Rice Plantation as Revealed in the Papers of R. W. Allston* (Chicago, 1945), 291.

50. The literature on women and emancipation is now considerable. For many of the main contributions see the books cited in note 3 above.

51. "Visit to 'Gowrie' and 'East Hermitage' Plantations," March 22, 1867, Manigault Family Papers, ser. 1, folder 5, Southern Historical Collection.

52. On women on plantations at the end of the war see especially Schwalm, *A Hard Fight for We*; Bercaw, *Gendered Freedoms*; and O'Donovan, *Becoming Free in the Cotton South*. For testimonies offered to the Southern Claims Commission, see, for example, Claim of Silvy Baker, December 4, 1876, Liberty County, Georgia, Southern Claims Commission Records, RG 217, National Archives. There are many other such statements in the Claims Commission Records. See also Kate Drumgoold, *A Slave Girl's Story, Being an Autobiography of Kate Drumgoold* (Brooklyn, N.Y., 1898), accessed at http://docsouth.unc.edu/neh/drumgoold/menu.html (February 5, 2009).

MICHAEL VORENBERG

Abraham Lincoln's "Fellow Citizens"— Before and After Emancipation

Did Abraham Lincoln's Emancipation Proclamation, which promised freedom to almost 4 million enslaved African Americans, also assure them citizenship? The question seems so basic—what did Lincoln assume to be the citizenship status of those freed by the war?—but it evades an easy answer. When Lincoln used the expression "fellow citizens," which he did in almost one hundred of his speeches (and that is just the published ones), did he imagine free African Americans in that group? He did not use the expression during the two times that he addressed an audience of African Americans—in August 1862, when he touted a plan of colonization to free black leaders, and in October 1864, when he responded to a group of newly free Maryland African Americans who had come to serenade him. But had he nonetheless come to regard free people of color as his "fellow citizens"? Or were they something less than that?

The question is as important for our own day as it was for Lincoln's. We remain perplexed by how and when people gain citizenship, and how and when they can lose it. The subject was arguably more critical in Lincoln's time, but the definition of citizenship during the era was hazy, and the vocabulary consisted of fewer terms than we have today for those caught between personhood and citizenship. Today people in the middle might be neatly categorized as "guest workers" or "resident aliens," but in the Civil War era, newly freed African Americans were formless shadows on the spectrum from person to citizen.[1]

Making the matter of citizenship more complicated, the commonly held definitions of the concept at the time, and the terms associated with it, do not neatly correspond to current definitions and nomenclature. Regardless of the words that nineteenth-century Americans used to describe citizenship, their understanding of the term tended to fall into three categories. The specific words I use to describe these categories would be familiar to nineteenth-century lawmakers and legal theorists, but the categories themselves, porous and interrelated, are of my own devising. First, there was *legal citizenship*: Was a person or group of people categorized as citizen explicitly by statute or legal decision? Second, there was *civic citizenship*: Did a person or group of people exercise certain rights, such as property owning or voting, that would suggest that they were citizens, even if the law did not use the word "citizen" to describe them? Third, there was *affective citizenship*: Did a person or group feel themselves citizens of a place, even if that place might not have reciprocated by categorizing them explicitly as legal or civic citizens? Many people felt themselves tied to a place because of a common language, a common set of concerns, or simply a shared residency. They were members of an "imagined community," to use Benedict Anderson's well-known expression. They enjoyed affective citizenship, even if they might have been denied formal membership in the community that they imagined.[2]

LET US BEGIN with *legal* citizenship. Were slaves freed by the Emancipation Proclamation now legal citizens? The answer, for the most part, was no. The ruling of the *Dred Scott* decision of 1857, which remained in place during the war, was that no black people, free or enslaved, were legal citizens of their state or of the nation. They were "excluded" from the "political family" created by the Constitution, declared Chief Justice Roger Taney, who was still alive, barely, when Lincoln signed the Emancipation Proclamation.[3] Lincoln had accepted that decision, though tentatively. In 1857, he suggested that Americans "treat it as not having yet quite established a settled doctrine for the country."[4] Lincoln seems still to have accepted *Dred Scott* in 1862, even if he knew further settlement of the doctrine was needed. In his annual message of December of that year, he wrote, "Liberia and Hayti are, as yet, the only countries to which colonists of African descent from here, could go with certainty of being received and adopted as citizens."[5] The implication was that they could not be adopted as citizens in the United States, nor in any country with a nonblack majority.

Lincoln did not live to see the doctrine of legal citizenship finally settled. This came in the Civil Rights Act of 1866 followed by the Fourteenth Amendment of 1868, both of which declared birthplace as the basis of citizenship, making legal citizens of African Americans born in

"Now ready: the Dred Scott decision—Opinion of Chief-Justice Roger B.
Taney." Advertisement by Van Evrie, Horton & Co, 1859. The advertisement was
printed in *Harper's Weekly*, July 23, 1859, for a pamphlet that supports the Supreme Court's *Dred Scott* decision. Courtesy of the Library of Congress.

the United States, regardless of whether they were born free or enslaved. As for people of color *not* born in the country, they would soon be able to attain citizenship through the Naturalization Act of 1870, which finally opened up naturalization to people of African descent not born in the United States. Until that time, naturalization had been available to whites only—though the 1870 law kept naturalization closed to others, most significantly the Chinese.

All of that came well after Lincoln's death, of course. During his lifetime, the *legal* citizenship status of African Americans remained ambiguous at best, even after the Emancipation Proclamation. No one understood this ambiguity better than Lincoln's attorney general, Edward Bates. In the fall of 1862, in that precarious period between Lincoln's issuing of the preliminary Emancipation Proclamation and his signing of the final proclamation on January 1, 1863, Bates went in search of the meaning of American citizenship. It was not the proclamation that prompted Bates's search but another matter. A small schooner engaged in the coastal trade, piloted by a freeborn African American man and flying the American flag, had been captured by a U.S. Treasury ship. By law, only American citizens could pilot ships flying the American flag. Salmon P. Chase, the secretary of the treasury, saw an opportunity for the Union to declare freeborn African Americans as citizens—in effect, to overturn one of the key elements of the *Dred Scott* decision of five years before. He asked Bates to write an opinion about the legal status of the ship's pilot.

The crucial part of Bates's long opinion in response to Chase's request is fairly well known among historians: he declared that the man was indeed a citizen, but only by dint of his being born free in the United States. Bates thus took an important step toward reversing *Dred Scott*, though he left open the citizenship status of roughly 4 million African Americans born as slaves who might soon be free. On that issue, Bates ducked. He wrote to Chase, "of slavery, and whether or no[t] it is legally possible for a slave to be a citizen. . . . I make no question, because it is not within the scope of your inquiry," an inquiry that dealt *only* with a freeborn black person.[6]

In rendering this opinion, Bates underscored his frustration in trying to obtain a clear definition of citizen and citizenship. "I have often been pained by the fruitless search in our law books and the records of our courts, for a clear and satisfactory definition of the phrase citizen of the United States," he conceded. "I find no such definition, no authoritative

"Sec. Edward Bates,
Attorney-General."
Courtesy of the
Library of Congress.

establishment of the meaning of the phrase. . . . Eighty years of practical
enjoyment of citizenship, under the Constitution, have not sufficed to
teach us either the exact meaning of the word, or the constituent elements of the thing we prize so highly."[7] In other words, for all the times
that the law spoke of American citizens, it did not establish in any uniform way what constituted a citizen or what rights and obligations were
associated with that status.

Bates might have been consoled—though only slightly—had he known
that the definition of citizenship was just as elusive in the Confederacy.
Residents there had experienced the "practical enjoyment" of Confederate citizenship for only twenty months, rather than eighty years, but
prized the thing at least as much as their counterparts in the North. Not
that Confederate lawmakers were any more at ease than Bates about the
ambiguity of citizenship. Architects of the Confederate Constitution in
early 1861 had attempted to define the term, anticipating similar debates
over the creation of the Fourteenth Amendment five years later. One

delegate to the Confederate constitutional convention, for example, suggested a clause granting citizenship in the Confederacy to "every free white person who is a citizen of any one of the Confederate States . . . and every person born of parents domiciled in any of the States or Territories of the Confederate States." Another delegate tried to add clarity to the racial dimension of citizenship by excluding "aliens or persons having one-eighth or more of African blood in their veins." All such proposals were rejected, though the final Confederate Constitution did remove some confusion by clearly implying that, because of the sovereignty of the states, one's citizenship status in the nation depended entirely on one's citizenship status in his or her state. A number of states took the new opportunity provided them to pass laws defining citizenship. Georgia, for example, declared resident aliens there citizens unless they declared citizenship elsewhere within three months after secession.[8]

From the perspective of Confederate law, Bates's 1862 opinion declaring freeborn blacks as citizens might have represented a monumental step forward from *Dred Scott*—had it been applied widely. But the opinion had little direct effect and seems to have garnered little attention. Chase, who had requested the opinion in the first place, made much of it, as did his like-minded allies in Louisiana, who invoked the document to claim that freeborn African Americans there should be granted full citizenship rights, and that the adult men among them should be granted the vote.[9] Yet there is no evidence that Chase's superior even read Bates's opinion, much less expressed approval of it.

As for Lincoln, between the *Dred Scott* decision of 1857 and the Emancipation Proclamation of 1863, he retained a fairly consistent, skeptical view of what he called "negro citizenship." In at least two of his debates with Stephen Douglas, he answered Douglas's charge that he favored "negro citizenship" with an outright denial. "I am not in favor of negro citizenship," he said at Charleston, Illinois. To the extent that he disapproved of the citizenship part of the *Dred Scott* decision, it was only because it removed the power of granting or denying citizenship from the states and gave it exclusively to the national government. Then he went further: "If the State of Illinois had [been given] that power" by the *Dred Scott* decision—that is, the power to confer citizenship—"I should be opposed to the exercise of it."[10] Lincoln's white audience applauded the statement. They, like most so-called "butternuts," those whites from the lower Midwest who had strong ties to the South, tended to oppose any measure that hinted at the bugbear of "negro equality." Four years after that debate, when he spoke to free black leaders in August 1862 about his plan of colonization, he took a similar stance. "But even when you cease to be slaves, you are yet far removed from being placed on an equality with the white race," he told them. "The aspiration of men is to enjoy equality with the best when free, but on this broad continent, not a single man of your race is made the equal of a single man of ours. Go where you are treated the best [on this continent], and the ban is still upon you."[11] Even if one takes the most favorable view of Lincoln, and argues that he might have considered some African Americans worthy of formal, *legal* citizenship at the time before *and after* he signed the Emancipation Proclamation, he remained consistent in his position that the power to grant citizenship should lie primarily, if not exclusively, with the states, not the nation. This was a position that he made clear again and again in his reconstruction efforts, which were aimed primarily at changing state rather than national laws.

But what about Lincoln's position on those areas under exclusive *national* jurisdiction—namely, the District of Columbia and the federal territories? He never proposed or supported legislation that granted explicit legal citizenship to African Americans in those places, although he signed the 1862 act emancipating African Americans in Washington, D.C., which included habeas corpus rights for former slaves so that they could keep their former masters from denying them their freedom. And he signed a bill into law in March 1865 that prohibited racial discrimination on Washington, D.C., street cars.

Yet such measures merely granted specific rights to freed people rather than granting them explicit citizenship. That is, the measures represented not *legal* citizenship but a second type: *civic* citizenship. This was a different but not necessarily inferior type of citizenship. It was based more on the idea of *rights* than an older idea of *association*. Americans in 1800 tended to link their status to the associations they belonged to—church groups, mutual relief societies, reform groups, political parties, and, finally, one's town, state, and nation. Each association had rules of membership: one was either in or out. Thus citizenship was as much about exclusion of others as membership for oneself. By 1900, however, Americans tended to regard their status as tied more to rights—those legal guarantees that they would have equal opportunities as individuals—than to their membership in associations. The Civil War era represented a transitional moment, a time when rights consciousness was awakening but older ideas of association still held their place.[12] When Lincoln spoke disparagingly to the African American leaders in 1862 about colonization, it was because he was relying on older ideas of the law of association.

One such association was the army. Lincoln held the greatest disdain for deserters from the Union army, for they had broken the fundamental law of association of soldier-citizens. One of the few times that he invoked qualifications for citizenship came in his pardon proclamation of March 1865 dealing with deserters. He offered amnesty to many of them, but to those who failed to request amnesty within sixty days, he declared that they had "voluntarily relinquished and forfeited their rights of citizenship, and their rights to become citizens."[13]

Lincoln did not see how white Americans would accept free black people into their association, and thus he doubted African Americans' ability to become *legal* citizens. Had Lincoln relied more on the competing notion of *civic* citizenship, in which citizenship is about equality among each individual's rights rather than membership in a collective, then he might have been more optimistic, for from the start of the war, free African Americans were acquiring many rights that would eventually, after Lincoln's death, come to be called "civil rights."

What rights were these? Already I have mentioned a few of the *national* civil rights laws passed in Lincoln's lifetime—habeas corpus rights for freed people in the District of Columbia, and equal access to streetcars there—but most of the rights during the war were granted at the state level. The greatest change was in the midwestern states. There, the so-called "black laws" that prohibited free blacks from suing in court, from testifying in cases involving white defendants, and even from migrating to a particular state, began to fall away during the war. Lincoln's state of Illinois had all of these laws at the start of the conflict, and none of them by the end. Yet there is no reason to think that Lincoln paid any attention to this development, despite the fact that he had more correspondents in that state than in any other.[14]

Lincoln listened politely to Charles Sumner in the Senate and Salmon Chase in the Cabinet as they spoke about the need for laws to protect the rights of free blacks, but he never seemed to catch on. Take, for example, the apprenticeships for newly freed African Americans. Chase labored mightily in the last years of the war to convince Lincoln that if African Americans were apprenticed to their former masters, they might end up in relationships little different from slavery. Yet in his Reconstruction Proclamation of December 1863, and then consistently afterward, Lincoln favored apprenticeships as one way to avoid the problem of freed slaves becoming a "laboring [but] landless, homeless class."[15] Apprenticeships, he believed, would help freed slaves learn the ways of acquisitive capitalism from those who had experience as free wage-laborers. Lincoln's position on apprenticeships was not reactionary. He was simply slower than some to embrace explicit civil rights as preconditions for citizenship. Most Republicans took the same position. As they steered the amendment abolishing slavery through Congress in 1864 and early 1865, they said almost nothing about what specific rights should be attached to freedom. It would take Congress another year to begin to work out what those specific rights should be—a process that culminated in the passage of the Civil Rights Act of 1866.[16]

There is, of course, one famous exception to Lincoln's pattern of not expressly advocating specific rights for African Americans beyond the abolition of slavery: he supported limited black suffrage in Louisiana. First in private in 1864, then in public in his last address, Lincoln began to support voting rights for African Americans who had been soldiers for the Union and those who were, in his words, "the very intelligent."[17] When he spoke of the "most intelligent," he had in mind those African Americans who had been free *before* the war—that is, those who had not suffered what he regarded as the crippling effects of slavery on the intellect. He had a poor sense of how politically aware many slaves were. After all, many slaves had watched secession back in 1860 and 1861 with a better sense than white politicians that events were building toward war; thus scores of slaves arrived at Union forts in the South even before the firing on Fort Sumter had begun.[18] Lincoln had a higher regard for the political capacities of African Americans who had been free before the war. In his official capacity as president, Lincoln had the opportunity to meet African Americans who were at least as educated and politically aware as himself—black ministers, black educators, and even black officials from the newly recognized republics of Haiti and Liberia. In fact, it was his meeting with two highly educated leaders of the black community in New Orleans that probably did more than anything else to convince him that some African Americans should be granted the ballot. These men, Jean Baptiste Roudanez and Arnold Bertonneau, presented Lincoln on March 12, 1864, with a petition demanding black suffrage signed by over one thousand literate African Americans, some of whom had fought under Andrew Jackson at the battle of New Orleans in 1815. Impressed by Roudanez, Bertonneau, and the people they represented, he sat down the next day to write his now-famous though then-private letter to Governor Michael Hahn suggesting that intelligent blacks and black veterans be allowed to vote.[19]

Because legal theorists in Lincoln's time as well as our own tend to regard voting rights as a sign of full, legal citizenship, it would be natural to see Lincoln's endorsement of suffrage rights for some African Americans as tantamount to a belief that all African Americans might someday become legal citizens. But nowhere in Lincoln's words recommending limited suffrage rights for African Americans does he call them citizens. In his proposed Reconstruction plan for Louisiana, described in his proclamation of December 1863, he portrayed a system in which only those who could vote in 1860 would compose the new, loyal government of the state and create a new state constitution. Chase and others pressed him to expand membership in the new state to African Americans, but Lincoln showed no signs of moving in that direction. In his last public address, he urged Louisiana to give the vote to some African Americans, but he said nothing then, or at any other time, privately or publicly, about changing his proposed Reconstruction plan for Louisiana so that those given the vote at some point *after* 1860 might take part in the new state convention and help create the new constitution. Persuaded that some African Americans deserved the vote, Lincoln still had his doubts that even the "very intelligent" among them would be accepted as members into the body politic.

As for black Union veterans, Lincoln saw their claim to suffrage less as a sign of entrance into a community of citizens than as a fulfillment of a contract, much like the cash bounties that the government paid to volunteers. Consider the contrast in the way that he described foreign-born and African American soldiers for the Union. At the outbreak of the war, he supported the plan of someone he called "a Polish gentleman, naturalized, [who] proposes raising a Regiment of our citizens of his nationality, to serve in our Army."[20] Notice how he emphasized naturalization, an avenue toward citizenship not available for African Americans until 1870, and also how he spoke of "our" citizens, even though they were of "his"—the Pole's—nationality. Later that year, he made a similar endorsement, this time of a request for a Mexican-born Californian to raise a cavalry regiment of what Lincoln called "native Mexican citizens of California"—in other words, people born in Mexico but now citizens of the United States by way of California.[21] Lincoln came to think at least as highly of the soldiering abilities of African Americans. He endorsed their service in the Emancipation Proclamation and came to praise it on many later occasions. He never used the word "citizens" to describe black soldiers, though, even as he employed precisely that word to describe foreign-born soldiers. In contrast, William Whiting, his solicitor general who was the main authority on the citizenship status of soldiers, did use the word "citizen" to describe black soldiers. To a commander in the field in April 1863, Whiting said bluntly of black soldiers that "if they are in the army, then they are citizens." He told the commander that Lincoln approved of this principle, but there is no evidence that Whiting and Lincoln ever discussed the matter.[22] Nor is there evidence that Lincoln had anything to say about Whiting's other declarations, which he seemed to give out liberally. He declared that Indians and "half-breeds," as he called those of mixed Native American descent, could not be citizens unless expressly made so by treaty, and thus that they could not be accepted as volunteers.[23] He also said that slaves pressed into service by Union commanders were not citizens.[24]

Black soldiers deserved something, to be sure, thought Lincoln. He often expressed this sense of a debt to black soldiers. It was implied as early as August 1863, when he wrote in a public letter to an opponent of emancipation: "you say you will not fight to free negroes. Some of them seem willing to fight for you."[25] One could quickly earn the right to vote, thought Lincoln, perhaps by proving one's intelligence, perhaps by serving in the military. But earning citizenship was a different matter. That required a capacity for long-term association, which, as he told the African American leaders in August 1862, he did not believe blacks could have with whites. If, as Lincoln may have thought, black soldiers could vote but could never really be citizens, then they would have had the strangest legal status of anyone. Maybe it was with this odd status in mind that Lincoln said to Maj. Gen. Benjamin Butler sometime near the end of the war that it might make sense, instead of mustering out the black soldiers, to send them abroad on some project in the service of the country, such as the building of a canal between the Atlantic and Pacific. Mark Neely has shown convincingly that this conversation could not have taken place when and where Butler said it did, but I remain open to the possibility that some conversation of this sort did occur. I agree with Neely that Lincoln had given up on the idea of colonizing freed people by this time. But this was not a plan for colonization. It was a plan for black soldiers in peacetime, black soldiers who were owed something but who, in Lincoln's mind, were unlikely ever to become citizens of the nation.[26]

So far, this essay has dealt almost exclusively with only one side of the issue of whether African Americans became Lincoln's "fellow citizens" through emancipation—namely, the side of the lawmakers. But what about African Americans themselves? Did they regard themselves as citizens? To put it another way, did they show evidence of *affective* citizenship—that sense of belonging to a polity, even if that polity does not reciprocate with *legal* citizenship or *civic* citizenship? As many historians have shown, many free African Americans, and perhaps even some enslaved ones, had long regarded themselves as U.S. citizens, regardless of what any particular law did or did not say. In the antebellum era, African Americans frequently discussed the matter of citizenship as they engaged with such issues as colonization and emigration, fugitive slave laws and personal liberty laws, and segregation and desegregation. By the time of the Civil War, most African American leaders, Frederick Douglass foremost among them, assumed that black military service, if not emancipation alone, would secure citizenship for African Americans. But ordinary African Americans by the time of the Civil War were still not necessarily certain about their citizenship status.

Consider, for example, the responses given by a handful of black sailors who were captured by Union warships and asked directly to identify their citizenship. Blockading warships regularly captured commercial ships suspected of trading with the Confederacy, seized the goods, and deposed or even imprisoned the sailors. Although historians have written much about the impact of these actions on the Constitution—the legality of the seizures was ultimately tested and upheld in the Supreme Court Prize Cases of 1863—they have had little to say about their effect on the sailors who were detained. All of these sailors were asked a set of questions, or "standing interrogatories," the first of which asked them to specify their citizenship and allegiance. Had they not been stopped by the blockade, these sailors might never have had to identify for themselves and their interrogators their citizenship and allegiance, or whether these two terms, citizenship and allegiance, even meant the same thing. But because of these circumstances, we get to hear firsthand the answers of men such as

Samuel Robinson, a long-time merchant sailor who had been born in New York City and who gave not a thought to the *Dred Scott* decision when, in June 1861, he told the prize commission interrogator that he was a "citizen of New York and owe[d] allegiance to the United States of America." On further inspection of Robinson's testimony, it becomes clear that he regarded citizenship merely as a *descriptive* term of one's birthplace—in this case, the state of New York—whereas allegiance was an *ascriptive* term of affiliation—in this case, to the United States exclusively, and against all other political entities, such as the Confederate States of America. For Robinson, allegiance was a matter of volition, whereas citizenship was linked to birthright; and neither was necessarily connected to the other. To the extent that Robinson thought of himself as a citizen in the way we think of that term, it was as a civic citizen— someone who was loyal to a political entity and might benefit from that loyalty—but that meaning was embedded not in the term "citizen," which he used as a synonym for birthplace, but rather in the term "allegiance."[27]

Other African Americans used "citizen" as more than simply a descriptive term of birthplace. James Edwin Simpson took the view common among lawmakers in the mid-nineteenth century that allegiance required only the loyalty of a person, but citizenship required a mutual obligation of the person and the state. Thus Simpson testified that he "owe[d] allegiance to the government of the United States of America," but he could not determine whether "I am a citizen of the United States because I am a coloured man, but I was born and bred there." Probably without meaning to do so, Simpson had responded to the interrogatories as one who had read the *Dred Scott* decision might. He seemed to think that civic citizenship, the existence of some sort of mutual obligation between a person and the state, which he embedded in "allegiance," did not correspond to the narrower category of legal citizenship.[28]

Charles Hall, an African American from the same ship as Simpson, worked from similar premises but reached a different conclusion. As for his allegiance, he stated, "I owe allegiance to the Northern Country. I belong to the United States." On his citizenship, he declared, "I must be a citizen of the United States of America if I am a citizen at all."[29] The first statement suggested that allegiance was an expression of civic citizenship. He "belonged" to the nation of the United States and thus owed allegiance to it and was protected by it, much as he might once have belonged to a slave owner and thus owed allegiance to him while deserving protection from him. On legal citizenship, he determined that he was a legal citizen of the United States. He did not assume that civic citizenship translated neatly into legal citizenship: here his reasoning was much like James Simpson's, or like Chief Justice Taney's, for that matter. But he did assume that every free person had to have citizenship in some country—an argument that Taney and other lawmakers had rejected, resulting in the strange antebellum phenomenon of some free African Americans, when asked to declare their citizenship, simply inventing one.[30] To the extent that Hall believed he was an American citizen, it was by default alone.

Hall may have been an affective citizen of the United States, but the affection did not run deep. Had the war not broken out, his affective citizenship might have stayed latent. Instead, like many others during the war, he had to identify himself with a nation for the first time in his life. Wars stir up currents of nationalism, and the Civil War, which unleashed patriotic fever on both sides of the Mason-Dixon line, was no different. But Hall's self-identification as a U.S. citizen did not come from being battered with patriotic rhetoric. Rather, it came from direct engagement with an instrument of national power: a prize court. Such was the case with much affective citizenship during the war. It may have complemented burgeoning nationalism, but it was triggered less by spontaneous emotion than by force. Hall was one of many caught in a previously unthinkable situation that demanded a pledge of allegiance—or at least of affection—to a country on which he had little claim, and which had not yet claimed him. If people during the Civil War were part of an imagined community, it may have been only because the situation forced them to imagine their community. As is usually the case with ordinary people caught up in the process of nation making, force precedes affect.

Regardless of whether or not people's declared affection for the nation was forced, their opportunity was now greater than ever to earn citizenship by declaring affection—so long as they were white. The African Americans in the prize courts who declared themselves loyal to the United States, even citizens of the United States, did not become legal citizens simply by demonstrating affective citizenship. In contrast, the many whites who took oaths of allegiance, as opposed to mere declarations, did affirm, earn, or even restore their legal citizenship.

To be sure, many African Americans did believe that a demonstration of affective citizenship might lead to civic or even legal citizenship. Witness the publicity received in August 1861 by Henry Highland Garnet, who took the oath of allegiance, was awarded a United States passport, and was celebrated in *Douglass' Monthly* for demonstrating his status as a legal citizen.[31] Less fanfare attended the awarding of passports to less famous African Americans, such as Benjamin C. Taylor of Buffalo, New York, and Pedrona Wright of Philadelphia, both of whom were described by passport officers as having "mulatto" complexions.[32] But they, no less than Garnet, must have thought that their affective citizenship gave them some claim to legal citizenship. Only a handful of applications from African Americans exist in the passport records, so it is hard to extract much from the evidence. Most, like Taylor and Wright, were described as light in complexion, and all had to declare a place abroad to which they were traveling. Small was the universe of possible African Americans who might have their legal citizenship affirmed through the passport application process. They would have to be freeborn and have the means to travel abroad. A light shade of skin might help, too.

Enlisting in the army required an oath of loyalty, and provided another opportunity for African Americans to take a step toward legal citizenship. But that universe was again small: it was limited to freeborn African Americans (the citizenship status of former slaves who served remained uncertain until the Fourteenth Amendment) and to men of military age. The number of freeborn African Americans who earned citizenship by swearing an oath during the war, either in the enlistment or passport process, may have numbered more than 100,000, but not much more than that.

By contrast, the number of whites who took the oath to earn or restore their citizenship must have numbered at least a million; certainly it reached that number if whites in the Confederacy and Union are included. The ranks of oath takers included men and women on all sides of the struggle. Historians have made much of the Civil War as "the Era of the Oath," an expression coined by Harold Hyman, whose 1954 book of the same name remains the best study of the subject of loyalty oaths imposed by the Union during the sectional conflict.[33] When Hyman wrote that book, he was concerned mainly with the constitutionality of such oaths. And well he should have been, for loyalty oaths in the McCarthy era were assaulting the foundation of American civil liberties. Historians after Hyman followed his lead, concerning themselves mainly with the legal propriety of the oath, especially the oath as administered to whites in the Union during and after the Civil War. Neglected in this angle of inquiry is the meaning of the oath for African Americans.

For African Americans who felt themselves citizens of the United States but whose opportunity to take an oath demonstrating that feeling was limited, the oath-taking by one-time traitors must have stung. It was another reminder of whites' faith in the moral capacity of their own race and their suspicion of soullessness in all others. In mid-1864, a Florida correspondent of the *Christian Recorder*, the organ of the African Methodist Episcopal (AME) Church, marveled at "how easy [it was] for a rebel to come in [to Union lines], give himself up, take the oath, and get a pass to go home, twelve or fifteen miles off, and transmit information which might be fatal to us!" Just over a year later, the same man, an African American, put a sharper point on the commentary: he said it was disgraceful for former Confederates to be allowed to testify in court while African Americans were denied the right of taking the witness oath. The discrepancy led courts to be complicit in white violence against African Americans. "Negro citizens although they have been the only true and avowed friends of the United States Government in this section of the country," the correspondent reported, "are still compelled to feel that they are black, and the smooth oily tongue of the white planter is enough to condemn any number of them to a tying up for twenty-four hours."[34]

Yet, unbeknownst to the *Christian Recorder's* correspondent as well as many other commentators, and for that matter later historians, many former slaves had begun taking oaths in southern courts. Freeborn African Americans had usually had this right in northern courts, and in southern courts where the defendant was black, but during the Civil War increasing numbers of ex-slaves were being allowed to testify in cases involving white defendants. The first courts to move in this direction in the South were the Union courts-martial, some of which began allowing the testimony of black witnesses against whites as early as 1862. Federal and state civil courts would not officially adopt the practice for at least another two years.

Being allowed to take the oath and testify in court against whites may not have been the same as a declaration of allegiance leading to legal citizenship, but certain elements were similar: Americans publicly declared their coupled faith in God and nation, and they were admitted into a restricted community. If this was not legal citizenship, it was certainly civic and affective citizenship. And it was yet another avenue opened by the Civil War to allow African Americans to become full legal citizens.

Consider the statement of Sylvester Deeds, a white man court-martialed in July 1864 whose fate rested on the determination of a judge advocate to accept or reject the testimony of two female African American witnesses who were ready to declare that Deeds had acted in self-defense but whose testimony had not been allowed at the first hearing. By the witness laws of the state of Missouri, blacks were not allowed to testify in cases with white defendants. According to Deeds, the two black women in question had kin who were fighting for the Union army. "The two colored women whoes [sic] testimony was rejected by this court," Deeds explained, "are represented—one by three brothers and a father, and the other by two brothers—jeopardizing their lives, and fighting to help save our country from ruin. And must they be deprived of the common rights of a human being?" The judge agreed. The women, he declared, "may be presumed to feel the obligations of an oath."[35] In other words, the judge was acknowledging the authority of these women's affective citizenship. They felt as citizens feel. And thus they *belonged* in this community and should enjoy the rights of those within it. African Americans were pushing the law forward, even as Lincoln and other lawmakers lagged behind. The time had come for Americans to rank the loyal black oath above the dubious oath of the white southerner. This was a step that Lincoln had never taken. For southern allies in reconstruction, he had always looked first to loyal white southerners and only grudgingly and hesitantly to black southerners, or to be more precise, a subset of them: veterans and the most "intelligent." Yet the manifest commitment of all free African Americans demanded reciprocal obligation. They were ready to take oaths to the Union, to risk eternal damnation for the sake of a citizenship that was unacknowledged by law, that was at best affective. Lincoln, for his part, did require all southern whites wanting their U.S. citizenship secured to take an oath to the Union, the Constitution, *and* the Emancipation Proclamation. He did not take the next step of inviting the people freed by the proclamation to take their own oath of citizenship. But they were ready to do so. He would have done well to let them.

Notes

For research assistance in the examination of Lincoln's use of the word "citizen," I am grateful to David Beyer.

1. "Address on Colonization to a Deputation of Negroes," August 14, 1862, in *The Collected Works of Abraham Lincoln*, 9 vols., ed. Roy P. Basler (New Brunswick, N.J.: Rutgers University Press, 1953–55), 5:370–75 (hereafter cited as *CW*); Noah Brooks, dispatch of November 2, 1864, in Michael Burlingame, *Lincoln Observed: Civil War Dispatches of Noah Brooks* (Baltimore: Johns Hopkins University Press, 1998), 141–42. For a more detailed examination of Lincoln's racial views, see Michael Vorenberg, "Slavery Reparations in Theory and Practice: Lincoln's Approach," in *Lincoln Emancipated: The President and the Politics of Race*, ed. Brian Dirck (DeKalb: Northern Illinois University Press, 2007), 117–29.

2. Benedict Anderson, *Imagined Communities: Reflections on the Origin and Spread of Nationalism*, rev. ed. (London: Verso, 1991). I am grateful to Michael Les Benedict, who, in his comments on an earlier version of this essay, used these terms to describe the categories of citizenship.

3. *Scott v. Sandford*, U.S. Reports (1857), 60:406.

4. *CW*, 2:401.

5. *CW*, 5:520.

6. See Edward Bates, "Citizenship" (letter of November 29, 1862, to Salmon P. Chase), in *Official Opinions of the Attorneys General of the United States*, 10:382–413; reprinted in *U.S. AG Lexis*, 4, quote at p. 26.

7. Ibid., 2–3.

8. James H. Kettner, *The Development of American Citizenship, 1608–1870* (Chapel Hill: University of North Carolina Press, 1978), 337 (including note 9).

9. James P. McClure, Leigh Johnsen, Kathleen Norman, and Michael Vanderlan, "Circumventing the *Dred Scott* decision: Edward Bates, Salmon P. Chase, and the Citizenship of African Americans," *Civil War History* 43 (December 1997): 279–309.

10. *CW*, 3:179.

11. *CW*, 5:372.

12. William J. Novak, "The Legal Transformation of Citizenship in Nineteenth-Century America," in *The Democratic Experiment: New Directions in American Political History*, ed. Meg Jacobs, William J. Novak, and Julian E. Zelizer (Princeton, N.J.: Princeton University Press, 2003), 85–119.

13. *CW*, 8:349–50.

14. Michael Vorenberg, *Final Freedom: The Civil War, the Abolition of Slavery, and the Thirteenth Amendment* (Cambridge: Cambridge University Press, 2001), 219–21.

15. *CW*, 7:55.

16. Vorenberg, *Final Freedom*, 234–39.

17. Letter to Michael Hahn, March 13, 1864, *CW*, 7:243; last public address, April 11, 1865, *CW*, 8:403.

18. David W. Blight, "They Knew What Time It Was: African-Americans," in *Why the Civil War Came*, ed. Gabor S. Boritt (New York: Oxford University Press, 2006), 51–78.

19. James M. McPherson, ed., *The Negro's Civil War: How American Negroes Felt and Acted during the War for the Union* (Urbana: University of Illinois Press, 1982), 277–90.

20. *CW*, 4:374.

21. *CW*, 4:519.

22. William Whiting, "Dear Sir," April 23, 1863, Record Group 107, entry 64, vol. 1, copy of letter following opinion 127, National Archives, Washington, D.C.

23. William Whiting, "Citizenship and Enrolment of Indians," June 1863, Record Group 107, entry 63, vol. 2, opinion 465, ibid.

24. William Whiting, "Enrollment of Slaves . . . ," December 31, 1863, Record Group 107, entry 64, vol. 3, opinion 410, ibid.

25. *CW*, 6:409.

26. Mark E. Neely Jr., "Abraham Lincoln and Black Colonization: Benjamin Butler's Spurious Testimony," *Civil War History* 25 (March 1979): 77–83.

27. "Deposition of Samuel Robinson," *U.S. v. Crenshaw*, box 5, file A16-415, Record Group 21, entry 106, U.S. District Court, Southern District of N.Y., "Prize Case Files— Civil War," National Archives Northeast Regional Research Center, New York, N.Y.

28. "Deposition of James Edwin Simpson," *U.S. v. Tropic Wind*, box 4, file A16-384, ibid.

29. "Deposition of Charles Hall," ibid.

30. Kunal M. Parker, "Making Blacks Foreigners: The Legal Construction of Former Slaves in Post-Revolutionary Massachusetts," *Utah Law Review* 75 (2001): 75–124.

31. McPherson, *The Negro's Civil War*, 249.

32. Passport application of Benjamin C. Taylor, October 29, 1863, reel 119, frame 11983; and passport application of Pedrona Wright, November 5, 1864, reel 125, frame 16016, Record Group 59, National Archives, Washington, D.C.

33. Harold M. Hyman, *The Era of the Oath: Northern Loyalty Tests during the Civil War and Reconstruction* (Philadelphia: University of Pennsylvania Press, 1954).

34. *Christian Recorder*, April 9, 1864, Oct. 21, 1865.

35. "Trial of Sylvester Deeds" (March 1864), folder nn 1582 (1), Court Martial Records, Record Group 153, National Archives, Washington, D.C., quotations at p. 52 of handwritten transcript and p. 6 of typewritten opinion of Gen. E. B. Brown.

LOUIS GERTEIS

Slaves, Servants, and Soldiers

Uneven Paths to Freedom in the Border States, 1861–1865

Secession defined the border states. In the immediate aftermath of Lincoln's election, South Carolina, followed by Mississippi, Florida, Alabama, Georgia, Louisiana, and Texas, declared themselves out of the United States and created a new central government, the Confederate States of America. Abraham Lincoln took office as President of the United States of America in the midst of this secession crisis and promised all loyal citizens, and particularly slaveholders, the full protection of the federal government. In his inaugural address of March 4, 1861, Lincoln assured Americans that "the property, peace, and security of no section are to be in any wise endangered by the now incoming Administration." To this pledge, Lincoln added his endorsement of the Fugitive Slave Law of 1850. Although the president promised stability and security for slave property, he acknowledged key difficulties in this arena when he suggested the need for legislation to insure "that a free man be not in any case surrendered as a slave." Lincoln also suggested the need for congressional legislation to enforce the privileges and immunities clause of the Constitution. Clearly, the new Republican administration could not ignore conflicts associated with the enforcement of the federal Fugitive Slave Law and the controversial Supreme Court decision in the *Dred Scott* case, both of which inflamed northern public opinion. But, Lincoln made his central point plain: his administration would protect the "property . . . peace and personal security" of the "people of the Southern States."[1]

Within weeks, Lincoln's hopes for peacefully restoring the Union were dashed. In April 1861, Confederate forces attacked the federal garrison at Fort Sumter in Charleston harbor and the secession crisis became a war of rebellion. Lincoln's call to the states to send troops to support the national government led to secession in the Upper South, as Virginia,

Arkansas, Tennessee, and North Carolina all joined the Confederacy. The remaining slaveholding states—Delaware, Maryland, the western counties of Virginia (that became the state of West Virginia in 1863), Kentucky, and Missouri—held fast to their conservative Unionism. Lincoln viewed these loyal slave states as essential to the eventual restoration of the Union and his so-called border state policy attempted to appease the Unionist majorities in these states. To maintain the support of the border states, Lincoln pursued limited war aims against the Confederacy and held out the possibility that a relatively swift restoration of the Union could leave slavery substantially intact. For a time, Lincoln tried to maintain the distinction between loyal and disloyal masters everywhere in the South. This policy made sense only if loyal slaveholders brought seceded states back into the United States. Increasingly, as Confederate resistance stiffened, the distinction between loyal and disloyal masters had meaning only in the border states where Unionists prevailed.

In this setting, border state Unionists supported both Lincoln's September 1861 revocation of John C. Frémont's emancipation proclamation (announced in Missouri on August 30, 1861) and the First Confiscation Act previously passed by Congress in July. Confiscation allowed Unionists to punish disloyal persons and potentially profit from a redistribution of wealth. Frémont's emancipation edict delighted abolitionists and drew praise from Radical Republicans, but emancipation raised issues, including citizenship, that Lincoln and conservative Unionists would not entertain. Nevertheless, in the spring of 1862, as the war entered its second year, Lincoln began to consider emancipation as a war measure capable of transforming the character of the conflict. In those areas of the South that continued to resist federal authority, Lincoln now considered adopting a more radical course, in which the South's enslaved labor force became a valuable military asset. Lincoln continued to defer to loyal masters in the border states and, indeed, intended to reward them with federal compensation. At the same time that Lincoln developed his emancipation policy for the seceded South, he secured the passage of a congressional resolution offering compensation to "any state which may adopt gradual abolishment of slavery." The resolution passed because the Republican majority supported it unanimously. At this point, Lincoln's courtship of the loyal masters of the border states grew sour. Border state Unionists strongly opposed the compensation measure and resisted Lincoln's efforts to persuade them otherwise.[2] As Lincoln fashioned the preliminary

Emancipation Proclamation, slaveholders in the border states expressed their bitter displeasure with the prospect that a war against southern rebellion might destroy an existing system of racial subordination and erect nothing to replace it. Slaveholders in the border states rejected Lincoln's offer of compensation and explored instead systems of apprenticeship intended to extend their control over the labor power of "servants" for another generation, or more.

In terms of developing federal policy, the Emancipation Proclamation is pivotal because with its promulgation, Lincoln committed his administration to a total war against the southern rebellion. Before the proclamation, Lincoln's cautious policy prevailed for the border states. After the proclamation, Lincoln spoke not of the loyalty of individuals but of the loyalty of states and regions. The areas exempted from the final proclamation—all of the border states together with Tennessee and several eastern counties in Virginia and the southern parishes in Louisiana— were deemed sufficiently loyal by the president to be allowed to continue to debate the future of slavery. Nevertheless, the nature of the discussion had changed. With the issuance of the proclamation, Lincoln acquiesced in the military necessity of enrolling black troops. Earlier, when he had urged the border states to accept gradual compensated emancipation, Lincoln had warned that not to do so left loyal slaveholders vulnerable to unforeseen "incidents" related to the prosecution of the war. The decision to enlist black troops proved to be an "incident" with profound consequences. Lincoln continued to offer support to loyal slaveholders in the border states, but the slaves did not distinguish between loyal and disloyal masters, and slaveholders in the border states witnessed a steady erosion of slavery even as they clung tenaciously to their human property.

FOR LINCOLN, THE change in perspective had been substantial. Before the Emancipation Proclamation, he had accommodated and seemed to embrace much of the conservative racial ideology articulated most prominently by former Jacksonian Democrats whose political evolution had carried them into the Republican Party. A leading popularizer of this racial ideology was Francis "Frank" P. Blair Jr. of Missouri. As a member of a powerful political family, Frank Blair's opinions carried a good deal of weight. His father, Francis P. Blair Sr., traced his political roots back to Andrew Jackson's "kitchen cabinet." With Missouri's senator Thomas Hart Benton, the elder Blair led the fight against the rising Southern

"Hon. Montgomery
Blair, half-length
portrait." Courtesy
of the Library of
Congress.

Rights wing of the Democratic Party. As Southern Rights partisans gained
control of the Democratic Party (and defeated Benton in Missouri in
1850), Francis P. Blair led antislavery Democrats into the new Republican
Party. The elder Blair presided over the first Republican national convention in 1856 and enthusiastically supported the party's first presidential
nominee, Benton's son-in-law, John C. Frémont.

From the Blair House, across Pennsylvania Avenue from the White
House, and from "Silver Spring," his Maryland estate, Francis P. Blair led
the conservative wing of the Republican Party. His son Frank Blair led
Republicans in Missouri. Another son, Montgomery Blair, began his law
career in St. Louis before moving to Washington, D.C., in the early 1850s.
Montgomery Blair gained national attention as one of the attorneys for
Dred Scott before the Supreme Court. And Montgomery Blair became
Lincoln's choice for postmaster general. For his part, Frank Blair took
center stage in the late 1850s as he worked to revive support for coloniza-
tion as a means of promoting emancipation. The Blair family shared

Frank's enthusiasm for colonization, as did another conservative Republican leader, Edward Bates of Missouri. Bates had been Francis P. Blair's first choice for the 1860 Republican presidential nomination. Lincoln brought Bates into his cabinet as attorney general.[3]

What made Frank Blair's colonization argument compelling to many people was the manner in which he linked the older Jeffersonian dream of a white republic with a mid-nineteenth century preoccupation with the expansion of American influence in Central America. Blair focused his colonization discussion on the growing American interest in controlling a passage to the Pacific across the isthmus of Central America. Blair proposed the creation of a black republic on the isthmus. It would be peopled by emancipated American slaves, and the new nation's loyalty to the United States would promote American interests in the region. Drawing from an earlier speech by Senator Benton, Blair insisted that it was the "Destiny of the Races" that the Negro, like the Indian, would disappear from the "temperate zone" of North America. In Blair's imagery, Indians fled in advance of the expansion of Anglo-Saxon civilization and migrated steadily to the far north of the continent. In the same imagery, African Americans settled naturally and willingly in the tropical region to the south. It was prudent to promote this destiny with subsidized colonization because it served American interests in the hemisphere and left the United States the exclusive domain of the Anglo-Saxon race.[4]

This racial ideology permitted conservative Republicans to support the antislavery plank of the party's platform. All Republicans agreed that there should be no new slave states. Conservative Republicans like the Blairs made this commitment without giving ground on the necessity of linking emancipation to racial separation. In May 1862, when Republicans in Missouri began to discuss the possibility of emancipation in the state, Frank Blair returned to his colonization argument. He described himself as a "friend" of emancipation who had always embraced Jefferson's view that the American republic had no room for slaves. Like Lincoln, Blair supported gradual emancipation accompanied by "compensation to loyal owners of slaves." But he opposed emancipation unless provision could be made for the "separation of the white and black races." Blair insisted that "the people of Missouri will require the removal of the blacks as a condition precedent to their liberation."[5]

Before issuing the Emancipation Proclamation, Lincoln embraced this colonization plan with a sincerity that disheartened many African Americans and enraged abolitionists. When Lincoln met with African American leaders in the White House on August 14, 1862, colonization dominated his comments. "You and we are different races," said the president. "We have between us a broader difference than exists between almost any other two races." Echoing Frank Blair, Lincoln continued: "It is better for us both, therefore, to be separated." The president wanted these leaders to work with his administration to create a colony in Central America.[6] Lincoln made this appeal as he prepared to issue the preliminary Emancipation Proclamation and as he offered compensation to loyal masters in the border states. Like Bates and the Blair family, Lincoln appeared to believe that the promise of racial separation and compensation for loyal masters could promote an emancipation policy. Abolitionists were incensed. Emancipation without expatriation and without compensation to slave owners had been the central tenets of their cause for thirty years. On the colonization issue in particular, abolitionists insisted that it was they who stood on practical ground while conservatives such as Blair and the president promoted what Edmund Quincy termed a "wild, delusive and impractical scheme."[7] If "the removal of the blacks" became a precondition for emancipation, abolitionists believed that slavery would never end.

The colonization idea is central to the perspective of Unionists in the border states. The principle that emancipation required racial separation signaled that their defense of the Union in no way implied moral hostility to slavery or sympathy for equal rights across racial lines. They opposed secession because it promoted the interests of a "slave power" that elevated property rights in slaves above all other aspects of the nation's domestic and foreign policy. In this sense, they were antislavery, and they generally opposed the extension of slavery into the western territories. Unlike southern-rights advocates, border state Unionists spoke of the future of the United States in language that was compatible with northern paeans to material progress and commercial expansion. This northern orientation reflected their interests. All the principal cities of the border states—Wilmington, Baltimore, Wheeling, Louisville, and St. Louis—integrated significant portions of the economies of each state with the North. Despite Unionist sympathies and northern economic ties, however, support for slavery remained strong in the border states. The colonization argument allowed border state Unionists to speak about a future without slavery, but the implausibility of achieving a total separation of the races also justified discussions about how African American servitude could be extended into future generations. In none of the border states did Lincoln's plan for compensated emancipation take hold. Each state had its distinctive character, but they held in common a strong reluctance to end slavery and a bitter resistance to incorporating African Americans into civil society.

Lincoln's border state policy sustained the expectation that slaveholders in the border states would emerge from the conflict with firm legal control over the labor power they had owned before the war. After the Emancipation Proclamation, Lincoln's engagement with the border states continued, but he viewed the issues with which they struggled in a significantly different light.

When Lincoln issued the final Emancipation Proclamation on January 1, 1863, he moved decisively away from the colonization argument. In the proclamation, Lincoln announced that freed slaves would be enrolled as soldiers. According to Lincoln's biographer David Donald, the president arrived at this position "reluctantly, and after great hesitation." "An unstated corollary of the President's new position," observed Donald, was the abandonment of Blair's colonization scheme. "Henceforth," Donald concluded, "Lincoln recognized that blacks were to make their future as citizens of the United States." As Lincoln biographer Richard Carwardine observed, the president had concluded that victory required emancipation and recruitment of black soldiers. Even as he faced the possibility of defeat in the presidential election of 1864, Lincoln rejected suggestions from border state conservatives that he retract the Emancipation Proclamation.[8]

Historians continue to debate whether Lincoln's final proclamation significantly changed the course of the war or simply acknowledged a wartime process of emancipation already under way.[9] In either case, however, the Emancipation Proclamation and the public policies that followed from it provided a measure of discipline and direction to the energies unleashed by war.

Of the energies unleashed by war, none was more powerful than the determination of enslaved African Americans to press for freedom wherever they could. The Emancipation Proclamation did not create this energy, but the federal policies that followed from the proclamation— particularly the decision to enlist black men as soldiers in the Union army—added discipline and direction to the struggles of the slaves. Slave-

"Company E, 4th U.S. Colored Infantry, at Fort Lincoln." The photograph shows twenty-seven African Americans in two lines with rifle butts resting on the ground. Approximately 175 regiments of nearly 200,000 free blacks and freed slaves fought for the Union Army as part of the United States Colored Troops. Courtesy of the Library of Congress.

holders in the border states fought doggedly and effectively to maintain their human property. Lincoln's border state policy aided this effort, and the rising wartime rebelliousness among slaves might have dissipated as slaveholders fought to maintain control of slave families. The decision to enlist black troops provided a structure within which individual acts of rebelliousness became a powerful, history-altering force. The decision to enlist black troops proved to be pivotal in the destruction of slavery. Without that choice, slavery might have survived for some time in the loyal slave states. But, it was the struggles of the slaves and not the structure of public policy that generated the energy necessary to dismantle slavery.

THE CENTRAL WARNING of Lincoln's first inaugural address had been that the safety and security of persons and property lay in adhering to constitutional government. Rebellion and war brought uncertainty. Particularly unfathomable were the effects of wartime emancipation. As Lincoln abandoned Blair's colonization scheme and accepted the necessity of incorporating the former slaves into postwar civil society, he looked to the border states, including his home state of Kentucky, for insight into how this could be accomplished as safely as possible. The border states provided the president with a somewhat controlled setting in which emancipation-related issues, including labor and race relations, could be examined and public policies devised. They also provided Lincoln with an opportunity to examine the process of emancipation without the artificial constraints of direct military occupation.

By exempting the border states from the terms of the Emancipation Proclamation, Lincoln continued to extend to them some of the autonomy they had enjoyed during the first years of the war. Civil governments continued to function in Delaware, Maryland, Kentucky, and Missouri and in the new state of West Virginia, but Lincoln also authorized the imposition of martial law in these states. Lincoln consistently defended his middle course and rejected repeated pleas to resolve the tensions in the border states, either by placing them entirely under federal military control or by deferring to the authority of their civil governments. Lincoln's middle course helped to insure that the Civil War in the border states earned its name. Conflict in these states raged at the most intimate levels of civil society.

For all of the border states, a defense of slavery became a central concern in the Civil War. Even in Delaware, where slavery had declined steadily in the antebellum decades and where Unionists overwhelmingly rejected secession, hostility to emancipation became a dominant sentiment. On January 3, 1861, the Delaware state legislature voted against secession by a wide margin. To emphasize the strong vote favoring the Union, the legislature added the statement that since "Delaware was the first to adopt, so will she be the last to abandon the Federal Constitution." Although untouched by the violence of the Civil War and firmly devoted to the constitution, Delaware refused Lincoln's offer of compensated emancipation. Delaware struggled to maintain slavery even though fewer than 2,000 of the state's 20,000 African Americans were slaves in 1860 and fewer than 600 households owned slaves. It was not until the ratification of the Thirteenth Amendment in December of 1865 that slavery finally ended in Delaware. And it ended without Delaware's assent: in 1865, the Delaware legislature rejected the Thirteenth Amendment and did not endorse it until 1901.[10]

Confederate sympathies ran considerably higher in Maryland, where pro-Confederate riots and sabotage threatened to isolate Washington from the free states. But the arrival of federal troops in the area around the District of Columbia soon suppressed secessionist tendencies in Maryland. The riots of April 19, 1861, were followed by a reassertion of Unionist sentiment. Thousands of federal troops secured the nation's capital, and on May 13, Maj. Gen. Benjamin Butler of Massachusetts occupied Baltimore without opposition. On June 13, Maryland voters went to the polls to choose representatives to serve in the special session of Congress called by President Lincoln. Unionists won all of the seats and did so facing very little opposition. Only five counties—Talbot and Worcester on the Eastern Shore and St. Marys, Charles, and Calvert in southern Maryland —supported non-Unionist candidates. The remaining sixteen counties delivered Unionist majorities and assured the election of Unionist congressmen. Of the 67,000 votes cast, less than 25,000 went for non-Unionist candidates. Unionists won with more than 63 percent of the vote. As in neighboring Delaware, however, Unionist strength in Maryland did not translate into antislavery sentiment. Maryland, too, rejected Lincoln's plan for compensated emancipation. Nevertheless, in November 1864, about a year before the ratification of the Thirteenth Amendment, Maryland adopted a new state constitution that ended slavery in the state.[11]

Unionists created West Virginia out of the twenty-five Virginia counties that lay west of the Shenandoah Valley and north of the Kanawha River. Always restive under Richmond's rule, western Virginians took advantage of the secession movement to declare their own independence. When Virginians went to the polls on April 17, 1861, western Virginians rejected secession by a three-to-one margin. The Unionist Virginia government led by Francis Pierpont in Alexandria (under the protection of federal troops defending Washington, D.C.) met the conditions of Article IV, section 3, of the U.S. Constitution and authorized the western counties to form a separate state.

West Virginia became a state on June 20, 1863, after its legislature met the demand of the U.S. Congress that it adopt a constitution that ended slavery. As in Delaware, there were few slaveholders in West Virginia, and only about 4 percent of the population was enslaved. Nevertheless, without the specific conditions set by Congress, West Virginians would have maintained slavery. Even with the congressional requirement, the West Virginia legislature outlined a very gradual emancipation policy. Under the new constitution, the children of slaves born after July 4, 1863, would be free. Slaves born before that date would be emancipated on their twenty-fifth birthday. Adult slaves would not be freed, and their lifetime of labor would compensate their owners for the gradual ending of slavery. However, West Virginia cast its vote to ratify the Thirteenth Amendment, and slavery in the new state ended completely in December 1865.[12]

Kentucky proclaimed its neutrality in the struggle between North and South, but by September 1861 Confederate forces began fortifying Columbus, Kentucky, on the Mississippi River. Ulysses S. Grant countered by locating federal forces at the mouth of the Tennessee and Cumberland rivers. Kentucky soon resembled Missouri, with a Unionist government in the state capital and a Confederate government in exile. But Kentucky had nearly twice as many slaves as Missouri, and only Virginia and Georgia had more slave owners than Kentucky. As in all of the border states, Kentucky rejected Lincoln's compensated emancipation plan. And, like Delaware, Kentucky refused to ratify the Thirteenth Amendment. Slavery ended in Kentucky only with the ratification of the Thirteenth Amendment in December 1865.[13]

In Missouri in 1860, Claiborne Jackson and Thomas Reynolds ran for governor and lieutenant governor respectively as Democrats supporting Stephen A. Douglas for president. Missouri delivered its electoral votes to Douglas (the only state to do so) and Jackson and Reynolds were elected to office by voters who overwhelmingly supported the Union. In the secession crisis, however, Jackson and Reynolds favored the Confederacy and maneuvered as best they could to take Missouri out of the Union. Jackson refused to comply with Lincoln's call for troops after the attack on Fort Sumter and called instead for the state militia to muster to protect Missouri from attacks by enemies. The militia muster in the St. Louis Military District took place on the western edge of the city and became the focal point for a clash between Confederate sympathizers and the Unionists. With the approval of General of the Army Winfield Scott and President Lincoln, Frank Blair organized a group of Unionists as a "committee of safety" and worked with the new federal commander in St.

Louis, Gen. Nathaniel Lyon, to raise several regiments of "home guards," drawn largely from the German immigrant population.

Under these circumstances, the militia muster in St. Louis drew mostly Confederate sympathizers. Those who answered Governor Jackson's call to arms named their camp in his honor and "Camp Jackson" raised the hopes of Confederate sympathizers that the federal arsenal in St. Louis could be captured to aid the rebel cause. Early in May 1861, determined to end this defiance of federal authority, General Lyon led a small force of regular United States army soldiers and an overwhelming force of home guards to surround Camp Jackson and force its surrender. In June, Lyon forced Jackson to abandon the state capital at Jefferson City. A state constitutional convention (ironically called by Jackson to promote secession) declared the office of governor and other state offices abandoned and voted to appoint the proslavery Unionist Hamilton Gamble provisional governor pending a new election. Gamble, son-in-law of Attorney General Bates, served as governor throughout the war. Gamble shared the conservative racial views of Bates and the Blair family and led loyal slaveholders in Missouri in opposition to Lincoln's compensation plan and in designing a lengthy period of African American postwar apprenticeship.[14] Eventually, however, and somewhat in advance of the passage of the Thirteenth Amendment, Missouri adopted a new constitution that abolished slavery immediately and without compensation.

Determined as Unionist slaveholders were to maintain control over their labor force, slavery in the border states crumbled during the Civil War. The erosion continued even as federal military forces tried to avoid disrupting the institution. As federal forces moved through Maryland, for example, Butler and his successor, Gen. John A. Dix, ordered their troops to do nothing to disrupt existing labor relations. But, as Dix soon noted, slaves left their masters, whether loyal or disloyal, and made their way to Union lines. At Fortress Monroe, Virginia, Dix reported that a large number of the black refugees gathered there "are fugitives from the service of Union men, who have been persecuted by the secessionists for their fidelity to the Government of the United States." Dix clearly sympathized with the plight of Unionist slaveholders. "Some Union families in this neighborhood have lost all their negroes," Dix observed. At Secretary of War Edwin M. Stanton's direction, Dix provided camps for all of the refugees, observing that it would be "troublesome to separate one class from the other."[15]

During the first two years of the war, Lincoln routinely deferred to the requests of loyal slaveholders in the border states. Nevertheless, growing numbers of slaves discovered that the war offered new opportunities for them to secure their freedom. John Boston, a fugitive from Maryland, reported his whereabouts to his wife in January 1862. He had found refuge and work with a New York regiment encamped in Virginia. The Brooklyn soldiers treated him well, Boston reported, but he worried about the wife and child he had left behind. He urged his wife to speak to her mistress. "I trust that she will continue her kindness to you and that God will bless her." "Kiss Daniel for me," Boston wrote in closing, and, "Give my love to father and mother." The fact that Boston's letter became a part of the North's military records suggests that a loyal slaveholder presented it as evidence that Union troops harbored fugitive slaves.[16]

By the second year of the war, conservative Unionists clearly tried the patience of Lincoln and his administration. In March 1862, Congress adopted an article of war stating that it was no part of the duty of an officer to capture and return fugitive slaves. In April, Congress abolished slavery in the District of Columbia and, at Lincoln's behest, approved a plan for voluntary, compensated emancipation for loyal slaveholders. The border states rejected the plan in the face of mounting evidence that masters could not easily maintain their hold on their slave property. In April 1862, a Maryland congressman complained to Secretary of War Stanton that large numbers of slaves owned by loyal masters found refuge in army camps. The congressman noted that federal commanders had earlier issued orders excluding slaves from their camps. The congressman warned that if the slaves were not immediately sent out of the camps they would be lost to their owners when the army moved. Two weeks later the congressman received a brief reply from the assistant secretary of war stating that "the pressure of more urgent and important business connected with the operations of the army" prevented Stanton from "considering this subject."[17]

Nevertheless, when Lincoln issued the final Emancipation Proclamation on January 1, 1863, he exempted from its terms all of the border states. Despite the exemptions, slaves continued with varying degrees of success to find pathways to freedom. Emancipation in the District of Columbia created a haven for slaves escaping from nearby Maryland and Delaware. In Kentucky, where such a safe haven did not exist, slaveholders and their agents captured and returned fugitives to bondage.

Sheriffs in Kentucky vigorously enforced that state's slave laws. In the fall of 1862, when the army of Gen. Don Carlos Buell returned to Kentucky, county sheriffs near Louisville arrested slaves that followed the federal troops out of Tennessee despite their status under the Second Confiscation Act as freed slaves of disloyal masters. Sold at public auctions in Kentucky, these briefly freed people fetched prices ranging from $200 to $450. Clearly, slaves retained significant value, indicating that masters expected to maintain ownership of their labor power for some time to come. Buell appointed a commission to correct this violation of federal law, but only direct intervention by federal troops succeeded in freeing a few of these re-enslaved people.[18]

The persistence of civil governments in the border states aided the efforts of slaveholders to resist the advance of emancipation. Missouri offered a particularly clear picture of what masters had in mind when they discussed and rejected Lincoln's compensated emancipation plan. Missouri's provisional governor Hamilton Gamble proposed to begin a gradual plan of emancipation in 1870. In that year, slaves aged between twelve and forty would become servants "subject to the authority of their late masters" until 1876. Slaves under twelve in 1870 would remain servants until they reached the age of twenty-three. Under Gamble's plan, a slave child born in December 1869 remained a servant until December 1892. Slaves older than forty in 1870 would remain slaves for life. In Gamble's mind, the plan was a balanced one that served the "interest of the masters" as well as the interests of the slaves. Gamble rejected arguments for immediate emancipation as "Utopian notions" that assumed that by breaking the shackles of the slaves, the freedman "becomes an angel—becomes at once an intelligent man capable of sustaining himself under all the trials of life."[19]

Missouri did not enact this plan because emancipationists defeated conservative Unionists at the polls in 1864. A stern new loyalty oath contributed to a sharp decline in Missouri voters (52,000 fewer citizens voted in 1864 than in 1860). Missouri quickly adopted a new constitution that abolished slavery without compensation and without Gamble's gradualist features. In Kentucky and Maryland, however, slaveholders turned to existing laws of apprenticeship to maintain control over the labor power of their former slaves. In Maryland, Union general Lew Wallace attempted to shield freedmen from this abuse by placing them under military protection. Even so, in the absence of a military presence in the countryside, former slaves were easily intimidated into accepting conditions that fell short of freedom. A provost marshal reported from Easton, Maryland, that since the adoption of the new state constitution, land owners compelled their former slaves "to bind their children to them, under the old apprenticeship law."[20] Governor Augustus Bradford supported the apprentice system and denied that it led to abuse. Bradford's successor, Governor Thomas Swann, concurred and supported a related practice of sentencing freedmen to slave labor for petty crimes.[21] Kentucky passed a new apprenticeship law in February 1866, and county judges facilitated the practice of binding former slave children to former masters.[22]

WHEN LINCOLN AGREED to enlist African Americans as Union soldiers, he and federal authorities generally understood that a broad new pathway to freedom had been opened. As a result, despite Lincoln's efforts to appease loyal slaveholders, the intensity of the conflicts between federal forces and conservative Unionists increased significantly. By the summer of 1863, enlistment of black troops began in the free states and in the occupied portions of the Confederacy. In October, the War Department ordered recruitment to begin in Delaware, Maryland, and Missouri. Kentucky was spared, ostensibly because so many black men in the state worked as military laborers. But in January 1864, recruitment began in the area west of the Tennessee River (part of the military Department of the Tennessee), with recruitment centers located in Paducah and in the federally occupied town of Columbus.

Throughout the border states, owners resisted recruitment with every means at their disposal, and Lincoln continued to try to appease them. In Maryland, federal authorities initially restricted recruitment to free blacks. As late as March 1864, Lincoln agreed with Kentucky governor Thomas Bramlette that black soldiers would not be enlisted in counties where the federal quota for troops was met by white enlistees. Moreover, Lincoln agreed that blacks who joined the army of their own volition would be removed from Kentucky for training. The president agreed to avoid the embarrassment slaveholders experienced in the presence of black recruits and the attendant insubordination that masters experienced from slaves who became soldiers. The Bramlette-Lincoln agreement failed when not enough white recruits came forward.

Although Bramlette continued to protest the enlistment of black troops in Kentucky, large numbers of slaves braved the violence of angry masters to enlist as Union soldiers. When the Kentucky slave Elijah Burdett joined the Union army his master beat his wife so severely she fled the plantation distraught that she had left her four children behind. Mary Wilson, also the wife of a Union soldier, found that her master enjoyed the full support of Lexington policemen, who captured her, returned her to her master's house, and whipped her. In June 1865, Minerva Banks, the mother of a black solider from western Kentucky, found employment in Nashville, stating that she regarded herself as free. Her master and an armed companion tracked her down and whipped her. She then learned from her "employer" that he could not pay her "as he was obliged to pay my wages" to her former master.[23]

Black troops violated every tenet of Kentucky governor Bramlette's conservative Unionist faith. In September 1864, Bramlette wrote to Lincoln announcing his opposition to the president's reelection: as the governor, he was not willing "to sacrifice a single life, or imperil the smallest right of free white men for the sake of the negro." Deeply embittered by the course of federal policy, Bramlette expressed his fervent but futile wish *"that the negro be ignored."*[24]

Enlistment provided the surest path to freedom for border state slaves and their families. The Militia Act of 1862 freed the families of black men employed by the military. At the time, such employment was limited to slaves of disloyal owners. As federal enlistment expanded to include all able-bodied black men, soldiers and Union officers claimed freedom for the soldiers' families. In March 1865, Congress specifically provided for the freedom of soldiers' families regardless of the loyalty of the masters.[25]

In Missouri, guerrillas as well as slave owners worked to disrupt the recruitment of black troops. One black man who succeeded in getting to Jefferson City from an outlying plantation reported that he had hidden during the day and traveled at night to avoid bushwhackers. This new recruit reported seeing three black men killed by bushwhackers on his way to the state capital. Near Mexico, Missouri, a Unionist protested to a St. Louis friend in December 1863 that slave patrols (technically illegal under martial law) prevented blacks from entering the town to enlist. When black men succeeded in enlisting, they often left behind families that were vulnerable to abuse by angry masters. Richard Glover, a slave near Mexico, successfully enlisted in December 1863. When he wrote to his wife, Martha, from his post at Benton Barracks in St. Louis, he received a prompt but distraught reply. "I have had nothing but trouble since you left," she lamented. "You recollect what I told you how they would do after you was gone." Her fears had proved to be well founded. Her master threatened not to feed her children. He had beaten her "scandalously," as she put it. She concluded by begging her soldier husband to return: "You ought not to left me in the fix I am in & all these little helpless children to take care of."[26]

Black soldiers angered by these conditions threatened retaliation. Sam Bowmen, stationed at Benton Barracks Hospital in St. Louis, wrote to his wife near Tipton, Missouri, in May 1864, promising to protect her. At the same time, he warned his wife's master of dire consequences if he mistreated her. He told his wife that he had orders from his commanding general to bring her to St. Louis if she wished to come. "So it lays to your own choice to stay or come," he wrote. "If You donot want to stay tell Mr. Wilson in a decent manner, that You do not." He then addressed his comments to his wife's owner: "General Pile[27] says if You Mr. Wilson is as good a Union man as Sam Hannah recommends you to be you will let her come on good terms and give her a piece of writing to shew that You are what you profess to be." He then warned Wilson about the consequences of any mistreatment:

> If you do not . . . we will shew You what we intend to do.—We are not expecting that this will insult a Union man. You know that a Soldiers wife is free. Read this letter to her and let her return her own answer. I will find out whether this has been read to her in afull understanding with her or not, and if I should find out that she has never heard of her deliverance I will undoubtedly punish you. . . . You can See I have power. . . . I write You with this determination that by the 20th day of May this matter must & will be closed so you can rest till Then or doit sooner as it will be better for You. . . . I want you to understand that we hav labord in the field to Subdue Slavery and now we mean to protect them.[28]

Private Spotswood Rice wrote similarly from Benton Barracks Hospital to his daughters and their owner in Glasgow, Missouri, in September 1864: "Dear Children, be assured that I will have you if it cost me my life." "Your Miss Kaitty said that I tried to steal you," he continued, "but I'll let her know that god never intended for man to steal his own flesh and blood."

To his daughter Mary's owner, Kittey Diggs, Private Rice had this to say:

I want you to remember this one thing that the longer you keep
my Child from me the longer you will have to burn in hell and the
quicker you get there for we are now making up about one thousand
black troops to come up through . . . Glasgow and when we come
woe be to Copperhead rebels and to Slaveholding rebels. . . . I want
you to understand kittey diggs that where ever you and I meets we
are enemies to each other. . . . I have no fears about getting mary out
of your hands this whole Government gives cheer to me and you
cannot help yourself.[29]

Rice's letters to Kitty Diggs deeply angered her brother, Frances W.
Diggs, who promptly wrote the federal commander in Missouri, Gen.
William Rosecrans, and insisted that Rice be sent "down to the army" to
get him out of the state. Diggs claimed that he had freed several of Rice's
children as well as the soldier's wife. Diggs told Rosecrans that his loyalty
to the United States had cost him dearly throughout the war and that this
insult "by such a black scoundrel is more than I can bear."[30]

Rice's owner, Benjamin Lewis of Glasgow, exemplified the wealthy
proslavery Unionists in Missouri. He had migrated to Missouri in the
early 1830s from Virginia, evidently bringing Spotswood Rice with him as
a skilled cigar maker. Benjamin Lewis and two brothers formed a large
and profitable tobacco company and by 1860 employed more than 500
slaves on several plantations and in tobacco factories. Benjamin Lewis
personally owned fifty-five slaves in 1860. A wealthy slave owner, Lewis
was also an unconditional Unionist and suffered at the hands of guerrillas
during Sterling Price's invasion of Missouri in October 1864.[31]

Through his philanthropy, Lewis left Glasgow a handsome public library that bears his name and displays his portrait. In a late nineteenth-
century celebratory history of Missouri, Lewis is described as a "kind"
master and "outright" Unionist who displayed his "liberal humane spirit"
by freeing his "colored people" a year before Lincoln issued the final
Emancipation Proclamation, "and then employing at wages those who
chose to remain in their service." In fact, Lewis retained his slaves well
after the issuance of the final Emancipation Proclamation, although he
clearly hoped to create the impression that his devotion to the Union
cause made him sympathetic to emancipation. In September 1863, eight
months after Lincoln issued the Emancipation Proclamation, a St. Louis
newspaper printed a story with the heading "Manumission of 100 slaves

—A Generous Deed." According to the story, Lewis told his slaves that "if they would work faithfully till the stock of tobacco on hand was manufactured they should be free." The story added that Lewis promised to charter a steamboat at his own expense "and transport the whole number, men, women and children—or at least all who desire to avail themselves of the opportunity—to Kansas," where the men could join the army if they wished.[32]

No record of such a grand act of emancipation exists. The records that do exist show that Spotswood Rice, together with other slaves from Howard County, ran off to enlist in the Union army. Army muster rolls show that Rice joined the Union army at Glasgow on February 9, 1864. "This recruit presented himself for enlistment," reads the entry next to his name. As a loyal slaveholder, Lewis could have delivered Rice to the federal recruiters and received $300 in compensation. Lewis never sought compensation for Rice. He died in February 1866, reportedly from the effects of injuries he had received from the guerrilla attack in 1864. In December 1866, Lewis's brother sought compensation for Spotswood Rice, indicating that the soldier had been the property of a loyal slave owner at the time of his enlistment.[33]

Lewis's reputation for liberality survived in the memory of white Missourians, but not in the memory of the descendants of Spotswood Rice. Rice's daughter, Mary, interviewed in St. Louis in 1936 as part of the federal Works Progress Administration's Slave Narrative project, recalled stories of cruelty that caused Rice to be separated from his wife and children and that led to his being beaten before he escaped to be a soldier.[34]

SLAVERY DIED SLOWLY and painfully throughout the border states. Kentucky and Delaware refused to abolish slavery and refused to ratify the Thirteenth Amendment. Although they were slow to do so, Maryland and Missouri managed to abolish slavery before Congress passed the Thirteenth Amendment.[35] Lincoln had hoped for swifter action but encouraged emancipation in any case. On October 19, 1864, Lincoln wrote at the request of Henry W. Hoffman, chairman of the Maryland Unconditional Union Central Committee, to urge adoption of a new state constitution. As the president noted, the only feature of the document that raised any controversy "is that which provides for the extinction of slavery." Lincoln presumed that his view on the matter was well known. He would be "gratified exceedingly," he wrote, if Marylanders ratified the new constitution. On October 29, Governor Bradford announced the ratification of the new constitution. The vote had been exceedingly close. Out of the nearly 60,000 votes cast, Marylanders ratified the constitution by a narrow margin of 375 votes. Proponents of emancipation had gained 50.3 percent of the vote; their opponents had won 49.7 percent. The constitution went into effect on November 1, 1864. The previous day, Lincoln delivered a brief speech to the Forty-Second Massachusetts Regiment in Baltimore. The regiment had completed its term of service, and the soldiers were going home. Lincoln recalled the violence that another regiment of Massachusetts soldiers had encountered in Baltimore in 1861. "I congratulate you upon having a better time today in Baltimore than that regiment had," said the president. As he thanked the troops for their service, Lincoln remarked that "tonight, midnight, slavery ceases in Maryland, and this state of things in Maryland is due greatly to the soldiers." At sunrise on November 1, troops at Fort McHenry fired a sixty-five gun salute and church bells rang in Baltimore. Throughout the day and evening African Americans in Baltimore celebrated the day of emancipation.[36]

On January 11, 1865, the members of the Missouri constitutional convention quickly amended the state constitution to abolish slavery. From his St. Louis headquarters, Missouri's federal commander, Gen. Grenville Dodge, ordered a sixty-gun salute. "The sonorous voices of the great guns," reported the *St. Louis Democrat*, "sent their reverberations far and near, telling people for miles around that Missouri was free." The celebration continued into the evening.[37] A few weeks after the celebration, in February 1865, the Missouri General Assembly ratified the newly passed Thirteenth Amendment to the U.S. Constitution.

Although Kentucky refused to ratify the Thirteenth Amendment, African Americans in Louisville chose to celebrate their pending freedom on July 4, 1865, using Independence Day to commemorate congressional passage of the Thirteenth Amendment. Ten thousand participants paraded through the city.[38]

Celebrations of emancipation continued on various dates into the late nineteenth century and beyond. St. Louisans continued to celebrate emancipation on January 11 at least through 1872. Each year, often in bad weather, members of black benevolent societies and Sunday schools paraded through the streets accompanied by bands. In the evening, celebrants gathered in Turner's Hall to listen to speeches.[39]

As the historian Donald R. Shaffer has shown, black veterans played centrally important leadership roles in postwar black communities. The forms of compensation received by black veterans and their families (particularly pension income) provided a degree of financial stability not generally available in the postemancipation black community. More than 80,000 black veterans successfully applied for pensions and received, on average, nearly $4,000 each from the federal government over the course of two decades after the war. Shaffer estimated conservatively that black veterans received a total of $313 million in the form of Civil War pensions. When millions of dollars in Civil War bounties and other claims are added in, Shaffer concluded that the total represented a "sizable infusion of money into the post–Civil War black community." These resources aided veterans such as William Simmons in Kentucky and Spotswood Rice in Missouri. Simmons became president of a black university in Louisville, edited the *American Baptist*, and presided over the State Convention of Colored Men in Kentucky. Rice became an ordained minister in the African Methodist Episcopal Church, led congregations in St. Louis, and then became a missionary in the West.[40]

The memory of what it meant to become a soldier also survived in the African American community. Spotswood Rice succeeded in freeing his family from slavery and made St. Louis his postwar home. His daughter, Mary, had been twelve years old when he wrote to her mistress in 1864. Seventy-two years later, Mary was eighty-five and told her family story to an interviewer from the Federal Writers' Project. Mary recalled that her owner had been "an old maid named Miss Kitty Diggs." Most of all she remembered the story of her father fleeing from a cruel master and joining the army. As Mary related her father's story, Spotswood Rice had suffered badly as Lewis's slave. She described her father as the "head man" on Lewis's plantation. Rice cured all of the tobacco and made all of "twists and plugs of tobacco." According to Mary, Lewis beat her father severely in an effort to keep him on the plantation and away from federal lines. At one point, Rice ran away from the Lewis plantation and hid out for three days from the slave patrols. He appealed to a slave dealer to buy him from Lewis, but when the dealer tried to make the purchase, "Mr. Lewis said there wasn't a plantation owner with money enough to pay him for Spot." Rice then told Lewis that if he whipped him again he would run away and eventually make good his escape from bondage. Lewis knew he could not hold onto his slaves much longer, "so he sat down and talked with my father about the future and promised my father if he would stay with him and ship his tobacco for him and look after all of his business on his plantation after freedom was declared, he would give him a nice house and lot for his family right on his plantation." Lewis knew that Rice had a good deal of influence over the other slaves, and he urged Rice to persuade the workers to stay on the Lewis plantation rather than take a chance with strangers who did not know them. Lewis "pleaded so hard with my father" that Rice agreed to stay. In his heart, however, Rice distrusted Lewis. "Lewis had been so mean to father," Mary recalled, that Rice "felt Lewis did not have a spot of good in him." Lewis, said Mary, had "no place for a black man." So Rice stayed on Lewis's plantation for another six months, at which point he took "eleven of the best slaves on the plantation" and joined the Union army. Eventually, Rice secured Mary's freedom from Kitty Diggs. Mary recalled that she went to St. Louis when Lincoln was assassinated and attended school for the first time at Benton Barracks.

As she came to the end of her interview, Mary emphasized the dignity of the African American soldier: "I told you my father's name was Spot, but that was his nickname in slavery. His full name was Spotswood Rice and my son's full name is William A. Bell. He is enlisted in the army in the Phillipine [sic] Islands. I love army men, my father, brother, husband and son were all army men. I love a man who will fight for his rights, and any person that wants to be something."[41]

Notes

1. Roy P. Basler, ed., *The Collected Works of Abraham Lincoln*, 9 vols. (New Brunswick, N.J.: Rutgers University Press, 1953–55), 5:263–64 (hereafter cited as *CW*).

2. James M. McPherson, *Battle Cry of Freedom: The Civil War Era* (New York: Oxford University Press, 1988), 498–99.

3. Doris Kearns Goodwin, *Team of Rivals: The Political Genius of Abraham Lincoln* (New York: Simon & Schuster, 2005), 23–25.

4. Francis P. Blair Jr., *The Destiny of the Races of This Continent. An Address Delivered Before the Mercantile Library Association of Boston, Massachusetts, on the 26th of January, 1859* (Washington, D.C.: n.p., 1859).

5. Blair is quoted in the St. Louis *Missouri Democrat*, May 10, 1862.

6. David Herbert Donald, *Lincoln* (New York: Simon & Schuster, 1996), 367.

7. Quincy is quoted in James M. McPherson, *The Struggle for Equality: Abolitionists and the Negro in the Civil War and Reconstruction* (Princeton: Princeton University Press, 1964), 156.

8. Donald, *Lincoln*, 429–30; Richard Carwardine, *Lincoln: A Life of Purpose and Power* (New York: Alfred A. Knopf, 2006), 231–33.

9. See, for example, James M. McPherson, "Who Freed the Slaves," in *Abraham Lincoln and the Crucible of War: Papers from the Sixth Annual Lincoln Colloquium*, ed. George L. Painter (n.p., n.d.), 59–69; and Ira Berlin, "Who Freed the Slaves? Emancipation and Its Meaning," in *Union & Emancipation: Essays on Politics and Race in the Civil War Era*, ed. David W. Blight and Brooks D. Simpson (Kent, Ohio: Kent State University Press, 1997), 105–21. On the political awareness of slaves, see Steven Hahn, *A Nation Under Our Feet: Black Political Struggles in the Rural South from Slavery to the Great Migration* (Cambridge, Mass.: Harvard University Press, 2003), 65–66.

10. Patience Essah, *A House Divided: Slavery and Emancipation in Delaware, 1638–1865* (Charlottesville: University Press of Virginia, 1996), 161–62, 186; James M. McPherson, *Ordeal by Fire: The Civil War and Reconstruction*, 2nd ed. (New York: McGraw-Hill, 1992), 156.

11. Charles Lewis Wagandt, *The Mighty Revolution: Negro Emancipation in Maryland, 1862–1864* (Baltimore: Johns Hopkins University Press, 1964), 18, 264.

12. McPherson, *Battle Cry of Freedom*, 297–99, 303–4.

13. Victor B. Howard, *Black Liberation in Kentucky: Emancipation and Freedom, 1862–1884* (Lexington: University Press of Kentucky, 1983), 2.

14. Dennis K. Boman, *Lincoln's Resolute Unionist: Hamilton Gamble, Dred Scott Dissenter and Missouri's Civil War Governor* (Baton Rouge: Louisiana State University Press, 2006), 214.

15. Major-General John A. Dix, Headquarters, Department of Virginia, to Hon. E. M. Stanton, November 11, 1862, *The War of the Rebellion: A Compilation of the Official Records of the Union and Confederate Armies*, 128 vols. (Washington, D.C.: GPO, 1880–1901), ser. 1, 18:461.

16. John Boston to Mrs. Elizabeth Boston, January 12, 1862, in Ira Berlin et al., eds., *The Destruction of Slavery*, ser. 1, vol. 1 of *Freedom: A Documentary History of Emancipation, 1861–1867* (New York: Cambridge University Press, 1985), 357–58.

17. Assistant Secretary of War to Congressman Chas. B. Calvert, April 14, 1862 (copy), in Berlin et al., *The Destruction of Slavery*, 364n.

18. Howard, *Black Liberation in Kentucky*, 43–44.

19. Gamble is quoted in Boman, *Lincoln's Resolute Unionist*, 214.

20. Captn. Andrew Stafford to General, November 2, 1864, in Berlin et al., *The Destruction of Slavery*, 390.

21. Wagandt, *The Mighty Revolution*, 263–64; Barbara Jeanne Fields, *Slavery and Freedom on the Middle Ground: Maryland during the Nineteenth Century* (New Haven, Conn.: Yale University Press, 1985), 152–53.

22. Howard, *Black Liberation in Kentucky*, 125–26.

23. Affidavit of Clarissa Burdett, March 27, 1865; and Affidavit of Minerva Banks, September 19, 1865, in Berlin et al., *The Destruction of Slavery*, 615–16, 654–65.

24. Thos. E. Bramlette to His Excellency A. Lincoln, September 3, 1864, in ibid., 604–6.

25. Ibid., 513.

26. Martha to My Dear Husband, December 30, 1863, in Ira Berlin et al., *The Black Military Experience*, ser. 2 of *Freedom: A Documentary History of Emancipation, 1861–1867* (Cambridge: Cambridge University Press, 1982), 244. The following discussion of wartime emancipation in Missouri is drawn from Louis S. Gerteis, *Civil War St. Louis* (Lawrence: University Press of Kansas, 2001), 284–90.

27. Brig. Gen. William A. Pile.

28. Sam Bowmen to Dear Wife, in Berlin et al., *The Destruction of Slavery*, 483–85.

29. [Private Spotswood Rice] to My Children [September 3, 1864]; and Spotswood Rice to Kittey Diggs [September 3, 1864] in Berlin et al., *The Black Military Experience*, 689–90.

30. F. W. Diggs to Genl. Rosecrans, September 10, 1864, in ibid.

31. *History of Howard and Cooper Counties* (St. Louis: National Historical Company, 1883), 452–53; Howard L. Conard, ed., *Encyclopedia of the History of Missouri: A Compendium of History and Biography for Ready Reference*, 6 vols. (St. Louis: Southern History Company, 1901), 4:32.

32. Conard, *Encyclopedia*, 4:32; "Manumission of 100 slaves—A Generous Deed," *St. Louis Union*, reprinted in the *Columbia Statesman*, September 18, 1863.

33. Descriptive Recruitment List of Volunteers for U.S. Colored Troops for the State of Missouri, 1863–1865; and Spotswood Rice's Compiled Service Record, Record Group 977381, National Archives, Washington, D.C. I have benefited from the University of Missouri at St. Louis graduate seminar paper on Spotswood Rice written by Joshua Meyers (2004).

34. George P. Rawick, ed., *The American Slave: A Composite Autobiography* (Westport, Conn.: Greenwood Publishing Company, 1971), ser. 2, 2:25–31. The WPA slave narratives can also be found online at the Library of Congress website American Memory, <http://memory.loc.gov/ammem/snhtml/snhome.html> (accessed December 27, 2007).

35. Wartime reconstruction governments in Louisiana, Arkansas, and Tennessee also adopted state constitutions that abolished slavery before the ratification of the Thirteenth Amendment. See McPherson, *Ordeal by Fire*, 395.

36. *CW*, 8:41–42, 84; Wagandt, *The Mighty Revolution*, 264.

37. The January 14 celebration of emancipation is described in the *Missouri Democrat*, January 15, 1865.

38. Howard, *Black Liberation in Kentucky*, 63–64, 88–89, 146–47.

39. See, for example, *Missouri Democrat*, January 11, 1875. On emancipation celebrations, see William A. Blair, *Cities of the Dead* (Chapel Hill: University of North Carolina Press, 2004); and Mitch Kachun, *Festivals of Freedom: Memory and Meaning in African American Emancipation Celebrations, 1808–1915* (Amherst: University of Massachusetts Press, 2003).

40. Donald R. Shaffer, *After the Glory: The Struggles of Black Civil War Veterans* (Lawrence: University Press of Kansas, 2004), 89, 91, 98–99, 133.

41. Rawick, *The American Slave*, 30. Mary recalled that her father and his compan-

ions had gone to Kansas City to join the army. That memory may have reflected Lewis's promise to free his slaves and send them to Kansas if they labored faithfully through the 1864 season. Lewis's emancipation promise had been reported in September 1863. Rice and several companions enlisted in Glasgow, Missouri, on February 9, 1864. In the quoted passage above, I have taken the liberty of dropping the use of "dare" for "there" and "de" for "the."

WILLIAM A. BLAIR

Celebrating Freedom

The Problem of Emancipation in Public Commemoration

When historian David Brion Davis presented his seminal study on the rise of abolition in the modern world, he characterized the effort as coming to grips with a problem. It was not a problem in the sense of meeting a crisis, but of solving a puzzle. In doing so, he revealed the contradictions that lay at the heart of Atlantic world slavery. The first concerned the origins of abolition. What made a group of people wake up one morning and conceive that the ownership of human beings and their coercion for labor was something wrong? For millennia slavery had been the way of the world and a fundamental means of organizing life and work. While critics of the system always existed, new ideas about individualism and government, coupled with revolutions, gave abolition more currency in the late eighteenth century. Davis exposed the striking fact that slavery needed no explanation; the expansion of freedom did. Second, he observed the contradiction that has intrigued historians for some time now—that the freedom offered by the founding of the Americas coincided with the creation of an African slave trade that forced more than 12 million people to the western hemisphere. Davis wanted to know how to reconcile the story of slavery as "an intrinsic part of the American experience" with the image of the New World as a place to fulfill aspirations for expanded opportunity and greater equality.[1]

The problem of fitting the story of slavery with that of freedom has not ended with emancipation. If we consider the way we remember the coming of freedom, especially by using public commemorations as a gauge, it becomes clear that the need remains to reconcile past with present, slavery with freedom. Emancipation celebrations do exist in the United States and especially in the British Caribbean. But it is still a challenge to place enslavement within national stories that tend to feature triumphant achievement, to commemorate it in public ceremonies endorsed by a government and recognized by the fuller population. This holds true even when ceremonies emphasize abolition, which features the advance of human rights and international efforts to stop the perpetuation of chattel slavery. For even in this context, freedom forces a remembrance of slavery. The broken shackles on statues in the Caribbean celebrate a moment of triumph, but those same bonds signify the despair, the suffering, and the resistance that led up to that moment. The representations of slavery and abolition in public statuary and commemorations underscore that questions remain over racial issues today that affect our ability to fully embrace this part of the past. There is also a reluctance to revive memories that some consider embarrassing, painful, or damaging to national reputations.

The United States has days designated for an incredible array of other causes. We celebrate many landmarks of the nation's creation and endurance, beginning with Independence Day. The calendar also awards service to the country in the form of tributes to important presidents (Lincoln and Washington), recognition of sacrifice on Veterans' Day and Memorial Day, and reminders of patriotism through Flag Day. We feature various expressions of personal relationships by setting aside days to honor parents, sweethearts (Valentine's Day), ethnicity, and even important members of the workforce such as secretaries and administrators. The calendar has not ignored African Americans. In January, we have Martin Luther King Day; February has become recognized as the month for black history, especially in schools. But we do not routinely close schools, stop mail, or shut down banks to observe one of the most important advances in our national growth, or emancipation day. Which raises the question: should we set aside a national public holiday to commemorate emancipation? Is this the way to promote fruitful national discussions of slavery and its legacies, something we have few regular opportunities to pursue as a society?

Even though this question flirts with social commentary, it is possible to gain insights from a historical analysis of the evolution of public commemorations of slavery and emancipation. The exercise provides a way to consider how Lincoln's proclamation continues to have relevance today. We have not come to grips with slavery as a nation, and a better understanding of the past may provide one baby step toward breaching the racial divide. Too many Americans do not understand the process of

"Emancipation," by Thomas Nast. Published by S. Bott (Philadelphia, 1865).
Nast envisions an optimistic future for free blacks with the end of the Civil War.
The central scene shows a content and happy freedman's family gathered around
a "Union" woodstove. On either side of the central picture are scenes contrasting black life in the South during slavery with visions of the freedman's
life after the war. Courtesy of the Library of Congress.

emancipation, both its limitations and its achievements. The Emancipation Proclamation is a document that most people do not really understand. Greater reflection on the transition to freedom can help us, in
Lincoln's phrase, bind up the nation's wounds, or at least realize that
while we all share the same history of a nation we do not enjoy the same
experiences of that past. Attention to Lincoln and emancipation exposes
the fact that we need to develop a vocabulary that crosses boundaries in
order to consider the legacy of the document for people from a variety of
backgrounds.

Further, by looking at commemorations of freedom, and their presence or absence, we can appreciate the complicated history and legacy
of emancipation in the countries around the Atlantic rim, which were
shaped by the forced migration that was the African slave trade. The facts
of enslavement and emancipation are understood by academic special-
ists, but even scholars of Atlantic world slavery are only beginning to take
studies of memory and celebrations of emancipation from within national borders to a broader comparative world that spans the nineteenth

and twentieth centuries. When they do, they have found that abolition and commemorations of it typically reveal a consciousness that transcends traditional national borders, although this consciousness has been deployed to promote a variety of social issues within a nationalist framework. A cursory examination of public commemorations of emancipation indicates that a significant portion of the Atlantic world finds itself facing similar ambiguities and issues as the United States whenever trying to remember slavery and freedom. The difficulty of commemorating emancipation calls to mind the counsel of two historians writing more than two decades ago on the interconnections of slavery with capitalism. The burden of slavery, Elizabeth Fox-Genovese and Eugene Genovese observed, "fell not upon our country alone, not upon the slaveholding countries of the Western Hemisphere alone, but upon the world."[2]

IN THE UNITED STATES, there are signs that remembrances of emancipation are gaining a new life. On April 16, city workers in the District of Columbia—if not employees of private companies—can stay at home and still be paid. Legislation there has set aside the day as a public holiday in recognition of Emancipation Day. The anniversary marks the end of slavery in the district, which was the earliest emancipation during the Civil War. Coming in 1862 as the conflict raged, it was the most significant abolition in the United States that involved compensation to the masters. Because the legislative branch has sovereignty over the district, Washington was the one place where Congress, and not a state, controlled slavery's existence. The legislation supplied $1 million and set up a commission to award funds to masters in compensation for freeing their human property. Consequently, district residents commemorate an important moment when the war started to take a turn toward a new birth of freedom. Yet even this remembrance is not unanimous—private businesses are largely exempt from the legislation. For much of Washington, the day passes like any other business day.[3]

This observance in the nation's capital remains rare in the United States as perhaps the only government-sanctioned remembrance of slavery that involves a holiday, no matter how limited. Yet there are other signs that sensitivity to emancipation has been increasing. For instance, activists in the district were responsible in the early 1990s for convincing the National Archives to display the five-page original manuscript of the Emancipation Proclamation (although not the one Lincoln composed).

Prior to the efforts of Loretta Carter Hanes—a cofounder of Reading Is Fundamental—the document had lain in a vault, with concerns for preservation preventing its exposure even on a limited basis.[4] Elsewhere in the country, observers have noticed efforts to remember emancipation days especially through Juneteenth ceremonies in honor of when slaves in Galveston, Texas, received word of their freedom on June 19, 1865. The Texas legislature has endorsed the day as one for celebration. This has become an observance with considerable name recognition among African American communities across the country (including in the North), although it is not observed consistently.[5] Juneteenth celebrations typically have the feeling of a summer festival that treasures ethnic cultural legacies—song, dance, food, and art—rather than resurrecting memories of slavery and emancipation.

Nonetheless the popularity of the day is ironic because Juneteenth in its nineteenth-century origins was never more than a regional affair, confined primarily to Texas and parts of the southwestern United States.[6] Most Americans have forgotten the thriving celebrations of emancipation that existed in their own communities well into the twentieth century, especially in urban settings containing significant numbers of black people. The amnesia extends to the two times that African Americans attempted to create a national holiday for emancipation: once during the late nineteenth century and another time squarely in the twentieth century.

Emancipation Days tied to Lincoln's proclamation have had a remarkable career, if underappreciated by today's public. Beginning with the issuing of the proclamation in 1863, African Americans in the Union-occupied Sea Islands off the coasts of South Carolina and Georgia gathered in ceremonial events to mark what they hoped was the destruction of slavery. Many participants were former slaves involved in one of the first rehearsals for Reconstruction, abandoned by planters as the Union military captured the Carolina seacoast early in the conflict. These freedpeople were watched closely by white northerners to see whether they would embrace free labor (translation: grow cotton for the U.S. Treasury) and thus prove themselves "worthy" of freedom. Others were freshly recruited black soldiers. If there were doubts among white people about the abilities of black men and women, there was little doubt about their loyalty. The first ceremony had been organized by the military but was widely attended by African Americans. At one point, they took over the ceremony in a spontaneous outburst. Beginning with the voices of two women, others joined in singing "My Country, 'Tis of Thee." Col. Thomas Wentworth Higginson, who was recruiting black soldiers, said he "never saw anything so electric; it made all other words cheap; it seemed the choked voice of a race at last unloosed."[7]

Emancipation immediately became an important event for commemoration among Northern free blacks as well. Mitch Kachun has detailed in his study of freedom festivals that black and white abolitionists held "watch nights" on December 31, 1862, in order to keep tabs on whether Lincoln would fulfill his promise to issue the proclamation. January 1 contained some suspense for these Americans. Lincoln did not sign the proclamation until mid-afternoon, and it took even longer for the news to reach places such as Boston. When it did, abolitionists—often in biracial groups—greeted the news with resounding cheers. In many places cannons fired, bells rang, and people sang hymns, delivered orations, or listened to readings of the Emancipation Proclamation. Although Frederick Douglass had shared the reservations that abolitionists held about the limited nature of the proclamation, he immediately ranked the day among the hallowed dates in the history of the country, along with July 4. The next year showed that January 1 was on its way to remaining an important occasion. Commemorations continued in certain areas of the North. These observances invariably featured martial displays—parades with black veterans or militia groups—that highlighted the fighting ability of African Americans and their claim on the rights of citizens.[8]

With the end of the war, the pace picked up on these celebrations until Emancipation Day became arguably the most important holiday in black communities throughout the United States. Wherever African Americans constituted significant proportions of the population, businesses (at least black-owned ones) were shuttered for the day as residents conducted a parade. Participants listened to orations from prominent members of the community. A central ritual was the reading of the Emancipation Proclamation, an honor awarded to a person who had earned recognition within the community. Increasingly, the parades featured workingmen's societies, fraternal organizations, educational groups, women's groups, and other associations that signified the progress that African Americans were making as business owners and workers. Lincoln was a part of the events in the form of portraits that hung in prominent locations. Orators used these occasions to highlight the contributions of black people to

American civic life and, consequently, press the case for the advancement and protection of their rights.[9]

These public rituals announced a remarkable change in American political and social life. Before the war, the principal procession made along southern streets by these same black people had been in a slave coffle. Participation in public ceremonies of any kind had been tightly controlled. In the immediate postwar world, African Americans emphasized in emancipation parades that 180,000 black soldiers had fought not only for their liberation but also to help maintain the Union. At this same moment in Reconstruction, U.S. military officers were forcing Confederate southerners to put away their arms, their uniforms, and their military identities whenever conducting similar memorial ceremonies; yet black veterans openly marched in the streets, sometimes bearing their arms and always wearing their Union uniforms or something that mimicked military garb. The day signified an incredible rupture with the antebellum period as African Americans invented a public tradition that honored freedom, their sacrifice in achieving it, and their loyalty as national citizens.

Not surprisingly, it was a day that could spark controversy and sometimes violent backlash. Here, the observations of Jimmy Carter remind us of the problem of remembering the war in the former Confederacy. Looking back at his childhood, the former president recalled growing up "in one of the families whose people could not forget that we had been conquered, while most of our neighbors were black people whose grandparents had been liberated in the same conflict."[10] There were two Civil Wars in the South, with different meanings. Black commemorations of emancipation, even those on January 1, at least indirectly celebrated Confederate defeat in communities still trying to absorb the immediate meaning of the loss. More to the point, certain of the anniversaries of freedom corresponded with either the arrival of federal troops or the surrenders of Confederate soldiers. For instance, Richmond's African Americans organized celebrations around April 3 to commemorate the evacuation of the southern army from the Confederate capital. Others marked April 9, or the surrender of Robert E. Lee's army to Ulysses S. Grant. As one man in the 1890s put it, that day was when "the dog was killed."[11] It was not unusual for the first anniversaries to stir up hard feelings from the white Confederate population. Two days before one such affair in Richmond, arsonists burned down a black church that had served as a meeting point

THE RIGHT OF CITIZENS OF THE UNITED STATES TO VOTE SHALL NOT BE DENIED OR ABRIDGED BY THE UNITE

BALLOT BOX

EDUCATION

CELEBRATION AT BALTIMORE ON MAY

"The Fifteenth Amendment and Its Results." Drawn by G. F. Kahl. Lithograph by E. Sachse & Co.; published by Schneider & Fuchs (Baltimore, c. 1870). The print commemorates the celebration in Baltimore of the enactment of the Fifteenth Amendment and is full of symbolism and significant references. On either side of the central picture are two columns, "Education" and "Science," on top of which rest ballot boxes. At left, beside the "Education" column, is a classroom scene in which a black man teaches two black children geography. Below this scene is a bust portrait of Frederick Douglass. At right, near the "Science" column, are two black men at work as a stonemason and a blacksmith. Below this scene is a bust portrait of Mississippi senator Hiram R. Revels. At the top of the print is a portrait of Lincoln, decorated with an eagle and American flags and flanked by seated figures of History or Learning (left) and Columbia or Liberty (right) with a shield, Phrygian cap, and sword. At the far left are busts of President Ulysses S. Grant and Vice President Schuyler Colfax, and at far right busts of abolitionist martyr John Brown and Baltimore jurist Hugh Lenox Bond. Courtesy of the Library of Congress.

for people coordinating the event. During another celebration in Hampton, Virginia, snipers fired at the procession.[12]

The events grew in popularity and changed in their nature over time to reflect the evolving political situation in the North and South. From the beginning, they were biracial affairs that reflected the alliance of white and black Republicans in the postemancipation South. As the nineteenth century wore on, they contained fewer manifestations of military processions, although military heroes were lionized by speakers. They also became more segregated and racially specific, with speakers stressing the need for independent black political action. Black leaders used the occasions as a forum for spreading political strategies to resist the erosion of rights that occurred after Reconstruction. They stressed the ideal of self-help—that African Americans needed no support from the government but merely the ability to pursue economic, social, and political goals on a level playing field, without facing violence and intimidation that went unprosecuted. Lincoln remained an important figure, but not as the Great Emancipator—meaning the most important single figure responsible for freedom. Black people respected the president as an important part of the story of freedom, but they did not consider him the whole story. There were other heroes to include—such as Medal of Honor winners in the U.S. Colored troops, key black political leaders, and John Brown. Often speakers portrayed Lincoln as acting as an extension of God's will, with thanks due primarily to a divine hand. A black minister said, "I believe that while Lincoln wrote the emancipation proclamation, he wrote, not knowing what he did, but that the angel of God came down and guided his hand." Additionally, they were aware that the Thirteenth Amendment was needed to end slavery forever in this country.[13]

In the United States, Emancipation Day celebrations faded from African American communities with the convergence of a number of factors taking place over decades. Embarrassment over the slave past provided one ingredient. This attitude manifested itself in the late nineteenth century, especially among the younger generation of men and women who had not been enslaved. This should be no surprise: it is common among African descendants throughout the hemisphere to have conflicted views about remembering slavery. The sentiment in the United States persisted enough to warrant periodic reprimands from Emancipation Day speakers deep into the twentieth century. At a gathering in 1932 in Pittsburgh, Dr. J. Max Barber admitted to the audience, "There are quite a number of people of our group who feel embarrassed at emancipation celebrations." He added: "They are simple enough to imagine that if we forget, the world will also forget."[14] Embarrassment alone, however, cannot account for the demise of Emancipation Day celebrations, for it was present for too long of a time without diminishing the repetition of the custom.

The address by Dr. Barber provides clues into other elements at work. Tensions always existed among black people over how to commemorate the occasion, with two distinct modes of performance associated with these events: didactic and festive. The first one consisted of commemorations such as Barber's, which tended to be connected to schools, churches, or black clubs. They were organized by community leaders sensitive to public displays that might undercut claims that the race was ready for full rights as citizens. These organizers favored didactic events featuring instruction on how the race should advance socially and politically. Emancipation Days in this category might feature parades and picnics, but they were accompanied with speeches that underscored proper behavior, as well as readings of Lincoln's proclamation.

By describing opponents to the day as "simple," Barber perfectly captured the condescension with which participants viewed their less-educated comrades or African Americans who failed to behave with the appropriate decorum. This was evident in a column that pondered, " 'Emancipation Day' . . . Why Keep It?" H. S. Bynes, editor of the *Sunday School Worker*, wrote:

> Ignorance is to be pitied, but superstition, with all her hideous and satanic nets, will look one squarely into the face and say: "I ain't got time to go to 'Mancipation Day—I got ter work." Some will tell you: "Well, it looks like a big show off and I ain't going." Still others will say: "I can't get off de job—my boss won't let me off, and I might lose de job." God speed the day when the standard of Jesus Christ will be lifted up so high that these disintegrating and damning elements of the race will be reduced to chaff in the blowing winds of racial progress.[15]

Bynes certainly did not entice recruits into the fold by calling them ignorant and superstitious, but his parody unwittingly revealed additional dimensions to the eventual loss of Emancipation Days. There were external pressures to take into account. Economic coercion by white employers did take place against black workers. Jobs at times were threatened if African Americans asked for time off to attend a commemorative event. Additionally, white leaders might shut down the occasions if they promised to become too threatening. When black people in Warrenton, Georgia, scheduled Atlanta newspaper editor B. J. Davis to give the emancipation address, white people from the town told the sheriff that Davis could not be protected if he spoke about "social equality." White community leaders withdrew the use of the courthouse for the event. Under the circumstances, black organizers considered it better to cancel the appearance.[16]

African Americans wishing for fewer constraints on their commemorations by either black or white leaders found alternatives in more festive affairs. These might be holidays similar to Memorial Day today: a time for picnics, food, and other leisure pursuits. For instance, African Americans in Wheeling, West Virginia, staged emancipation dances around the anniversary of the preliminary proclamation in September. In 1931, the featured star was Blanche Calloway, sister of the famous jazz artist Cab Calloway.[17] In 1935 Roberta Clay, a columnist in Chicago, could not help but notice the plethora of days to commemorate the end of slavery across the country. She pondered why there should be eleven different times and such a variety of ways in which to remember emancipation. She noted that many states had formal programs at a church or school with speeches and readings of the proclamations. But she gave the impression that the more formal affairs were becoming a minority as the parades, baseball games, picnics, and other rituals that had no didactic content grew more frequent. She also noticed that the events without emancipation customs and lectures tended to have more support from white people in the communities, and thus caused fewer incursions against them.[18]

Time and the changing political climate likely applied the final straws to these internal tensions and external pressures. The celebrations appear to have sustained their last gasp with the increasing success of the civil rights movement. During the centennial observances of the Civil War, Congress proclaimed January 1, 1963, as Emancipation Proclamation Day. But as the title suggests, the day was more about the proclamation and Lincoln than recognition of African Americans. The centennial programs, in fact, excluded black people from the officially sanctioned national activities. In the dominant culture, the Civil War had become a war for Union, with the struggle for freedom often overlooked.[19]

We are left to surmise what happened because few people comment on a ceremony or ritual that disappears, and fewer still take the time to analyze the downfall. It is possible that the ceremonies appeared to be outdated or out of step with the more militant strands of black activism in the 1960s. Also, for a long time the Emancipation Day ceremonies had provided an important platform for political expression, one that was not really needed anymore. Or it could simply be that, as with many such situations, the rituals began to wane with the passing of the people most committed to the more formal, didactic forms of remembrance.

Yet there were efforts to make the commemoration of freedom into a national event. The dedication of the statue to Robert E. Lee in Richmond prompted one such attempt in 1890. Alarmed at what they saw in the public expressions of the Confederate past among white southerners attending the monument dedication, black leaders tried to forge a consensus for a national emancipation celebration. One African American from Lynchburg hoped for "a gathering of the clansmen like unto the Lee unveiling some time ago. Let every body talk the matter up."[20] It was a difficult task, with overtures to join with white politicians slapped aside by indifference or racism. Nothing was stated publicly. But the governor of the state, as well as other politicians, suddenly found that their schedules prevented them from attending the convention and the Emancipation Day parade. The governor gave a ridiculous excuse, at least to black people, saying that he would "visit his old home in Farmville on that day." Even President Benjamin Harrison did not keep a promise to come.[21]

It was also difficult to choose which day to observe. Lincoln's proclamation offered two options: September 22 for the preliminary version and January 1 for the actual. Then there were the days held as locally sacred—when black people in a particular state or region won their liberation. Virginia residents tended to favor events tied to defeat of the Confederates in their region, such as April 3 for evacuation day and April 9 for Appomattox. Delegates from beyond Virginia, however, favored different commemorative times. One scholar of these practices has traced at least fifteen different celebrations thriving around the country.[22] When John Mitchell, editor of the *Richmond Planet*, polled African Americans on this issue, he found many suggested January 1 as a possibility, but there was no overwhelming consensus. Nor did everyone agree that the Emancipation Proclamation should serve as the catalyst for commemoration. In addition to dates tied to Confederate defeats, dates were chosen to honor the passage of the Fifteenth Amendment, which prohibited race from determining eligibility for suffrage.[23]

The movement for a national Emancipation Day led to a convention that attracted roughly a couple hundred delegates from across the country. Beginning with ceremonies on October 15, they settled down to business in Richmond, Virginia, on October 17, 1890. Their mission was to choose a national day for commemorating freedom and fostering race pride. After great deliberation, the delegates chose January 1 to support as a national day of thanksgiving for emancipation.[24] Yet the effort seems to have had the impact of a pebble dropped into a lake. Scarcely a ripple made its way to any shore, whether local, regional, or national. Nothing happened in the Congress, which hardly would have greeted the idea warmly. Furthermore, the decision apparently changed nothing in the commemorative habits of African Americans, who continued to mark days important to local calendars. The men who gathered in Richmond were from the upper classes and represented churches, fraternal organizations, and newspapers. These were the same people who chided African Americans for improper deportment during holidays, which—they said—reinforced white claims that black people were not ready for full political rights. They also were undoubtedly older men who were meeting with resistance from a new generation less willing to consider memories of slavery as a means to advance public causes or instill pride. The movement also may have seemed to the broader community to be seeking rather small gains in the face of many larger problems.

Whether the Richmond movement could have enjoyed a different outcome by adopting different methods is doubtful. We actually have a day that recognizes the end of slavery, and still we do not observe it. Success came not in the 1890s but in the 1940s as the government began to lean toward ending segregation. Harry S. Truman signed into law such a bill in 1948 that designated February 1 as National Freedom Day. The day included Lincoln as part of the remembrance, but not for his proclamation. February 1 was the day that the president signed the joint congressional resolution that framed the Thirteenth Amendment, which ended slavery. Richard R. Wright Sr., a former slave from Georgia who became a successful banker in Philadelphia, led the charge for Freedom

Day. His father had served in the Union army during the Civil War. Wright sought to untangle the differing commemorative traditions by selecting the amendment for signifying the end of slavery. By doing so, the day could be shared by white people, and Lincoln could remain part of the story. Wright succeeded in getting a three-cent stamp printed to honor the Thirteenth Amendment. In 1947, he pushed Congress to designate February 1 for the commemoration. He triumphed, but he did not live to see Truman sign the bill in 1948.[25]

What happened since has not been recovered by scholars. No one appears to have recognized the occasion in any meaningful way as a celebration of slavery's demise in the United States. Just as with the Richmond convention in 1890, Wright's campaign failed to spark parades or sustained public observances. The government partly was to blame by paying only lip service to the event. Offices remained open, and the government supplied no other muscle to draw attention to Freedom Day. But the day remains on the books. By law, presidents still can issue an annual proclamation in its honor.[26] Yet as of this writing, there is no coordinated effort to commemorate the amendment that ended slavery in the United States.

So the question that launched our investigation is a trick one. We *have* an Emancipation Day in the United States. It has been disassociated from its historic roots in African American communities, and it exits on the calendar more often as a remembrance of freedom in general. If a poll were taken on the subject, it likely would reveal that 99 percent of Americans have no clue that this date of remembrance even exists. There is more publicity for Punxsutawney Phil on Groundhog Day—the day following February 1—than for the anniversary of the legislation that changed the meaning of freedom in this country.

IN DESCRIBING THE failure to create a national day for commemorating emancipation it would be wrong to assume that this is unique to the United States—that we are the only ones who have difficulty including slavery in the nation's civic traditions. Looking around the Atlantic world for those who celebrate emancipation presents a mixed story, shaped by the complicated process of abolition and the difficulty of having a sensitive subject embraced by a national public. There are examples of widespread observances of emancipation, but these exist alongside numerous countries in which remembering freedom from slavery remains muted at best. The reasons for this vary by country and region with other variables including a particular history and contemporary social issues. The examination here can only be suggestive, taking note of who does and does not observe an emancipation anniversary without presenting a conclusive analysis of the content of these commemorations, the issues that may prevent them, or the fervency of the participants.

At first glance, it may seem that others do much better with this than the United States. There are, in fact, very evident commemorative traditions that immediately strike an observer as signifying a healthy appreciation for the ending of slavery. One such example is Haiti—always an exceptional case. The other is the recognition of West Indian Emancipation, or when freedom came to the British holdings in the Caribbean. Finally, the bicentennial of the ending of the Atlantic slave trade has garnered an incredible amount of attention, but mostly confined to the United Kingdom and parts of the Caribbean. Interestingly, West Indian Emancipation has a long-standing history of celebration in the northern United States and, as we will see, was adopted by abolitionists both black and white to press their claims for ending slavery before the American Civil War.

Haiti, of course, represents the most remarkable situation. It featured the only slave revolution that also achieved independence from colonial dominion, in this case from the French. This revolution sent shock waves throughout the Atlantic world. Planters in the U.S. South paid careful attention to see if it would spark unrest in their own domain. The Haitian Revolution also had profound repercussions on the course that other nations adopted for emancipation. Most countries facing this issue chose to control its contours by enacting gradual freedom—not only to preserve labor but also to avoid similar violent ruptures. Haiti's origins provide a dual purpose to the celebration of freedom in the country, which occurs on January 1. It may be the only place that simultaneously marks both the end of slavery and the emergence of a republic in one of the most decisive moments of world history.

The slave revolution in St. Domingue has inspired a contemporary effort to remember the Atlantic slave trade and its crucial influences in shaping four continents. Beginning in the early 1990s, the United Nations Educational, Scientific, and Cultural Organization (UNESCO) established a Slave Route project to raise awareness of the ways in which the transatlantic slave trade still affects lives today. An offshoot of that project has been a K–12 education initiative called Breaking the Silence, which raises the proficiency of public school teachers for working on this topic with students in the hopes that better understanding of the past will make us better equipped to reconcile today's problems. The project adopted August 23 as an International Day for remembrance of the slave trade. This honors the uprising in St. Domingue, which broke out during the night of August 22–23, 1791. The organization has sponsored some annual remembrances, and at one point the schools project had involved people from twenty-four nations; however, the effort has been hard to sustain and lacks a significant funding partner. Still, there have been noticeable achievements, particularly in the establishment of World Heritage Sites and the organization's cooperation with programs concerning the 200th anniversary of the abolition of the African slave trade.[27]

When we look at the British-speaking areas of the Caribbean, we find a vibrant commemorative culture that observes the end of slavery. The United Kingdom abolished slavery through legislation in 1833, which took effect August 1, 1834. Places such as Jamaica and various islands in the Bahamas and elsewhere commemorate the occasion by holding public festivals or remembrances in early August. Trinidad and Tobago holds national celebrations, and its prime minister in 2005 boasted that the country was the first to create a national holiday for emancipation.[28] Government officials make speeches to remind their constituents of the forebears who shaped the world in which they now live. Menissa Rambally, minister for Social Transformation and Culture of St. Lucia, told his audience at the Emancipation Day gathering in 2002 that he had conflicting emotions about such a day, but declared it was impossible to enjoy the fruits of freedom "if we do not understand the pains and suffering of the past."[29]

The history of these occasions, and especially their transnational appeal, has received new attention from scholars. Jeffrey Kerr-Ritchie has taken the most recent look at the rise and use of the West Indian Emancipation rituals. Just as with Emancipation Day tied to Lincoln's proclamation, observances began almost immediately in the Caribbean. The rituals started out as white-organized commemorations during the four-year period of apprenticeship that led up to the total abolishment of slavery in the empire. The idea at first was to control the celebrations, for officials were concerned about the possibility of social disruption. So the earliest events tended to toast white paternalism and recognize the British Empire's role in abolition, with the chief heroes being the monarchy and key public officials. Yet the freedpeople quickly began to assert themselves more strongly into these commemorations. Increasingly after the end of apprenticeship arrived in 1838, the affairs moved out of the churches and into the public thoroughfares of communities. In the process, they were claimed by Afro-Caribbean communities and refashioned to announce goals important to them. Kerr-Ritchie concludes that "official commemorations became increasingly transformed into former slaves' own shouts of freedom."[30]

Kerr-Ritchie correctly sees the August 1 anniversaries as offering a contested vision over emancipation as well as a means of conducting protest over political issues. Historians who have dissected celebrations over the past few decades have tended to reach similar conclusions. Through public rituals, groups fashion the stories and interpretations of events that become one of the means for explaining who they are and where they stand in a nation. Memory constructed by a group validates certain power relations. Authority becomes reinforced through a commemorative calendar, with the people who can make decisions about such things, and the contents of ceremonies, sending messages about the values of the group. Most often this is conveyed through the heroes whose examples are to be treasured and followed. There also exist counter-rituals, or the use of public events as a way to present a different narrative, especially where people are contending for equality or to end forms of oppression.[31] In this case, August 1 became a symbolic day adopted by black people throughout the Atlantic world, including in the United States. In the Caribbean, the day became a part of a triumphant recognition, although it took time for the descendants of Africans to impart their own meaning to the occasion. In places where slavery still existed, the day became an expression of dissent or an affirmation of how the body politic could be enriched by expanding the parameters of freedom.

A number of things are noteworthy about this remembrance of West Indies freedom by people in the United States. First of all, black communities in northern America did not tie public events for freedom to the revolution in Haiti. It is impossible to prove why this did not happen, but a plausible reason for this has been suggested. Trying to convince a white majority to end the ownership of human beings meant resorting to other tactics than promoting the violent uprising of slaves. Abolitionists must have been aware that they were not going to muster white society to the cause of a black revolution.[32] Holding up the British Empire as a hero in the march toward abolition rubbed against nationalist sentiments that were on the rise and that were very much in opposition to the United Kingdom. If Britain could emancipate, why not the country that prided itself on liberty?

The process of emancipation in the northern United States reinforced the utility of reaching out to overseas for a more unified day of symbolism. Our first emancipation shared some dimensions of what occurred in Latin America, meaning it emerged as the byproduct of an anticolonial independence movement. Over the next fifteen or so years, northern states began to adopt gradual emancipation plans that freed children born to slave parents after reaching a certain age. Consequently, choosing one date for celebration was virtually impossible, and it was not unusual by the 1850s for antislavery organizations to adopt August 1 as the most logical day for unifying their efforts.

Finally, it is remarkable how long West Indies Emancipation Day endured in importance for many black people as a point of contrast for emancipation in the United States. During the Civil War, a year after Lincoln's proclamation, one of the members of the 54th Massachusetts—the famed unit of black soldiers raised in the North—expressed his exasperation to a newspaper over the lack of equal treatment in the military. The soldiers were particularly angry over receiving less pay than white soldiers. On August 1, 1864, George Stephens could not help but compare emancipation as it was unfolding in the Civil War with the British version. To him, living in that moment at that particular time, the proclamation seemed a lesser measure because it allowed for slavery in the border states. Stephens considered Lincoln's version "an abortion wrung from the Executive womb by necessity."[33] Even the adoption of the Thirteenth Amendment to the Constitution in 1865 did not set aside August 1 for African Americans, although it appears to have been more important in the North, especially parts of New England and New York. In 1887, some New Yorkers observed West Indian Emancipation Day, although the celebration was fused with elements from the Civil War, including a reading of Lincoln's proclamation. African Americans in Harrisburg, Pennsylvania, have recently launched a project to resurrect the commemoration of this anniversary, which the community first celebrated in 1857.[34]

In terms of commemorations of emancipation, Haiti and the British-speaking Caribbean remain the most recognizable successes and are ahead of the curve compared to much of the western hemisphere. Many of the nations that grew and developed because of the labor of enslaved Africans either have no commemoration at all or have only local commemorations that are kept alive by black associations and social clubs. This includes most of Latin America. Part of the reason is that although abolition in many of these countries came about through independence movements against a colonial power, emancipation was not necessarily tied to the primary goal of freedom from European control, as it was in Haiti. By 1825, almost every country in Spanish America had banned the importation of Africans and enacted programs of emancipation. Most of Latin America adopted gradual emancipation plans that came about as secondary to the emergence of new republics. Often these plans involved compensation to the masters in the form of periods of apprenticeship, in which owners retained the labor of their former chattel until a certain time. "Free womb" laws were created, indicating either that children born after a certain date were emancipated or, more typically, that they earned freedom after reaching a certain age. As in the northern United States, this process muddied the emancipation day waters somewhat, as the day on which legislation enabling freedom was enacted was not the actual moment of emancipation.[35]

There is evidence that some of the leading countries in the African slave trade have attempted to commemorate emancipation with a holiday, although the efforts have been decidedly mixed. Unlike the United States, the last countries in the western hemisphere to abolish slavery did so peacefully, although the laws for abolition came about in part from agitation from slaves and free allies. Puerto Rico abolished slavery on March 23, 1873, followed by Cuba in 1886. Brazil finally came to abolition on May 13, 1888. It had been the world's largest importer of African slaves, with estimates indicating it consumed 40 percent of the entire slave trade over nearly four centuries. The country gave it up because of mass movements from within. Brazil and Cuba also were the two most significant countries for the importation of slaves after the British tried to halt the African trade after 1807. Perhaps as much as one-quarter of the total number of Africans to cross the Atlantic during the nearly 400 years of the trade did so from 1808 to 1867, with Brazil and Cuba as the leading destinations.

Among the countries that retained slavery after it died in the United States the commemorative landscape is fairly uneven. Puerto Ricans appear to have the advantage. The country has March 23 on the calendar as a holiday—government offices and schools close for the day, but the celebrations are primarily small-scale academic affairs. One observer writes that like most other national holidays, Abolition Day in Puerto Rico is "more taken for granted than observed through celebratory or ceremonial acts." He added that issues of race, slavery, and African heritage "still arouse varying degrees of discomfort and ambivalence."[36] Cuba has a monument to the Runaway Slave and plans for a museum on slavery in the copper mines. At one point, Brazil tried to do something to recognize abolition. It took until the centennial of abolition in 1988 before officials organized both academic and public functions. The day was seized by Afro-Brazilians protesting employment and other discrimination, and the government scurried to head off further displays.[37]

For the remainder of Latin America, it would probably be incorrect to say that no remembrances of slavery or emancipation take place. Historian George Reid Andrews suspects that if scholars dug more deeply they might encounter evidence of traditions of observing the end of slavery in various locales, but little work has been done to test this assumption. The studies that exist show that in some places such as Brazil vernacular rituals took place beneath the "official" plane, with contention over how to mark emancipation.[38] Overall, then, the silence in scholarship and national rituals likely indicates unresolved issues over the insertion of the history of slavery into national narratives.

WHAT ABOUT AFRICA, which had an internal slave trade and has been in the center of debates concerning the impact of the slave trade on the economy and society? Slaves and the slave trade are not talked about much in West Africa, where it remains a sensitive subject. Roughly 12 million Africans were forced across the Atlantic by the slave trade, but the number of captives ranged much higher, with considerable numbers retained for internal use. One estimate suggests from one-third to one-half of all captives over the course of four centuries were not sent out of Africa. This should not serve as an apology for the European nations that fed on the internal African slave trade—it was the Atlantic trade that turned Africa from an importer to an exporter of this human commodity.[39] Slavery continued in Africa into the twentieth century, although the African institution was different from U.S. enslavement in that it tended to be geared toward domestic labor and generally ended with a slave's adoption into a family or clan. This has created a difficult situation today for untangling personal histories and allowing for the release of memories. Many families in West Africa have a slave branch, and people still may refer to a free person's slave ancestry to note the different backgrounds. Some stories have been repressed partly from the fear that their resurrection can tear families apart, although there are obviously more reasons behind the ambivalence that exists over this topic.

Even when remembrances of slavery come to fruition, they can be a problem, especially when they intend to capitalize on heritage as a commodity. One of the leading phenomena concerning remembering slavery in Africa has been the creation of heritage tourism. Ghana in particular has encouraged tourism to its central region, which contained dungeon-forts that Europeans used to protect their trade and collect enslaved Africans for transport to the Americas. This has been a boon to tourism there and attracted numerous people wanting to re-create their ancestors' part of the diaspora—what is called roots tourism. This is not necessarily a bad thing; in fact, quite moving and memorable experiences have been one of the benefits as patrons come to grips with the horrors of the past. But the practice also raises issues of how to represent such trauma, and from whose perspective. The targeted audience remains Europeans and black people from the Caribbean and the Americas, not the residents of Ghana. Some are concerned that consumerism will invariably chase out the bad memories in favor of the good. Remembrance of pain, Sandra Richards has reminded us, "is generally unappealing and thus bad for business." The danger comes when people try to compensate for this by creating a story that is too optimistic and too filled with an emphasis on resistance and resilience.[40] Ama Ata Aidoo, a professor of literature, captures the dual nature of the preservation of this past. On the one hand, having Elmina Castle included on the UNESCO list of World Heritage Sites "can be seen as a fine international gesture: a recognition of the fact that the world's collective heritage is a mixed bag of both wholesome and ugly things." On the other hand, people fear that "a sanitation process is going on which, not necessarily intended, would eventually cover up, or even remove the more sickening, and damning, evidence of its gruesome history."[41]

These concerns are typical of trying to present many aspects of history with subtlety and depth in a public forum, and they speak of the way even the best of intentions can go awry. Even for those who feel that some form of commemoration is warranted, it remains to be seen whether this process will help us better incorporate slavery and freedom into civic memory in the United States. The law of unintended consequences guarantees that these occasions will be claimed by various groups for causes and concerns that may not be quite on point. The mayor in the District of Columbia, for instance, used Emancipation Day in 2007 to organize a march pressing for district residents to be allowed to elect congressional representatives and have a stake in the electoral college. Emancipation has a different meaning in this context—as freedom from congressional oversight without representation. Brazil in 1988 found out that contention is natural for these occasions, and that many of the historical discussions and displays organized for this moment were overlooked. On the other hand, historical commemorations have sometimes been used to paper over more incendiary, contemporary issues by honoring heritage in order to avoid meaningful change. White governments have supported presentations that acknowledged the cultural contributions of African Americans without conceding the problem of segregation. The fact is that these events often stir up confrontation and contradictory memories that can be pleasant or unpleasant, no matter where and when one lives.

Yet the effort to stimulate some form of national discussion of slavery and freedom certainly is worth the effort, whether it takes having a special commemorative day or some other vehicle. A documentary film on the slave trade provides an example of the potential rewards. Created by Katrina Browne, *Traces of the Trade* provides a personal view of a slave-trading family in Rhode Island. When Browne learned that she was a descendant of the largest slave-trading family in U.S. history, she convinced some of her family to travel to important points along the triangle trade. After making this journey that spanned New England, Africa, and Cuba, family members talked with African Americans to ponder what to do next. Browne captured one of her relatives, Tom, conversing about the experience with an African American. He said, "The most common phrase I can remember [from white people talking about slavery] is, 'Why can't they just get over it?'. . . I'm beginning to get the inkling that my definition of what 'it' is, is different than what your definition of 'it' is."[42] He had grasped the main point: we all share a history but have different experiences of the past that sometimes prevent us from starting from the same point.

This brings us back to the Lincoln statue by Thomas Ball with which we opened the volume. In some ways this representation of Lincoln is the perfect figure to illustrate that we do not always talk about the same historical experience—the same "it"—even as it provides us with common ground on which to learn this fact. One person can look at this statue and see Lincoln as the proud father of emancipation. Another can look at it and see a kneeling slave who has not yet risen even though beckoned by a paternalistic hand. Claimed to an extent by both races—although not in the same way or for the same reasons—Lincoln has the rare ability to provoke discussion about meaningful issues across racial boundaries, even if this does not lead to a mutual agreement about him. He and his Emancipation Proclamation can speak to us still. What is not certain is if, or how, we will listen.

Notes

1. David Brion Davis, *The Problem of Slavery in Western Culture* (Ithaca, N.Y.: Cornell University Press, 1967), 10. For a classic analysis of the intermingling of slavery and freedom, see Edmund Morgan, *American Slavery, American Freedom: The Ordeal of Colonial Virginia* (New York: W. W. Norton, 1975).

2. Elizabeth Fox-Genovese and Eugene D. Genovese, *Fruits of Merchant Capital: Slavery and Bourgeois Property in the Rise and Expansion of Capitalism* (New York: Oxford University Press, 1983), 392. J. R. Kerr-Ritchie's new work on West Indian Abolition Day argues for the transnational nature of the impulse. See his *Rites of August First: Emancipation Day in the Black Atlantic World* (Baton Rouge: Louisiana State University Press, 2007).

3. For some of the context to Washington's emancipation, see Elizabeth Clark-Lewis, ed., *First Freed: Washington, D.C., in the Emancipation Era* (Washington: A. P. Foundation Press, 1998). For enabling legislation for recent observances, see the website for the District of Columbia, Department of Human Resources, <http://newsroom.dc.gov/show.aspx/agency/dcop/section/2/release/10728> (accessed November 19, 2007).

4. *Washington Post*, December 19, 1992; ibid., April 16, 2006.

5. The Texas legislature did designate the day as a state holiday. It was effective in 1980, but I have not studied the impact on the state or whether the holiday remains vibrant today. See the African American Registry, <http://www.aaregistry.com/african_american_history/240/JunteenthNational_Freedom_Day_observed> (accessed November 13, 2007).

6. William H. Wiggins Jr., *O Freedom! Afro-American Emancipation Celebrations* (Knoxville: University of Tennessee Press, 1987), 1–7, 35.

7. Thomas Wentworth Higginson, *Army Life in a Black Regiment*, intro. by Howard Mumford Jones (East Lansing: Michigan State University Press, 1960), 31. For another description of this event, see Mitch Kachun, *Festivals of Freedom: Memory and Meaning*

in African American Emancipation Celebrations, 1808–1915 (Amherst: University of Massachusetts Press, 2003), 104–6; Kathleen Clark, *Defining Moments: African American Commemoration & Political Culture in the South, 1863–1913* (Chapel Hill: University of North Carolina Press, 2005), 20–24. For the seminal work on the Sea Islands and the experiment with free labor by the U.S. Treasury, see Willie Lee Rose, *Rehearsal for Reconstruction: The Port Royal Experiment* (New York: Bobbs-Merrill, 1964).

8. Kachun, *Festivals of Freedom*, 103–4, 109, 112.

9. The literature on these events has grown considerably in the past decade. The looming work continues to be David Blight's *Race and Reunion: The Civil War in American Memory* (Cambridge, Mass.: Belknap Press, 2001). Others who describe emancipation celebrations include Kachun, *Festivals of Freedom*; Clark, *Defining Moments*, esp. Chapter 1; William Blair, *Cities of the Dead: Contesting the Memory of the Civil War in the South, 1865–1914* (Chapel Hill: University of North Carolina Press, 2004), esp. Chapter 2.

10. Quoted in David Goldfield, *Still Fighting the Civil War: The American South and Southern History* (Baton Rouge: Louisiana State University Press, 2002), 15.

11. *Richmond Planet*, September 27, 1890.

12. Blair, *Cities of the Dead*, 34–38.

13. Ibid., 163. For comment on emancipation as the hand of God, see the *Richmond Planet*, September 6, 1890; and *Richmond Dispatch*, October 16, 1890 [quotation].

14. *Pittsburgh Courier*, January 16, 1932.

15. *Atlanta Daily World*, December 11, 1938.

16. *Pittsburgh Courier*, January 25, 1930.

17. Ibid., September 19, 1931.

18. *Chicago Defender*, September 14, 1935.

19. For the centennial, see Jonathan Weiner, "Civil War, Cold War, Civil Rights: The Civil War Centennial in Context, 1961–1965," in *The Memory of the Civil War in American Culture*, ed. Alice Fahs and Joan Waugh (Chapel Hill: University of North Carolina Press, 2004), 237–57; Robert J. Cook, *Troubled Commemoration: The American Civil War Centennial, 1961–1965* (Baton Rouge: Louisiana State University Press, 2007). For observations on when certain ceremonies died, see *Rappahannock Times*, April 7, 1994; and *Richmond Times Dispatch*, April 3, 1994.

20. *Richmond Planet*, September 27, 1890.

21. *New York Times*, October 14, 1890.

22. Wiggins, *O Freedom*, x.

23. *Richmond Planet*, October 11, 1890.

24. Ibid., October 25, 1890.

25. Michael Vorenberg, *Final Freedom: The Civil War, the Abolition of Slavery, and the Thirteenth Amendment* (New York: Cambridge University Press, 2001), 244–45; Kachun, *Festivals of Freedom*, 282n51.

26. See U.S. Code, 124, Cornell University Law School, Legal Information Institute, online at <http://www4.law.cornell.edu/uscode/html/uscode36/usc_sec_36_000 00124——000-.html> (accessed November 13, 2007).

27. For information, consult the project's website at <http://portal.unesco.org/

education/en/ev.php-URL_ID=9442&URL_DO=DO_TOPIC&URL_SECTION= 201.html> (accessed February 19, 2009).

28. Address of Prime Minister Patrick Manning, August 1, 2005, <http://www.opm .gov.tt/news/index.php?pid=2001&nid=s20050801> (accessed November 15, 2007).

29. Address to Nation by Menissa Rambally, August 1, 2002, <http:/6/www.stlucia .gov.lc/addresses_and_speeches/menissa_rambally/address_by_hon_menissa_ rambally_on_emancipation_day_august_1_2002.htm> (accessed November 15, 2007).

30. Kerr-Ritchie, *Rites of August First*, 14.

31. See Pierre Nora, *Realms of Memory: The Construction of the French Past*, 3 vols. (New York: Columbia University Press, 1996–98); Eric Hobsbawm and Terence Ranger, eds., *The Invention of Tradition* (New York: Cambridge University Press, 1983); Eric Hobsbawm, *Nations and Nationalism Since 1780: Programme, Myth, Reality* (New York: Cambridge University Press, 1990). For the U.S. context, see David Thelen, ed., *Memory and History* (Bloomington: Indiana University Press, 1990); Blight, *Race and Reunion*.

32. Kachun, *Festivals of Freedom*, 57; Mitch Kachun, "Antebellum African Americans, Public Commemoration, and the Haitian Revolution: A Problem of Historical Mythmaking," *Journal of the Early Republic* 26 (Summer 2006): 254.

33. Donald Yacovone, ed., *A Voice of Thunder: The Civil War Letters of George E. Stephens* (Urbana: University of Illinois Press, 1997), 324.

34. Richard White, "Civil Rights Agitation: Emancipation Days in Central New York in the 1880s," *Journal of Negro History* 78 (Winter 1993): 16–17.

35. Stanley L. Engerman, *Slavery, Emancipation & Freedom* (Baton Rouge: Louisiana State University Press, 2007), 6–8, 37–50; George Reid Andrews, *Afro-Latin America, 1800–2000* (New York: Oxford University Press, 2004), 56–57.

36. Lowell Fiet, "Puerto Rico, Slavery, Race: Faded Memories, Erased Histories," in *Facing up to the Past: Perspectives on the Commemoration of Slavery from Africa, the Americas and Europe*, ed. Gert Oostindie (Kingston, Jamaica: Ian Randle Publishers, 2001), 70. For more on these issues, see Ileana M. Rodriguez Silva, "A Conspiracy of Silence: Blackness, Class, and National Identities in Post-Emancipation Puerto Rico, 1850–1920" (Ph.D. diss., University of Wisconsin, 2004).

37. Oostindie, *Facing up to the Past*, 75–76, 87; Andrews, *Blacks & Whites in Sao Paulo, Brazil, 1888–1988* (Madison: University of Wisconsin Press, 1991), 218–24, 231.

38. Andrews, *Blacks & Whites in Sao Paulo*, 211–13; George Reid Andrews to William Blair, March 23, 2007, email.

39. Engerman, *Slavery, Emancipation & Freedom*, 14–15; Stephanie E. Smallwood, *Saltwater Slavery: A Middle Passage from Africa to American Diaspora* (Cambridge, Mass.: Harvard University Press, 2007), 15–20.

40. Sandra L. Richards, "What Is to Be Remembered? Tourism to Ghana's Slave Castle-Dungeons," *Theatre Journal* 57 (2005): 632. For a similar point, see Saidiya Hartman, "The Time of Slavery," *South Atlantic Quarterly* 101 (Fall 2002): 760.

41. Ama Ata Aidoo, "Of Forts, Castles, and Silences," in Oostindie, *Facing up to the Past*, 31.

42. <http://www.tracesofthetrade.org/> (accessed February 19, 2009).

CONTRIBUTORS

WILLIAM A. BLAIR is professor of American history, director of the George and Ann Richards Civil War Era Center at the Pennsylvania State University, and editor of *Civil War History*, the scholarly journal for the history of the sectional crisis through Reconstruction. Blair has written *Virginia's Private War: Feeding Body and Soul in the Confederacy, 1861–1865*, and *Cities of the Dead: Contesting the Memory of the Civil War in the South, 1865–1914*. He is currently working on *With Malice toward Some*, a study of the use of treason during and after the Civil War.

RICHARD CARWARDINE is the Rhodes Professor of American History at the University of Oxford. His work focuses on Abraham Lincoln and the place of evangelical Protestantism in nineteenth-century America. In 2004 he became the first British scholar to win the prestigious Lincoln Prize, America's most generous award in the field of history, for his book *Lincoln*. He is also the author of *Evangelicals and Politics in Antebellum America*.

PAUL FINKELMAN is President William McKinley Distinguished Professor of Law and Public Policy and senior fellow at the Government Law Center at Albany Law School and the author of more than a hundred scholarly articles and more than twenty books.

LOUIS GERTEIS is professor of history at the University of Missouri–St. Louis, where he also serves as chair of the Department of History. His most recent publication is *Civil War St. Louis*. He has also written on the antislavery movement and federal policy toward the freedpeople.

STEVEN HAHN is the Roy F. and Jeannette P. Nichols Professor of History at the University of Pennsylvania. He is a specialist on the history of the American South and on the comparative history of slavery and emancipation. He is the author of the Pulitzer Prize–winning book *A Nation under Our Feet: Black Political Struggles in the Rural South from Slavery to the Great Migration*. His numerous publications also include *The Roots of Southern Populism: Yeoman Farmers and the Transformation of the Georgia Upcountry, 1850–1890*, which received both the Allan Nevins Prize of the Society of American History and the Frederick Jackson Turner Award of the Organization of American Historians.

STEPHANIE MCCURRY is professor of history at the University of Pennsylvania and specializes in nineteenth-century American and gender history as well as southern and political history. McCurry's book *Masters of Small Worlds: Yeoman Households, Gender Relations, and the Political Culture of the Antebellum South Carolina Low Country* received five awards, including the Francis Butler Simkins Award for the Best First Book in Southern History, the Charles S. Sydnor Award, and the John Hope Franklin Prize for the Best Book in American Studies.

MARK E. NEELY JR. is McCabe-Greer Professor of the History of the Civil War Era and senior historian in residence at the Pennsylvania State University. He is author or coauthor of thirteen previous books, including the Pulitzer Prize–winning book *The Fate of Liberty: Abraham Lincoln and Civil Liberties*. His most recent publication is *The Civil War and the Limits of Destruction*.

MICHAEL VORENBERG is associate professor of history at Brown University and the author of *Final Freedom: The Civil War, the Abolition of Slavery, and the Thirteenth Amendment*. He is also the author of a number of essays on Lincoln's engagement with the issues of slavery, emancipation, and race. Currently he is at work on an edited document collection concerning the Emancipation Proclamation as well as a book examining the impact of the Civil War on American citizenship.

KAREN FISHER YOUNGER is managing director of the Richards Civil War Era Center and the managing editor of *Civil War History*, the scholarly journal for the history of the sectional crisis through Reconstruction. Younger has written on the colonization movement, nineteenth-century white and black missionaries in Liberia, and the illegal transatlantic slave trade. She is currently working on *A Work of God*, a study of northern female colonization support in antebellum America.

INDEX